Labor Arbitration

The Strategy of Persuasion

Second Edition

Norman Brand

Cover illustration by Quinn Kazamaki
Cover design and production coordinated by Kristin Ashton Kazamaki

Library of Congress Catalog Card Number: 2006900913

ISBN 0-9778134-0-1

Table of Contents

Table of Contents

Table of Contents

Table of Contents

Preface to the Second Edition

When I began the first edition of this book in 1983, private sector arbitration predominated; public sector arbitration was a relatively new phenomenon; interest arbitration was rare, and federal sector parties were mostly involved in unit determinations and negotiating first contracts. In private sector arbitration well-trained union reps and HR managers with years of collective bargaining and grievance handling experience argued the cases. Most of the public sector advocates were union veterans of organizing campaigns, who had begun in private sector unions, or management veterans of the civil service system. In those days, an arbitrator could usually expect experienced advocates at hearings.

Over the last 20 years the mix of advocates has changed substantially. With the decline of private sector unions, fewer arbitrations occur, and fewer experienced advocates attend. Law firms that represent labor and management do much more employment law, and young lawyers have few opportunities to hone their arbitration advocacy skills. While public sector unions have grown substantially, the representatives who started with the unions when collective bargaining laws passed -- and honed their advocacy skills over many years -- are retiring, as are their veteran management counterparts. In both sectors many disputes are now characterized as statutory claims and do not go to arbitration. The new labor and management representatives spend less time on arbitration and more time in other forums. That is why I decided to bring out a second edition of *Labor Arbitration: The Strategy of Persuasion*. The need for a straightforward training tool to help new arbitration advocates has never been greater. This book provides a comprehensive method for investigating, organizing, and evaluating a grievance. By following the basic rules set out in this book, you will be able to prepare and argue your case in arbitration. No book can turn a novice into an expert. But if you follow the instructions in this book time after time, you will get the kind of experience that makes a novice advocate competent and a competent advocate expert.

Please note: In order to create this compact teaching edition I have eliminated the appendices that were contained in the first edition.

Preface

It is customary for authors to talk about their reasons for writing a book. If the book is capable of being made into a movie, no further explanation is necessary. Visions of obscene wealth, public acclaim, and a fawning article in *People* magazine can sustain an author through the frustrating months at the word processor. But this book will never be a movie, and it is unlikely it will ever become a best seller. At best, it will reach a few thousand people involved in the business of presenting arbitrations.

But I want to reach those people. As a practicing arbitrator, I have watched new advocates struggle painfully through their first arbitration. I wished I could give them some advice before they began. I have struggled through arbitrations in which one side presented a good case in a confused way. I wished I could help them organize the case so it would be as compelling as the raw material demanded. I have watched good advocates reach a plateau of competent presentation. I wished I could provide them that little extra push that would turn them into great advocates. Eventually, I realized that if I wanted to do these things, I would have to write a book.

This desire to help, of course, amounts to nothing more than the universal human impulse to tell other people what to do because you think you can do it better. This impulse is particularly strong among arbitrators. We have all felt, at various times, that we could present the case better than the advocates. Successful arbitrators have learned to stifle the impulse to take over the presentation of a case. Instead, we participate in seminars and educational programs where advocates actually want to hear what we have to say (or at least get out of the office in a socially acceptable way.)

But seminars do not provide the time to set out a comprehensive theory about persuading arbitrators. And they are usually run by sensible people who tremble when they hear an arbitrator say he has a "comprehensive theory," and suggest he talk instead about how he views insubordination cases. Publishers are used to grandiose plans from authors. An arbitrator with an idea for a "how to" book barely affects their blood pressure. And sometimes the plan actually leads to a book. That is what happened here.

Although it is not apparent from the cover, this book was the result of more than one hand. It began as a collaborative effort with John E. Sands. We worked together drafting outlines for chapters, discussing contents, and arguing over methods. The first drafts of Chapters 1 and 3—as well as parts of 5—were John's. He is the progenitor of the "Case Evaluation Matrix." Unfortunately, the press of an enormously successful arbtitration practice, together with the birth and nurturing of Impartial Enterprises, Inc., did not permit him to continue working on the book. Much of the original material has changed, but the entire book has been influenced by those early collaborative efforts with John. I am grateful for the intelligence, wit, and grace that he brought to the project.

I am also grateful to some practicing lawyers in San Francisco who made the time to review Chapter 8. Alan Berkowitz of Schacter, Kristoff, Ross, Sprague and Curiale gave the chapter a close reading and offered useful ideas for improvement. Ronald Yank of Neyhart, Anderson, Nussbaum, Freitas and Reilly helped me avoid errors that would have marred the chapter. A former student from my law school teaching days,

Preface

David Mungo of the Internal Revenue Service Office of General Legal Services, became my teacher. He helped me through the Byzantine appellate procedures of the Federal Services Labor Management Relations Statute. David Handsher of the National Treasury Employees Union brought the experience of a seasoned advocate to bear on that same statute. Let me add the usual disclaimer. Despite the best efforts of four extremely bright people, there may be errors in the chapter. Any error reflects my own inconquerable ignorance, not their advice.

One peculiarity of style may strike you as you read this book. At times I have simply substituted the feminine pronoun "she" for the masculine "he." There is no particular reason that I used one rather than the other in any specific place. I wanted to avoid making this book sound as if all arbitrators, advocates, and witnesses are male. They are not. Unfortunately, there is no readily acceptable alternative to the masculine pronoun. The constant use of "he or she" is tedious. Eliminating all singular pronouns creates so many passive sentences that the cure is worse than the disease. And using the abominable "s/he" should be a capital offense in any civilized country. Thus, I have changed "he" to "she" in assorted places and left it at that.

If you have read all the way through this preface, you deserve a reward. I hope the book that follows provides it.

Introduction

This is a "how to" book. It is not intended as a treatise on labor arbitration, but as a guide for both the novice and the more experienced arbitration advocate. Some parts of the book may seem far too complicated to the novice, while others may seem simplistic to the experienced advocate. Each should approach the book in a different way. If you are a novice, I have provided a step-by-step guide for investigating, analyzing, preparing, and arguing your first labor arbitration. You should concentrate first on the aspects of case preparation and presentation contained in Chapters 1, 2, and 3. Leave the finer points of arbitrator selection and posthearing activities until later cases. If you have to write a brief in your first case, however, the section on brief writing in Chapter 6 will guide you through that process.

The evaluation matrices in Chapter 1 provide a useful device for insuring that you consider all aspects of your case. In addition, they are a tool for organizing what can seem initially like an unmanageable volume of information. Chapter 2 describes an organized way to dissect and understand contract language. It is critical for both the novice and experienced advocate to read contract language with an eye to understanding and untangling ambiguity. Chapter 3 helps the novice understand the advocate's role in preparing for a hearing, and provides the experienced advocate with a checklist that will insure no major aspect of case preparation is omitted. Studying the first three chapters can develop the novice's confidence, or strengthen the experienced advocate's grasp of fundamentals.

A few words of caution to the novice. Everything I describe in the first three chapters takes a lot of time when doing your first few cases. Not only do you proceed haltingly at first, but witnesses are not always available, documents do not come on time, and records are in a jumble. As you become more experienced, you will be able to do your part in preparing a case more quickly, but you will never be able to eliminate all the other delays.

For the more experienced advocate, much of the first three chapters will be confirmation of what you have been doing for years. Start with the portion of Chapter 6 on brief writing: you may find it liberating. The premise of the chapter is that there is precious little that is precedential in arbitration. You can stop wasting time by looking for cites in *Labor Arbitration* to support everything you say. You are writing an argument for an arbitrator, not a brief for a court, and there is an important difference.

As an experienced advocate you may be called upon to do different types of arbitration. While you already have the skills to do rights arbitrations, Chapter 7 provides useful information on the differences you will encounter in other forms of arbitration. Knowing what differences to expect will make you more comfortable in the new setting. Also, as an experienced advocate, you are more likely to run into the need for ancillary litigation. Regardless of whether you will be doing the litigation yourself, it is important for you to understand the system for enforcing arbitration obligations.

There are no absolute rules in arbitration. I have suggested approaches, methods, and techniques. For the novice advocate they can be useful guidelines to follow while learning the trade. As you become more experienced you will internalize some of these guidelines and adapt others to fit your own style. From time to time, when you have a thorny problem, you may want to reread some of the earlier chapters and use their techniques to work your way through that problem.

For the experienced advocate, many of the approaches, methods, and techniques will be familiar, while a few will be new. The new techniques may help you through a difficult case, or provide an alternative when one of your own techniques is not effective. The sections on arbitrator selection and brief writing will undoubtedly provide some different ways of looking at these subjects. Take what you find useful, ignore the rest. I know that the exigencies of practice often make it impossible to spend the time required by the preparation methods I have suggested. But I also know that experienced advocates have incorporated truncated versions of these methods into their own case preparation.

If you use this book well, there are two predictable results. First, by knowing your cases more thoroughly you will be able to settle more of the cases that should be settled—before incurring any arbitration costs. Second, you will be prepared to forcefully argue the cases that cannot be settled—so that you will have the greatest likelihood of winning. Both results are good for the process of arbitration and the labor-management relations system of which it is a part.

1

Investigating, Analyzing, and Evaluating Your Case

Introduction

As an advocate, you will usually get involved in a grievance just after a demand for arbitration has been made. You probably will have had little or no part in the case up to this point. Rather, you will be faced for the first time with a series of events that took place some months or even years ago. You will often find that little serious thought has been given the grievance. It will have perked along with each side maintaining its position, certain that any arbitrator with a lick of sense would have to see things its way. As you first examine the case an uneasy feeling may overtake you.

You may discover that there has been no thorough investigation or examination of the facts. Rather, your side has simply accepted as verifiable anything asserted by your own people. You may discover that no one knows precisely what contract language is said to have been violated, or how that violation is said to have occurred. You are likely to find that no one on your side has developed a theory of the case that can serve to help you prepare for arbitration. In short, you may discover that it is up to you to bring order out of chaos.

This chapter will show you how to begin that process. It will present a simple and effective system for determining in every case:

1. the nature of a claim,
2. the basis of a claim,
3. the merits of a claim, and
4. the likelihood of the claim succeeding in arbitration.

My purpose is to help you prepare your most persuasive case. In preparing your case you may, of course, discover that there is a good chance you will lose at arbitration. Armed with this knowledge, you will be able to argue persuasively to your own side that the case should be settled. In addition, if you follow the method suggested for preparing a case, you will know precisely where the weaknesses in your case—as well as your opponent's—can be found. This knowledge will enable you to negotiate the best possible settlement.

Investigating a Claim

The purpose of investigation is to collect all the documents that are sources of obligation (collective bargaining agreements, side-letters, memoranda), and all of the facts relating to the grievance, so that you can analyze and evaluate your case for arbitration.

Documentation

Your first step must always be to collect the basic documents that define the parties' mutual obligations and provide the source of any claim in arbitration. These basic documents include:

The Parties' Collective Bargaining Agreement
Under Which the Claim Arises

The contract is the basis for the entire proceeding. It establishes the subject matter over which an arbitrator will have jurisdiction. It creates the arbitration forum in which the case will ultimately be decided. It establishes the rights of the parties and the obligations that may entitle grievant to the relief he or she claims. Its grievance procedure defines the steps that grievant must follow to submit and appeal his claim. Finally, it may also establish the procedure that will be followed in an arbitration.

The Original Grievance and Appeals to Higher Steps
of the Grievance Procedure

These documents establish: (1) what it is grievant claims, and (2) how grievant processed that claim through the parties' grievance procedure. When read with the contract arbitration clause, these two matters will usually demonstrate whether grievant's claim is substantively and procedurally arbitrable.

Grievances are usually brought by employees or unions, although some grievance procedures permit employers access to the process. Because the latter seem more the exception than the rule, I will assume for purposes of this chapter that the cases were brought by the employee or union. I shall also assume that the parties' procedure requires, as most do, a written statement of the grievance at some stage of the process.

Written Responses at Lower Steps of the Procedure

These are employer responses to grievances at pre-arbitration steps of the grievance procedure. Usually in writing, they are valuable evidence of the employer's view of the claim at issue. They may contain admissions of relevant facts as well as reservations of important rights and arguments. They will usually be dated, so as to provide evidence of whether the parties followed the time requirements of the grievance procedure.

Demand for Arbitration

Depending on the administering agency, if any, the demand for arbitration may contain a concise statement of grievant's claim, the contract articles upon which it is based, as well as the relief sought. If the demand arises in New York State, it may contain a statutory notice that shifts to respondent the obligation to move a court, within twenty days, to stay the arbitration. This "7503(c)" notice, and your response to it, is discussed more fully in Chapter 8.

Format for Determining Facts

Arbitration, like litigation, is a forum for settling disputes about facts and obligations. The arbitrator determines, as a judge would, who owes what to whom, under the *facts* of a case. Since the arbitrator can only apply the contract's obligations to the facts he finds, you must do an exhaustive investigation to identify all the relevant facts and the resources available (or lacking) to prove each fact.

The format that I suggest here asks the five "reporter's" questions—one of them twice—to direct your inquiry. There is nothing magic about it. It is just one of the many available procedures to ensure that your investigation covers all of the ground and discovers all of the relevant facts.

Here are the questions and what they seek:

Who?

Who is the grievant? If it is a "group grievance", what is the common characteristic that links the grievants? Who else was involved or is affected? Who are the witnesses?

4

You need to get all relevant identifying data concerning *people* involved in the case. Names, clock numbers, departments, shifts, job assignments, pay rates, seniority dates, supervisory authority—all of these facts will enable you to identify (and to locate if they are needed as witnesses or parties) everyone *involved* in the case.

Be sure to keep in mind that, for the purposes of investigation, "involved" is a very broad term. You should include not only the claimant and those who participated in the incident at issue, but also witnesses, likely witnesses, and other employees whose interests will be affected if grievant wins what he claims.

When?

When did the grievance arise? When was the grievance filed? When did the relevant incidents occur?

You need to identify all *time* factors relevant to the merits and timeliness of the grievance. Dates, times of day, shifts, work schedules, overtime or regular-time assignments, postmarks, receipt stamps—all involve possibly relevant questions of *time* that may affect grievant's right to the relief he seeks. Considerations of time may determine whether grievant has met the contract's procedural requirements, whether work was performed under circumstances requiring payment of overtime, and what witnesses may be available to establish disputed facts. By examining work schedules and time records you can discover who could (and could not) have seen an event. There is nothing more devastating to your opponent than being able to prove that his prize witness was not there on the day in question.

Where?

Where did the incident occur? Where were the participants and witnesses located? Where were all relevant people supposed to be? Where were the machines, furniture, buildings, partitions, and other objects that played a role in the case? The area of the facility in which the incident occurred, as well as its layout of fixtures and objects, sets the stage on which the action of the case occurred. Physical factors may determine questions of what could have happened as well as who could have seen it happen. In researching the physical data, always be sure that what you are seeing today is what would have been seen when the events occurred.

What? (First Time)

What happened? What physical evidence exists? You need to secure a complete description of all *events and objects* relevant to the incident or situation from which the grievance arises. That will include any statements, spoken or written, made by anyone present or otherwise involved, videotape records of surveillance, police reports, correspondence raising or answering claims, letters confirming employment or pay status, paycheck records, photographs, and descriptions of how similar matters have been handled in the past. The purpose of this question is, ultimately, to produce the "story" of how the case developed and of how prior similar cases have been handled.

Why?

Why is this a "grievance?" You must identify the *obligations* that grievant claims the employer violated and how the employer violated them. You need to identify the specific contract provisions or specific past practices on which grievant bases his claim. How you answer this question will determine

6

the theory underlying grievant's claim of entitlement to the relief he demands. And grievant's claim will shape the employer's defense.

What? (Second Time)

What does grievant want? What is respondent willing to give?

You need to identify what *relief* grievant wants and whether the employer will resist giving it. The information is useful both to evaluate exposure and to generate settlements. Every litigator has his own favorite story of a plaintiff who wanted less than he was entitled to. If you do not ask these questions, you risk escalating the dispute and ignoring a coincidence of interests that can resolve the case before it becomes costly and time consuming.

Format for Determining Obligations

There are contractual and noncontractual obligations. Contractual obligations, with which we are dealing in arbitration, are those established explicitly and implicitly by the parties' agreement. Noncontractual obligations may be found in federal, state, and local statutes, and ordinances regulating employment and labor-management relations. Noncontractual obligations may be relevant to interpreting the parties' contractual obligation. If, for example, one of two possible interpretations of ambiguous contract language will produce a result that violates applicable law, an arbitrator will likely conclude the parties intended their ambiguous words to comport with their legal obligation.

To determine contract obligations you must first identify relevant contract language. Start by skimming the entire collective bargaining agreement and pulling and copying the following provisions:

    a. contract articles cited in the grievance,

    b. contract articles that have language dealing with the same subject matter as the grievance, and

    c. contract articles that are logically related to the subject matter of the grievance. (For example, if the grievance involves overtime, consider the contract's provisions defining working hours, workday, and workweek.)

As to each potentially relevant contract provision, you should identify the essential elements necessary to establish breach or compliance. Chapter 2 contains a full description of that process. For the purposes of this discussion, however, it suffices to say that the essential elements of an obligation are the minimum facts necessary to constitute compliance with that obligation. Conversely, the essential elements of a claim are the minimum facts necessary to establish the opponent's breach of an obligation to the claiming party.

For example, assume a collective bargaining agreement that provides, "On December 20 of each calendar year the employer shall pay a $50 cash bonus to production employees with more than ten (10) years seniority." For a grievant to prevail on a claim that the employer failed to pay the required bonus, he must establish the following essential elements:

    a. Grievant is a production employee;

    b. Grievant has more than ten years seniority;

    c. Grievant met those requirements as of December 20 of the calendar year in question; and

    d. The employer failed to pay him $50 cash on December 20.

For the employer to prevail, on the other hand, it must establish that grievant fails to meet any one of the essential elements of his claim; or it must undercut grievant's proof on that issue, so that an arbitrator will not be convinced by what grievant has shown.

Although the contract language in question seems fairly clear on its face, it requires little to imagine some of the factual and legal disputes that might arise in such a case. For example, what if grievant, who has twelve years' service in the plant, spent his first six years as a maintenance employee? The employer may dispute his "ten years seniority," claiming that all ten years must be as a production employee. The answer to that issue might depend on the words of another contract provision defining the term "seniority," or upon the testimony of the parties' negotiators concerning their statements across the table during bargaining for the disputed benefit. The point of this example is to illustrate the necessity of identifying the essential elements, or minimum facts necessary for the grievant to establish the employer's breach of a contract obligation or, conversely, for the employer to establish its compliance.

Analyzing a Claim

Following the steps listed above, you now have collected *all* of the facts and contract obligations potentially relevant to the claim at issue. To analyze the claim and determine its merit you must relate the available facts to the essential elements of the contract obligations you have identified.

The first step of this process is listing every essential element of each obligation. You must then list those relevant facts that must be proved to establish compliance or violation with each essential element. That process will identify the *minimum* facts that must appear on the record of the arbitration proceeding in order to sustain or defeat grievant's claim.

The second critical step of this analytical process is to list the available sources of proof for each necessary fact. If, for example, the necessary fact is our hypothetical grievant's date of employment more than ten years prior to December 20, possible sources of proof (depending on your initial investigation of facts) might be grievant's own testimony, a company letter dated more than ten years earlier confirming grievant's appointment and welcoming him to employment, the stub of grievant's paycheck showing a seniority date more than ten years earlier, or the employer's stipulation of grievant's employment date.

At this point you need not choose which source of proof you will actually use. It is enough to identify and list those that are available and, as important, to identify those necessary facts for which you have no available source of proof. Remember, a fact is not a fact unless it can be proved on the record of your arbitration proceeding.

I have found it useful to combine these analytical steps in an "evaluation matrix." This is a chart that lists for each contract obligation: (1) the essential elements in the left column, (2) as to each essential element, the necessary facts in the second column, and (3) as to each necessary fact, each source of proof in the third column. The final two columns, "probative value" and "persuasive impact," will be used for evaluating each source of proof and will be explained later.

Here is what the evaluation matrix will look like:

Contract Obligation: _____

Essential Elements	Necessary Facts	Source of Proof	Probative Value	Persuasive Impact

The next analytical step involves the use of "feedback loops." After you have filled in the elements, facts, and proofs of an evaluation matrix you may notice that there are missing facts, or proofs necessary to establish certain elements of the contract breach or compliance. Use the chart as a tool for further investigation. If a fact is unknown, or if you have no source of proof, conduct a more narrowly-focused investigation to learn that fact or to locate something or someone to prove it. If that further investigation is unsuccessful, you will have to explore alternative theories for which you do have facts and proofs available.

You should continue this feedback-loop process of using the essential elements of each theory to identify missing facts, using the available facts to generate new theories, using the new theories to identify newly-relevant facts, and so on until your investigation can take you no further. Always be sure to list the available sources of proof for each fact. A fact that cannot be proved on the record *is not a fact.*

Evaluating a Claim

To evaluate a claim you must anticipate what the arbitrator will do with the case if it is presented as you plan. You match your proofs to the necessary facts and assess the probative value and persuasive impact of the proofs you plan.

Probative value involves the directness with which a proof establishes an essential element. For example, if the parties dispute whether the employer in fact *paid* grievant's seniority bonus, *direct* evidence of that fact could be the canceled bonus check bearing grievant's endorsement. That document, "real" as opposed to "testimonial" evidence, directly proves the fact in dispute.

Indirect, or "circumstantial," evidence proves other facts from which the fact in question can be inferred. If, for example, the employer claims to have made the disputed payment in cash, circumstantial evidence of that payment would be attendance records showing grievant's presence on the day of payment, testimony of a supervisor who observed grievant in line for receipt of payment, and a receipt-of-payment form bearing grievant's signature. (In contrast, testimony of the employer's paymaster that she actually handed a fifty-dollar bill to grievant would be *direct*, testimonial evidence of the fact of payment.)

Persuasive impact, on the other hand, involves the credibility of your witnesses and the credence that the arbitrator is likely to give your proof. Credibility of a witness's testimony will depend on such issues as the witness's reputation for honesty, likely demeanor, and personal interest in the case's outcome. All of these considerations taken together will give you some sense of the impact her testimony will probably make on an arbitrator.

In addition, as I will discuss in Chapter 5 on preparing of witnesses, to bolster credibility you should be sure that surrounding circumstances support the planned testimony. If, for example, you are offering the paymaster's testimony that she handed grievant a $50 bill on December 20, make sure that company attendance records confirm her presence at work on that day. (They must, of course, confirm grievant's presence on that same day.) You will be embarrassed (as will be your witness) if your client's own records show she is lying.

Probative value of real evidence involves your assessment of the credence that an arbitrator is likely to give it. If, for example, you offer an endorsed, canceled check as direct evidence of payment, make sure you have the original available for inspection and that your copies are legible. Even an arbitrator willing to take evidence "for what it is worth" is likely to find worthless an illegible, dog-eared copy. After all, if you have to use a witness to tell the arbitrator what the illegible material says, you will be relying on the testimony of the witness, not the document itself.

After completing your evaluation matrix, you must evaluate the proofs that you will have available to make your case or break your opponent's. You must have proof for each essential element of each obligation. To the extent there are "holes" in the facts necessary to establish essential elements, or to the extent that some proofs have little probative value or persuasive impact, your case is in trouble. You must employ the feedback-loop technique to explore new directions. If those new directions prove equally unavailing, you should explore the possibility of a negotiated settlement.

Practical Exercises

Let's examine a hypothetical fact situation and use the evaluation matrix to analyze and evaluate the competing parties' cases.

Smedlap's Overtime Claim
Facts
The relevant contract language reads, (1) "Overtime shall be paid at time and one-half for all authorized work before 8:00 A.M. or after 4:00 P.M." and (2) "Grievances must be reduced to writing within five days."

On Thursday, June 15 at 3:30 P.M., Waldo Smedlap, a machinist, was working at his lathe. His foreman, Ralph Greensleeves, passed by and saw that a five-gallon can of lubricating oil had sprung a leak and that there was a large and growing oil puddle on the floor next to Smedlap's lathe, but out of his line of vision. The puddle extended beyond Smedlap's work area to the walkway, encircling several trash barrels that were there.

Greensleeves said, "Clean it up." Smedlap replied, "I'll leave a note for the cleanup guys." The foreman responded, "Whatever—but this better not be here when I come in tomorrow." (Greensleeves's usual arrival time is 7:45 A.M.) A co-worker, Ralph Rackstraw, overheard this conversation while working at his lathe next to Smedlap's.

The following day Smedlap encountered Greensleeves at lunch time and said, "Be sure to put in an overtime slip for me. I came in like you told me at seven o'clock and cleaned up the spill." Greensleeves replied, "The hell I will. I never authorized any overtime."

Following that oral refusal, Smedlap pulled his timecard and wrote, "You owe me one hour OT for Friday 7:00 A.M. to 8:00 A.M." When Greensleeves was reviewing that week's timecards on the following Monday, he saw Smedlap's note and wrote underneath, "Do not pay—Ralph Greensleeves, Foreman." On the following pay day, Thursday, June 22, Smedlap received no overtime pay in his check. He filed his written appeal the next day with the company's personnel director, who decides appeals at Step Two of the grievance procedure.

At Step Two the employer denied Smedlap's grievance for the following reasons:

1. The grievance is untimely, having been filed more than a week after Greensleeves's denial of overtime.
2. No one saw Smedlap do the cleanup. Smedlap claims he came in at 7:00 A.M. through the normally-open loading dock. No one, however, saw him enter.
3. The owner of the company's outside janitorial service claims his guys cleaned up the spill.

14

4. In any event, Greensleeves never authorized Smedlap's performance of overtime work.

Complications

1. There is no time clock. Smedlap signed in "7:00 A.M." on his time card on Friday, June 16.
2. The loading dock door is opened for deliveries at 6:00 A.M., but the receiving clerk is not stationed near the door.
3. At the company's request, the owner of the cleaning contractor asked his three-man cleaning crew, "Did you guys clean up the oil spill at Widget Company yesterday?" They answered, "Absolutely, boss. The place was spotless when we left."
4. That cleaning crew normally cleans the company's offices and walkways and empties its trash barrels. They have no responsibility for work areas beyond the walkways.
5. Smedlap's wife will confirm that he left for work an hour earlier than usual on June 16.
6. Smedlap's co-worker, Ralph Rackstraw, did not see Smedlap perform the cleanup work. He will testify, "I saw the oil spill when we left at 4:00 P.M. Thursday, but it was gone when I came in at 7:50 A.M. Friday. When I got there I found Smedlap sitting by his lathe dunking a doughnut in his coffee."
7. On a central bulletin board on which employer and union messages are posted is a National Safety Council poster that reads, "SAFETY FIRST! CLEAN UP YOUR SPILLS!" The company's personnel director will testify, "We believe in that message, but the poster is not ours."

Analysis and Evaluation

Relevant obligations in this hypothetical include: (1) Widget Co.'s obligation to pay overtime at time and one-half for all authorized work before 8:00 A.M. or after 4:00 P.M. and (2) grievant's obligation to reduce his grievance to writing within five days.

Let's consider the overtime obligation first. Here are the essential elements, which you should enter in the left column of your evaluation matrix:

CHART A
GRIEVANT'S EVALUATION MATRIX

Contract Obligation: _____ Overtime payment _____

Essential Elements	Necessary Facts	Source of Proof	Probative Value	Persuasive Impact
(a) Work				
(b) Authorization				
(c) Before 8 A.M. or after 4 P.M.				
(d) Payment				
(e) At time and one-half				

The essential elements at issue in any dispute, involving violation of—or compliance with—the contract's obligation to pay overtime, are listed in the first column. Grievant, who bears the burden of proving his entitlement and the employer's breach, must identify the facts necessary to establish his case. That will be the second column of the evaluation matrix:

16

CHART B
GRIEVANT'S EVALUATION MATRIX

Contract Obligation: Overtime payment

Essential Elements	Necessary Facts	Source of Proof	Probative Value	Persuasive Impact
(a) Work	Cleaning oil spill on June 16			
(b) Authorization	Greensleeves's words			
(c) Before 8 A.M. or after 4 P.M.	7 A.M. to 8 A.M.			
(d) Payment	No payment			
(e) At time and one-half	Nothing			

What this evaluation matrix shows is that the work Smedlap did was to clean up the oil spill. That it was authorized will be shown by Greensleeves's words to Smedlap. The time it was done fits into the contractual definition of overtime, and Smedlap was not paid.

Sources of Proof

The third step in completing the evaluation matrix for proving grievant's case is identification of the available sources of proof for each element of his claim:

CHART C
GRIEVANT'S EVALUATION MATRIX

Contract Obligation: _____Overtime payment_____

Essential Elements	Necessary Facts	Source of Proof	Probative Value	Persuasive Impact
(a) Work	Cleaning oil spill on June 16	Smedlap's testimony		
(b) Authorization	Greensleeves's words	Smedlap's test Co-worker testimony Greensleeves's cross Stipulation?		
(c) Before 8 A.M. or after 4 P.M.	7 A.M. to 8 A.M.	Smedlap's testimony Smedlap's timecard Stipulation?		
(d) Payment	No payment	Stipulation?		
(e) At time and one-half	Nothing	Same proofs as (d)		

We have now listed all of the sources of direct proof that grievant will have available to establish the essential elements of his claim. Our evaluation matrix shows that we will have to rely on Smedlap's testimony to establish directly that he cleaned up the oil spill. We have several possibilities to show

18

Greensleeves's words of authorization. Smedlap and a co-worker both heard the words spoken by Greensleeves. On cross-examination, we may be able to get Greensleeves to admit what he said. In fact, there may be no argument about what he said, so that we can get a stipulation on his words from the other side.

Our proof of when Smedlap did the work is twofold. First, we have his testimony. Second, we have the writing on his time-card, which is ordinarily the company's "official" time record. There will probably be no dispute over whether Smedlap was paid for the time he cleaned up the spill. Thus, we should be able to prove the lack of payment through a stipulation. We must now evaluate the probative value and persuasive impact of each of grievant's sources of proof. The evaluation matrix continues:

CHART D
GRIEVANT'S EVALUATION MATRIX

Contract Obligation: Overtime Payment

Essential Elements	Necessary Facts	Source of Proof	Probative Value	Persuasive Impact
(a) Work	Cleaning oil spill on June 16	Smedlap's testimony	Direct	Credibility problems: interest, pugnacity

Labor Arbitration: The Strategy of Persuasion

Essential Elements	Necessary Facts	Source of Proof	Probative Value	Persuasive Impact
(b) Authorization	Greensleeves's words	Smedlap's testimony	Direct	Credibility problems: reasonable understanding, interest, pugnacity
		Co-worker's testimony	Direct	Credible
		Greensleeves's cross	Direct	Credibility problem: reasonable
		Stipulation	Direct	Conclusive (eliminates cross)
(c) Before 8 A.M. or after 4 P.M.	7 A.M. to 8 A.M.	Smedlap's testimony	Direct	Same as (a)
		Co-worker's testimony	Indirect	Weak inference
		Wife's testimony	Indirect	Credibility problem
		Smedlap's time card	Direct	Conclusive of presence
(d) Payment	No payment	Smedlap's testimony	Direct	Credible
		Smedlap's pay stub	Direct	Conclusive
		Stipulation?	Direct	Conclusive
(e) At time and one-half	Nothing	Same proofs as (d)	Same as (d)	Same as (d)

This evaluation matrix reveals that there may be some problems in grievant's proof of his case. There are credibility problems with Smedlap's testimony about cleaning up the oil spill, because he has an interest in the outcome of the case. That is, he would have a motive to lie. He is also a pugnacious fellow, and may not do well on cross-examination. He may argue with your adversary and appear to be hiding the truth. On the

20

authorization issue we have other testimony that will support the assertion about what Greensleeves said. If we can get a stipulation on the words, that will be conclusive. This is likely, since the real issue is not likely to be the words themselves, but what they reasonably could be considered to mean. On the other hand, you may want to get Greensleeves on the stand so that you can cross-examine him. If he appears evasive, the arbitrator may conclude that the tone in which he said the words conveyed authorization. The time of the work can be proved indirectly through Ralph Rackstraw, who saw grievant there early and the spill gone. This is, however, extremely weak proof. The time of the work can also be proved through Mrs. Smedlap, but she is an interested witness. The time card, as a business record, conclusively shows—at the very least—that Smedlap was there that day. As to the payment, a stipulation will prove conclusively that he was not paid for the time.

Both grievant and the employer should analyze grievant's claim according to the above evaluation matrix. Although grievant will know what sources of proof are available to him, the employer must make some educated guesses in order to anticipate grievant's case and its own exposure. If, for example, the employer's analysis of grievant's claim demonstrates that grievant has absolutely no proof of an essential element, the employer may want to consider resting at the end of grievant's case-in-chief. In addition, the employer's analysis will provide a useful framework within which to understand and evaluate the significance of unanticipated testimony by grievant's witnesses. The employer should, in any event, consider and evaluate what sources of proof are available to it either to undercut grievant's proofs or to establish contrary facts. Here is what the employer's evaluation matrix might look like for its own case-in-chief:

CHART E
EMPLOYER'S EVALUATION MATRIX

<u>Contract Obligation:</u> <u>Overtime Payment</u>

Essential Elements	Necessary Facts	Source of Proof	Probative Value	Persuasive Impact
(a) No work	Done by others	Contractor's testimony	Indirect	Nil: hearsay
		Cleaning crew's testimony	Direct	Credibility problems: interest, responsibility
		Smedlap's cross	Direct	Credibility problems: interest, pugnacity, cheaper alternative
(b) Not authorized	Greensleeves's words	Greensleeves's testimony	Direct	Credibility problems: defensive, reasonable expectation
		Smedlap's cross	Direct	Credibility: reasonable, understanding
		Stipulation	Direct	Conclusive (may avoid cross)
(c) Nonpayment	no payment	Stipulation	Direct	Conclusive

Based on that matrix the employer may realize that neither side has conclusive evidence as to who did the work. At best, the cleaning crew is interested in looking good; at worst, it does not —technically—have any responsibility for cleaning around Smedlap's work area. Smedlap's testimony is undercut by the logical problem in his believing the foreman wanted to pay an hour of overtime, rather than have the cleaning crew do a little extra. Ultimately, the employer must realize that the question of authorization or non-authorization is a critical one. There may be no disagreement concerning Greensleeves's words. At best they are ambiguous, and an arbitrator might reasonably go either way. He could equally well conclude that Smedlap reasonably understood those words to authorize overtime work or that Greensleeves reasonably expected Smedlap to choose the cheaper alternative of making sure the cleaning guys noticed and took care of the spill.

Faced with an apparent toss-up the employer might consider a new feedback loop on the authorization question. For example, if there is a consistent practice that supervisors *always* confirm their orders to work overtime by written memoranda, proof of that fact, proof of the absence of a written memorandum, and proof that Smedlap himself had received such memoranda in the past, will make a much more persuasive showing that Smedlap's work was not authorized.

Similarly, the union might for its part pursue an authorization feedback loop that would establish to its advantage that the overtime authorization practice has been a loose one and that Smedlap and others had often been directed to work (and had received overtime payments) with even less explicit instructions than those of Greensleeves in this case.

For each feedback loop you must record the sources of proof and your assessments of their probative value and persuasive impact. Here are the evaluation matrices for the two feedback loops we have just considered:

CHART F
EMPLOYER'S EVALUATION MATRIX
Contract Obligation: Overtime Authorization Issue

Essential Elements	Necessary Facts	Source of Proof	Probative Value	Persuasive Impact
Non-authori-zation	Greensleeves's word	Greensleeves's testimony	Direct	Credibility: reasonable expectation? Ambiguity problem
		Smedlap's cross	Direct	Credibility: reasonable understand-ing?
		Stipulation?	Direct	Conclusive avoid cross
	Past practice—written memoranda to confirm OT assign-ment	Greensleeves's testimony	Direct	Credible
		Supervisor #2's testimo-ny	Direct	Credible
		Smedlap's cross	Direct	Credible
	—no memo-randum here	Greensleeves's testimony	Direct	Credible
		Smedlap's cross (subpoena duces tecum)	Direct	Credible

24

CHART G
GRIEVANT'S EVALUATION MATRIX

Contract Obligation: Overtime Authorization Issue

Essential Elements	Necessary Facts	Source of Proof	Probative Value	Persuasive Impact
Authorization	Greensleeves's words	Smedlap's testimony	Direct	Credibility problems: reasonable understanding? interest, pugnacity
		Co-worker's testimony	Direct	Credible
		Greensleeves's cross	Direct	Credibility problems: reasonable expectations, interest
		Stipulation?	Direct	Conclusive (eliminates cross)
	Past practice loose with OT paid on less explicit instructions	Smedlap's testimony	Direct	Credibility problems: interest, pugnacity
		Co-worker's testimony	Direct	Credible
		Greensleeves's cross	Direct	Credibility problems: interest, defensiveness

Having completed evaluation matrices for each side's case on the overtime issue, let us follow their likely evaluation. We will begin with grievant's case:

25

Evaluation by Grievant's Attorney

I must first prove that Smedlap did the cleanup work. He is the best and most direct source of proof. Smedlap will testify under oath and subject to cross-examination that he did the work. That proof is direct evidence of the facts he alleges, and its persuasive impact will depend on the arbitrator's perception of Smedlap's credibility. Smedlap has no prior convictions for perjury, and he speaks with the confidence born of self-righteousness. He should, therefore, have no problem being believed, although the arbitrator may react negatively to Smedlap's pugnacity. I have no idea, however, how Smedlap will hold up on cross-examination. He has never testified before, and he is frankly frightened. If Smedlap stumbles on cross-examination I can always call his co-worker to give circumstantial evidence confirming that the spot was cleaned up. That will at least serve to shift to the employer the obligation to go forward with its own witnesses to prove that Smedlap did *not* clean up the spill.

On the issue of authorization there seems to be no factual dispute as to what Greensleeves said. Perhaps I can consult with the Company's representative to see if he is willing to stipulate to the words Greensleeves used. That way we can avoid an extended and argumentative cross-examination on the reasonableness of Smedlap's expectation and understanding in light of Greensleeves's words—although that question will remain even if we stipulate Greensleeves's words. I will try to cut short that line of cross by objecting that the questions are argumentative, but they'll probably be allowed.

The arbitrator's conclusion on reasonableness will be dispositive. I did some additional investigation and learned that overtime authorizations are usually fairly informal. If I can prove that, I will have a stronger basis to argue the reasonableness of grievant's understanding of his foreman's words.

On the timing issue, we should have no problem. The employer chose the method for recording arrival, and Smedlap's compliance with it should be conclusive as to the time of day he did the work he claims. This will give grievant an opportunity to identify and put into evidence his time card, which will also be necessary to show he reduced his grievance to writing within five days of Greensleeves's having refused to issue an overtime slip. That is not critical, however, for we will argue in the alternative that his written complaint on June 23 came within five days of the company's failure to pay.

The final element, nonpayment of the proper rate, presents no problem. I'm sure the company will stipulate, since they only dispute Smedlap's entitlement to overtime not whether he in fact received it.

* * *

From this analysis grievant's attorney has identified proof of Smedlap's work and of Greensleeves's authorization as his two critical problem areas. Whether he will want to recommend settlement of Smedlap's claim will depend on his confidence: (1) in Smedlap's credibility as a witness, (2) in his own ability to undercut the cleaning crew's credibility on cross-examination, and (3) in the credibility of the union's other witnesses on the loose past practice for authorizing overtime.

Similarly, the employer will evaluate its case on the overtime issue using its own evaluation matrix, Chart E. Here is what the employer's attorney may be thinking:

My first opportunity to establish that Smedlap did no work will be on his cross-examination. His self-interest in claiming he did the work is clear, but that would require a strong cynicism on the arbitrator's part to find that interest, alone, is enough to undercut Smedlap's credibility.

Greensleeves tells me that Smedlap is a pugnacious fellow, and I may be able to needle him enough on cross to provoke hostile and evasive responses that may help the arbitrator along the credibility path. Possibly a more productive route with Smedlap might be to explore on cross his knowledge of the cleaning crew's responsibility and its availability as a cheaper alternative to Smedlap's doing the work himself on overtime. That consideration—that he could have left a note for the cleaning crew—would also go to the reasonableness of Smedlap's understanding of Greensleeves's words on the authorization issue. In addition, it might provide a "trap" in which Smedlap could stumble by claiming that he cleaned the oil from the walkway as well as from his machine area. Walkways are clearly the cleaning crew's responsibility, and it is unlikely they would have missed that portion of the oil spill during their evening work.

I had better keep at least one member of the cleaning crew available to testify affirmatively that they did clean up the spill themselves. Our principal exposure here is that the oil spill extended beyond the crew's area of responsibility. Rather than have that attacked on cross-examination, I had better raise it on direct so that the witness can explain his conscientiousness under friendly examination—at least initially.

On the authorization issue there is no question concerning what Greensleeves said. By stipulating to his precise words, I may be able to avoid setting him up for cross-examination on the reasonableness of his expectation that Smedlap would not do the work. Greensleeves seems a bit defensive about this incident, for his boss has recently counseled him on the necessity for more effective supervision. Since Greensleeves is so sensitive, I am concerned that he will be an easy target on cross-examination. If I can keep him off the stand, I will. I can use my cross-examination of Smedlap to undercut the reasonableness of *his* understanding of Greensleeves's words, given the cheaper alternative of the cleaning crew's availability to do the work.

Recognizing that this authorization issue is the thorniest one, I did some extra investigation and learned from Greensleeves that company supervisors *always* use written memoranda to authorize overtime work. I had better nose around to check with other supervisors for confirmation that they follow the same procedure. If that is true, and if I can establish on Smedlap's cross that he has always received written memoranda in the past, that will be powerful proof that Smedlap's work was not authorized.

Finally, there is no issue of payment. We only contest Smedlap's entitlement to overtime pay so we might as well stipulate that no payment was made. By offering that stipulation first, we might set a tone of cooperation that could help secure a stipulation on Greensleeves's words that will avoid the necessity of having him testify.

* * *

Like grievant's attorney, the employer attorney has identified his own critical problem areas. For him, too, the settlement option will be more or less attractive depending on his confidence in the credibility of the cleaning crew and in the credibility of his supervisory witnesses on the strict past practice for written authorizations of overtime. It is worth noting that the parties have overlapping interests in resolving some evidentiary issues by stipulation. On the other hand, the parties have antithetical views on the authorization issue, and each believes its view will be supported by the evidence. It is not unusual for advocates to be convinced they have the means to prove something and later discover they do not have that evidence. Obviously, one of these advocates is in for a surprise.

Here are possible evaluation matrices for each side on the timeliness issue.

CHART H
GRIEVANT'S EVALUATION MATRIX

Contract Obligation: Timely Grievance

Essential Elements	Necessary Facts	Source of Proof	Probative Value	Persuasive Impact
(a) Grievance	Failure to pay OT on 6/22; or Greensleeves's refusal to put in OT slip on 6/16	6/22 pay stub of Smedlap	Direct	Conclusive
		Smedlap's testimony	Direct	Credible
		Greensleeves's cross	Direct	Credible
(b) reduced to writing	Formal grievance on 6/23	Grievance form	Direct	Conclusive
	or			
	Time card endorsement on 6/16	Smedlap's time card	Direct	Conclusive
(c) within 5 days	Same as (b)	Same as (b)	Same as (b)	Same as (b)

30

CHART I
EMPLOYER'S EVALUATION MATRIX

Contract Obligation: _____ Untimely Grievance

Essential Elements	Necessary Facts	Source of Proof	Probative Value	Persuasive Impact
(a) Grievance	Greensleeves's refusal to issue OT slip on 6/16	Greensleeves's testimony	Direct	Credible
		Smedlap cross	Direct	Credible
		Stipulation		
(b) reduced to writing	6/23 grievance	Grievance form	Direct	Conclusive
		Personnel Director's testimony	Direct	Credible
(c) more than five days	seven days	Same as (b)	Same as (b)	Same as (b)

Assume, in turn, that you represent grievant and the company. Practice evaluating your case on timeliness. As attorney for the employer, consider whether you have a sufficient chance of success to warrant risking an arbitrator's inference from a frivolous timeliness challenge that you lack confidence in your case on the merits.

We have now completed investigating, analyzing, and evaluating your case. Chapter 2 will deal in depth with the techniques of interpreting contracts and just cause obligations necessary for the analysis process. The next step in case preparation is preparation of your proofs, and that is addressed in Chapter 3.

2

Interpreting and Applying Contract Language

Introduction

In Chapter 1 we talked about identifying potentially relevant contract articles when investigating a claimed contract violation. After you identify the relevant contract articles, you must identify the essential elements of these articles—the elements necessary to establish breach or compliance. You then use these essential elements in your evaluation matrix. I used a brief illustration of how to identify essential elements in contract language, leaving a fuller explanation of that process for this chapter.

The illustration used in Chapter 1 was a simple one, since the focus was on the evaluation matrix and the process of investigating and analyzing claims. The contract language relied upon in the grievance was "Overtime shall be paid at time and one-half for all authorized work before 8:00 A.M. or after 4:00 P.M." I did a separate evaluation matrix on the issue of "authorization," noting that the word "authorized" is ambiguous. That is, it covers both oral and written authorizations and leaves open the specific nature of the authorization and by whom it must be given. I focused on using behavior (past practice) to prove the meaning of "authorized" in Smedlap's case. Now we need to look at the problem in some of its other dimensions.

There are many forms of contractual ambiguity, several methods of untangling that ambiguity to extract the essential elements of a claim, and a few rules that arbitrators apply in sorting out the meaning of ambiguous contract language. There is a great deal of work that you need to do with the language of your contract before you have the proper essential elements for your evaluation matrix. In this chapter I will focus on how to do that work. In addition, I will focus on the special meaning of "just cause," as that term is used in discipline clauses of collective bargaining agreements.

I will begin with a classification system that gives you a method for spotting ambiguities in contract language. Advocates frequently fail to see, or understand, their opponent's argument because they convince themselves that the language in question is absolutely unambiguous. That can be a fatal error. We will then look at the methods for taking ambiguous contract language and breaking it down into its essential elements. This can serve three purposes: it can enable you to understand the precise obligation imposed by the language, it can help you make that obligation clear to the arbitrator, and it can help you avoid future disputes by conforming the behavior of the party you represent to the obligations under the contract.

Sometimes, however, despite your best efforts to untangle the contract language, it will remain ambiguous in its application. You will then have to convince the arbitrator that the language should be interpreted in a certain way. To help you in that effort, we will look at the rules usually applied by arbitrators in sorting out the meaning of ambiguous contract language. This will serve two purposes: first, at the hearing you will be able to put in evidence that is consistent with your argument as to how the language should be interpreted; second, after the hearing you will be able to frame your arguments in a way that an arbitrator is most likely to understand and accept. Finally, since many arbitrations are disciplinary arbitrations, I will give you an outline of the general rules used by arbitrators in interpreting the contract's "just cause" obligation.

Spotting Ambiguity in Contract Language

You do not have to become an expert in linguistics to spot ambiguity, but it is helpful to know the categories language specialists use so that you can identify and decipher ambiguities more efficiently. There are two general types of ambiguity in contract language: semantic and syntactic.

Semantic ambiguity exists because words can have many meanings. They have a "denotation," which we can think of as their "dictionary meanings," and a "connotation," which we can think of as the meanings that have grown up around words because of the way they are used by a particular group.

Syntactic ambiguity exists because English sentences rely heavily on word order and punctuation for their meaning. The position of a word or phrase in a sentence can be as important to the meaning of the sentence as the words themselves. In this section we will first identify types of semantic ambiguity and then syntactic ambiguity.

Semantic Ambiguity

There are three types of semantic ambiguity commonly found in collective bargaining agreements. First, the kind that occurs because a particular word may have more than one meaning. For instance, consider the word "day." A collective bargaining agreement says, "Any employee who works 180 days shall be entitled to 5 vacation days." What does "day" mean in that sentence?

Arguably, there are at least three distinct meanings. The parties could have meant "calendar days," so that after approximately half a year's employment an employee can take a five calendar day vacation. Alternatively, the parties could have meant "workdays," so that if the employing company has a six-day week, the employee would accrue five vacation days after approximately thirty weeks employment. Finally, the parties could have intended "days" to mean "shifts." Thus, if an employee worked only four shifts per week, he would not be entitled to five shifts off until after approximately forty-five weeks. Obviously, even more changes could be rung on the meaning of "day" in the contract language we've just examined. All these possibilities exist because a single word may have more than one meaning, and there may be nothing in the context of the contract clause that demands a specific meaning for the word. When you spot a word like "day" you have to ascertain, from your own side, whether people in the business normally use the word to mean something other than calendar days. You also need to determine whether any different meaning was given to the word when the contract was negotiated, or through the years. Finally, you need to decide whether you will be obligated to prove the meaning of "day" as one of your essential elements.

A second type of semantic ambiguity involves generalizations. While a word like "day" can have a fairly concrete meaning—usually a twenty-four-hour period—there are other words that can be more general. Consider, for example, the word "screwdriver." It is a concrete word describing a number of objects that have certain characteristics in common. Those characteristics are so well known that a picture of a screwdriver may well have come to your mind when you saw the word. You probably saw an object with a handle, a metal shaft, and a tip that had a straight or star design. A more general word that covers the category in which screwdriver is included is the word "tool." While you can have some assurance of the range of characteristics of the object in the mental picture created by the word "screwdriver," you cannot be sure of the mental picture evoked by the word "tool." Indeed, it may be very different for each person who hears the word. "Tool" is a general word that covers a defined category of concrete objects. Because the mental pictures evoked by the word "tool" are very different, the word itself is ambiguous. When you see a word like "tool" in the contract, your task is to determine whether the facts of the dispute are inside or outside the category created by the general word.

For instance, in the Smedlap case, the contract language said that "Grievances must be reduced to writing within five days." You recall that Smedlap wrote on his time card: "You owe me one hour OT for Friday 7:00 A.M. to 8:00 A.M." The word "writing" in the contract is a general one. Does it include any written communication, or only certain specific types of writing intended by the grievance procedure? Your job as an advocate will be to argue whether the note Smedlap put on his time card is included in the category created by the ambiguous general word "writing."

A third category of semantic ambiguity involves unqualified abstractions. For instance, a more abstract word that includes the categories "screwdriver" and "tool" is the word "implement." The word is an abstract one, and it is broad enough to describe "anything necessary to effect an end." Because "implement" is abstract, it is extremely difficult to tie a single concrete image to it. We can speak of trade restrictions as "implements" of foreign policy. It is likely that the last sentence evoked *no* mental images.

Most commonly, abstract words are used to express generalized good intentions in a contract. Consider this extreme example of language from a faculty contract: "It is the policy of the University to maintain and encourage full freedom, within the law, of inquiry, teaching, and research." Depending upon whether you represent a university or faculty member, the interpretations that you could give to this clause are almost endless. At one extreme, you could argue for a religiously affiliated college that God's "law" prohibits inquiry into the origins of man to the extent that inquiry is inconsistent with the biblical idea of creation. On the other extreme, you could argue that it is permissible to teach a college physics class how to make atomic bombs, since the data are not classified under statutory law. Because the quoted sentence is made up of so many abstract words, it is capable of conflicting interpretations in almost any concrete situation.

As an advocate you may argue that such abstract expressions of goodwill were not intended to have a specific contractual effect. Or, you may argue that everything in the contract was intended to have some effect—depending upon which side you are on. If you argue for effect, as I will describe more fully later, you will have to show that the effect you give the words in the abstract statement does not conflict with specific contractual obligations found elsewhere in the contract.

Syntactic Ambiguity

The second type of ambiguity, syntactic ambiguity, can be either simple or complex. Simple syntactic ambiguity can arise merely out of the way in which words, phrases, or marks of punctuation are placed in a sentence. Complex syntactic ambiguity arises out of the way in which a sentence is structured. Let us first look at the simple problems.

Simple Syntactic Ambiguity

Where you place a modifier can radically change the meaning of a sentence. Consider this example from Wydick's *Plain English for Lawyers*. The modifier is: "who was kicking and screaming." The sentence is: "The judge ordered the bailiff to evict the photographer." Notice the difference if you put the modifier after "judge," after "bailiff," or after "photographer." In each instance, the meaning of the sentence is changed considerably.

Sometimes, however, a sentence means two different things precisely because of where the modifier is placed. Consider the following sentence: "Stopping a car on the railroad tracks, under a New York statute, may be negligence *per se*." While it is amusing to think of a New York statute strung up above a railroad crossing, modifier problems are often the cause of some serious disputes. Consider the following example:

> No man covered by this agreement may leave the pier during working hours for the purpose of obtaining drink, or for any purpose whatever, except with the express permission of the supervisor involved.

As this sentence is written, it could be construed to allow the supervisor to give permission for men to leave the pier to get a drink. The parties may not have intended that result.

An additional form of simple syntactic ambiguity is caused by punctuation errors. The most common punctuation error in collective bargaining contracts is a failure to use the "series comma." When three items are contained in a series in which the last two are separated by the word "and," the series comma prevents ambiguity. Consider this sentence:

> All job security provisions contained in this agreement will be voided in the case of any strike affecting the company's operations, acts of God and emergencies brought about by fire, flood or storm.

By omitting the comma after "God," the writer suggests that both acts of God and emergencies are modified by "fire, flood or storm." Are the job security provisions in effect if there is an earthquake? While this may seem a frivolous question, this particular clause comes from a retail store contract in California. Thus, a real dispute could occur if an earthquake damaged a store and caused the employer to have to close it. If the drafters had included a series comma after "God," there would be no question about earthquakes being covered by the clause, since they are obviously "acts of God." As it stands, the clause is ambiguous.

Your most difficult task may be in recognizing this type of ambiguity in contract language. It is usually overlooked because your side has felt certain it "knew" what the language meant, and that it was unambiguous. When some action occurs so that the language is challenged, however, you will be obliged to prove the meaning you have ascribed to it. Later in this chapter we will examine the rules arbitrators are likely to apply in determining the meaning of these ambiguous clauses. What you need to note at this point is that the proof of the meaning of the ambiguous clause will be an essential element in your case.

Complex Syntactic Ambiguity

Complex syntactic ambiguity arises out of the ways in which sentences are structured. Let us consider four examples. First, syntactic ambiguity can be caused by a "shifted construction." Examine the following sentence:

> The Employer agrees to make available to the Union (1) bulletin board for the posting of the Union notices relating to meetings or other Union business, but no political, or propaganda, or other notices shall be posted without written permission of the Employer.

The drafter of this provision linked two slightly different ideas with a comma and a conjunction ("but") without thinking about the effect of each portion of the sentence on the other. The categories "other union business" and "other notices" overlap. One plausible interpretation of this language is that almost anything other than a notice of a union meeting, agenda, or election notice, requires employer approval. In fact, this interpretation led to an arbitration.

A second complex type of syntactic ambiguity is caused by "embeddings." These are phrases or clauses that modify the straightforward meaning expressed in a sentence. When embeddings interrupt the main thought of the sentence, they make it difficult to understand. For example:

> The Employer agrees to reimburse, on a per diem basis, in accordance with the previously promulgated rules and regulations, the actual and necessary expenses of employees, who are otherwise eligible for travel expenses, when they are incurred while in travel status, during the performance of their official duties, for hotel lodging, meals and incidental expenses related thereto (hotel tips, etc.), for a full day at the corporate rate generally available to other employees.

Notice how difficult it is to figure out both: (1) who the employer is agreeing to reimburse; and (2) the prerequisites for reimbursement. The problem is that nine clauses have been strung together in what appears to be the order in which they occurred to the drafter. The ambiguity results from the absence of a straightforward hierarchy among the clauses. It is impossible to easily grasp which clause prevails if there is a conflict.

When there is a conflict, you may wind up in an arbitration in which you must defend or attack the action taken by the employer. In order to do so, you will have to untangle this contract clause for yourself and the arbitrator. It will not be enough to simply set out the different requirements of the clause. You also have to put them in an order that makes clear their interdependency.

While we will be discussing methods for untangling sentences like this shortly, an illustration may be helpful. The fifth clause says: "who are otherwise eligible for travel expenses." When you are preparing your evaluation matrix to analyze a claimed improper payment, it is important to know that the universe is divided into those who are and those who are not eligible for travel reimbursement. An essential element, and one that may have otherwise gone unexplored, is the question of whether the complainant was "eligible for travel reimbursement." Once you have correctly analyzed this clause, it will be the first essential element in your evaluation matrix. After all, if a person was not eligible for travel reimbursement, any payment to that person was erroneous, regardless of the other rules. Thus, by sorting out the embeddings in this contract clause, you may be able to resolve a grievance at an early step in your analysis.

A third complex type of syntactic ambiguity is caused by "complex conditionals." These are rules that have many conditions that must be fulfilled before they operate. You will be faced with problems when the contract jams the rule and all its conditions into one sentence. Consider this sentence:

> An employee who has completed forty-five (45) workdays and who was injured on the job and reports the injury to his foreman or nurse, and who requires medical attention and is treated by the company doctor, shall be paid lost time on the day of injury, on the basis of gang hours and straight time and for additional days on the first week on the basis of eight (8) hours per day.

This sentence sets up a number of conditions for paying an injured employee for his lost time. If the conditions are met, then the employee will be paid at a certain rate. All of the conditions have been joined in a single sentence filled with "ands." It is possible to disentangle this sentence and identify its essential elements for your evaluation matrix; we will examine how later.

Because of the way this sentence was put together, the parties may have introduced unintended requirements that could form the basis for an arbitration. For instance, the employer would have a solid contractual argument if it withheld compensation from an employee who had completed forty-five workdays, was injured on the job, reported it to his foreman, and was taken to the local hospital for medical attention. After all, the employee was not "treated by the company doctor." After identifying the ambiguity in this sentence, however, you may still be able to argue—applying one of the rules we discuss later —that the arbitrator should not permit that result.

Finally, the contract may contain ambiguous sentences because its drafters crammed so many elements into a sentence that they lost sight of what they wanted to do. They wound up with an "overstuffed" sentence. Examine the following example:

> The Employer agrees to furnish their family status, new employees hired, employees whose services are terminated, and such other information as may be required by any underwriting insurance company, or by a Plan, for the proper administration thereof.

It is difficult to determine: (1) to whom the employer is furnishing information; (2) what is meant by the phrase "family status;" and (3) whether the employer has agreed to furnish information to insurance companies only if it is required for the proper administration of the plan. The drafters introduced ambiguity by tossing all of the agreement's elements into one sentence without thinking how they relate to one another. We will discuss methods for untangling this final type of ambiguous sentence later on in this chapter.

In this section I have identified different types of contractual ambiguity, but have not discussed the causes of this ambiguity. I prefer to focus first on identifying the ambiguity and developing tools for extracting the essential elements you will be using in your evaluation matrix. You may infer that I condemn poor drafting as the cause of all contract interpretation arbitrations. That is not the case.

I recognize that collective bargaining is a continuing process and that some ambiguity is intentional. For a variety of good reasons negotiators are reluctant to change language they have lived with successfully over the years. Consequently, when language must be added to cover a new technology or situation, they often add it without changing existing language to make clauses, sentences, or sections work together. The negotiators are carefully focused on the new problem. It is only hindsight that discloses the ambiguity they have created. Similarly, not every aspect of the workplace relationship is reduced to contract language. As a consequence, the parties may later be forced to infer some meaning from existing contract language to govern a dispute over activities not specifically mentioned in the contract.

There are also times when the parties agree to deliberately ambiguous language so that they can reach some agreement rather than wind up in an impasse. Frequently contracts use words like "reasonable," "practical," and "possible." The parties are well aware of the semantic ambiguity they are creating. But they are also aware of the need to bring negotiations to a conclusion.

Finally, few negotiators have the gift of being able to see the future. Over the years the background conditions against which particular contract language was negotiated may change. Then, at some point a new technology or reality is introduced, and the contract language does not clearly cover it. This is not a fault of the drafters, but an inevitable consequence of change.

For all of these reasons, I do not want to give the impression that all ambiguous contract language can be blamed on bad drafting. Rather than placing blame, I want to explore ways to untangle ambiguous language in order to identify its essential elements, use it in the evaluation matrix, and argue effectively to an arbitrator.

Converting Contract Language into Essential Elements

Before you can effectively investigate a case in which ambiguous contract language plays a role, you must convert that language into the essential elements of the contract interpretation portion of your case. In doing this conversion, you may discover that the actions taken by a supervisor violated the contract. If so, as a management advocate you will have the opportunity to settle the case. If you discover that your grievant's claim is dubious, in light of your interpretation of the ambiguous language, as a union advocate you will have a similar opportunity. Moreover, both sides will be left with a "rule" that can guide the future behavior of their clients.

Equally important, you can use the rule to argue your case to the arbitrator. Since the arbitrator has not lived with your contract, he does not know what meaning, if any, the language has been given. The graphic techniques that we will be using to clarify the ambiguous language will be extremely useful in *showing* the arbitrator what particular language means. That is, you will offer the arbitrator an interpretation of the language that comports with your view of the case. Of course, for one side this may be disadvantageous. Consequently, that side will not want to offer the arbitrator an untangled version of the contract language. Rather, it will muddy the waters and attempt to convince the arbitrator that the offered interpretation fails to comprehend the magnificent complexity of the contract language.

Let us examine three methods for turning rather complex language into the essential elements you need for your evaluation matrix. This piece of contract language might give difficulty to either side:

> An employee who has completed forty-five (45) workdays and who is injured on-the-job and reports the injury to his foreman or nurse, and who requires medical attention and is treated by his company doctor, shall be paid for time lost on the day of injury, on the basis of gang hours and straight time, and for additional days on the first week, on the basis of eight hours per day.

I can identify three methods for making this language comprehensible: structured enumeration, algorithms, and flowcharts. I will explain each method, illustrating it with the quoted language.

The easiest method is structured enumeration. It is also a useful method when writing the original contract language. The quoted section has two separate rules. One rule has a set of conditions that must obtain before it comes into effect (what I previously called a "complex conditional"). The other rule has further specifications clarifying how it is to be applied.

The simplest statement of the first rule is that "An employee shall be paid for time lost as a result of on-the-job injuries." There are several conditions, however, that must be met if the employee is to be paid. So after that first sentence, "An employee shall be paid for time lost as a result of on-the-job injuries," let us put the word "if." Now let us list the conditions under which the employee shall be paid. First, the employee must have completed forty-five workdays; second, the injury must have been reported to the employee's foreman or the nurse; third, the employee must require medical treatment; and fourth, the employee must be treated by the company doctor. Let us now set these conditions out as a series of indented "if" clauses, joined by the word "and," since the parties apparently intended that the employee must fulfill each and every condition in order to be eligible for the pay. The rule looks like this:

An employee shall be paid for time lost as result of on-the-job injuries if:

   a. he or she has completed forty-five workdays; and
   b. the injury is reported to his or her foreman; or
   c. the injury is reported to the nurse; and
   d. he or she requires medical treatment; and
   e. he or she is treated by the company doctor.

The payment rule can be abstracted in a similar way:

The payment shall be at straight time for:

   a. gang hours lost on the day of injury; and
   b. eight hours per day for additional days in the first week of injury.

When the language is set forth in this structured enumeration, a number of things become apparent. First, the language does not specifically cover employees whose on-the-job injuries are serious enough to require an immediate visit to the hospital, rather than initial medical attention from the company doctor. Second, the language does not indicate what the payment shall be, if any, when the disability period extends beyond one week. It is possible, of course, that this is covered in another section of the contract.

As you can see from the way we have restructured the contract language, each of the lettered statements, as well as the condition contained in the initial straightforward statement (that an employee lost time because of an on-the-job injury) forms an essential element for your evaluation matrix. Each of these essential elements requires proof before breach or compliance with the contract can be asserted. But you are now in the position to search for your proofs (or match them to the essential elements) in order to properly analyze your case.

Let us now consider a second method for turning this contract language into essential elements for yourself and the arbitrator. In order to create what we call a list algorithm, you must determine the logic of the language involved and convert it to a series of questions. The clause that we have been examining deals with time lost due to on-the-job injuries. It does not deal with off-the-job, work-related or non-work-related, injuries. Consequently, the first question you must ask is whether the employee who lost time was injured on the job. We know, however, that not all employees are covered by this clause. Therefore, the second question must be whether the employee has worked more than forty-five days. As you can see, if you answer the first question "no," i.e., the injury causing lost time was not on the job, you don't have to answer the second question, since the injury is not covered by this section. So, too, if you answer "no" to the question of whether the employee has worked forty-five days, you do not have to ask any further questions because the employee is not eligible for any coverage under this section. On the other hand, if you ask whether the employee has reported the injury to a foreman and the answer is "no," that does not mean the employee is barred from receiving payment. Rather, it means you must ask whether the employee reported the injury to the nurse.

By proceeding in this fashion, we can come up with the following list algorithm:

1. *Was the employee injured on the job?*

   If *Yes*, go to 2.
   If *No*, go to 8.

2. *Has the employee completed forty-five days of work?*

   If *Yes*, go to 3.
   If *No*, go to 8.

3. *Was the injury reported to the nurse?*

   If *Yes*, go to 5.
   If *No*, go to 4.

4. *Was the injury reported to the foreman?*

   If *Yes*, go to 5.
   If *No*, go to 8.

5. *Was medical treatment required?*

   If *Yes*, go to 6.
   If *No*, go to 8.

6. *Was employee treated by company doctor?*

   If *Yes*, go to 7.
   If *No*, go to 8.

7. *Employee to be paid for resulting lost time, according to formula below.*

8. *No compensation under this section.*

There are a number of aspects of this list algorithm worth further explanation. First, it helps those on your side to focus on the essential elements of the alleged contract violation. All too often, grievances are not settled because the people handling them do not focus on a precise meaning for the contract language early in the investigation. Second, this list algorithm can be used to structure your investigation at the earliest stages. Third, the list algorithm can be a useful tool in structuring your presentation at the arbitration. By initially providing it to the arbitrator, and then using it as an ordering device for either stipulating to facts or presenting evidence, the list algorithm can help you to focus the arbitrator on what is critical in the case. You can use it to object to the relevance of evidence offered by your opponent, suggesting that the test for relevance is whether evidence tends to answer one of the questions contained in the list algorithm. Thus, this tool has uses beyond those associated with developing your evaluation matrix.

The third method for clarifying complex contract language is the flowchart, a schematic representation of a list algorithm. Consider the following contract language:

> In the event an employee who would have been eligible for vacation pay resigns and provides at least one week's notice, or is laid off by reason of slack work, prior to his (her) vacation, but after the last business day of March of the same year, and has had nine months' service or more with the company, he (she) shall be entitled to vacation pay in the same manner and to the same extent as he (she) would have been had he (she) remained on the payroll. In no event shall vacation pay be paid to employees discharged for cause.

The language is Byzantine, to say the least. The best that can be said about it is that the parties probably knew to whom they did and did not want to give vacation pay. The problem is in the language they used to embody their agreement. Let's take a look.

One thing is quite clear: employees who are canned for cause get nothing. It is a group that can be eliminated immediately. The first question we might ask, then, is whether the employee was discharged for cause. If the answer is "yes," then that employee is not entitled to any vacation pay. If the answer is "no," there are several other questions we must ask. The next question is whether the employee was laid off for slack work. If the employee was laid off for slack work, he or she may have some entitlement. However, if the employee was not laid off for slack work, there are two other possibilities. Either the employee was discharged for cause (a possibility we have already dealt with) or the employee resigned. Therefore, we must ask whether the employee resigned. If the answer is "no," we have reached the limits of this contract clause. That is, we have an employee who neither resigned nor was discharged nor was laid off. That leaves only employees who have died, are out sick, or are still working. Those employees are not covered by the language of this clause.

Among people who resigned, we still need to know whether they provided one week's notice. If not, they have no entitlement to vacation pay. If so, they are in the same position as an employee who has been laid off for slack work. Figure One (below) illustrates what we have done so far.

FIGURE ONE

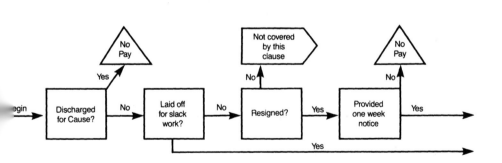

FIGURE TWO

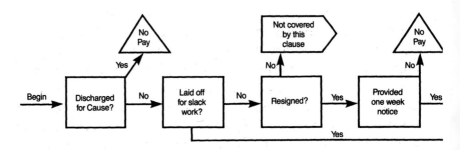

Up to this point, we have partially determined whether the employee is in the category of those potentially entitled to vacation pay. There are, however, two more questions. First, we must ask whether the person is someone who has been with the company nine months or more. Second, we must ask if they would have been eligible for vacation pay had they not quit or been laid off. Finally, having established eligibility, we must look at when the layoff or resignation occurred. Figure Two (above on this and following page) depicts a flowchart that puts all these aspects together.

As you can see, using this tool requires answering yes or no questions about an employee and an event. The answer to the previous question determines what the next question will be.

The flow chart is particularly useful for the visually oriented, since it lays out the essential elements of the contractual obligation in a graphic format. The logic of the flowchart is helpful in guiding the investigation and suggesting feedback loops. For instance, as Figure One shows, this contract clause has no literal application to a ten-year employee who dies in April, before taking his vacation for that year. Nor does it cover a disabled employee who is off the job from the middle of April to the end of the year. Thus, if the situation you are investigating

FIGURE TWO (Continued)

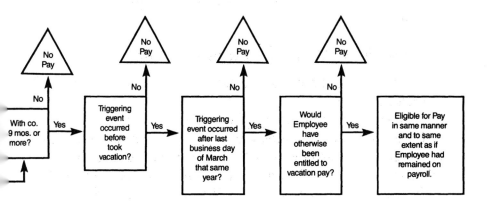

involves death or disability, this contract language does not apply. It may, however, provide an indication of the parties' intentions in those situations that they did not foresee.

Structured enumeration, algorithms, and flowcharts all offer you methods for dissecting complex contract language so you can discover the essential elements for your evaluation matrix. They can clarify your thinking when you are investigating a case, and structure the arbitrator's thinking when you are arguing the case.

How Arbitrators Decide the Meaning of Ambiguous Language

Sometimes, contract language is truly ambiguous. The arbitrator must attempt to ascertain the parties' intention when they wrote the ambiguous language, in order to decide the case before him. Arbitrators use many methods to do this. Some of these methods involve assumptions, either about the way people use language, or about how drafters operate when addressing a specific problem. Others consider how parties have acted, both during and after negotiations. All of these methods are important in planning what facts you are going to elicit at the hearing.

Assumptions About How People Use Words

Let us first examine some assumptions about the use of language.

1. Ordinary words are to be given their ordinary meaning.

If you use such common words as "day" throughout your contract, the arbitrator is likely to interpret them as they are ordinarily used. For instance, "day" ordinarily refers to a calendar day of twenty-four hours. If you mean "working day," you must say so. Thus, if your grievance procedure has time limits that are denominated in days, it is unlikely that the arbitrator is only going to count the days Monday through Friday, and exclude weekends and holidays when determining whether a grievance is timely.

2. Words with a technical meaning will be given that meaning unless indicated otherwise.

Where you use a term of art from your industry, trade, or profession, an arbitrator will assume that you have used it as it is specially used in your industry, trade, or profession. For example, among prison guards the word "watch" is used to signify the shift to which a guard is assigned. Thus, when speaking of the "guard's watch," the contract is not likely to be referring to a small clock owned by an employee.

3. The dictionary meaning of a word does not control.

Sometimes, in a search for authority with which to support a position about the meaning of contract language, parties introduce a dictionary definition. While the dictionary definition may provide some guidance as to the ordinary meaning of a word, it is not safe to assume that the parties intended the dictionary definition. This is especially true because the meaning of words is constantly changing, and a dictionary represents only what a word meant at a certain time. Whether that was what it meant at the time the contract was being negotiated is another question entirely. It is particularly inappropriate to use a dictionary definition where it varies significantly from the ordinary import of the word. In that instance, other proof is necessary to convince an arbitrator that the parties meant something different. For example, one dictionary definition of "shift" is a "change in place or position." It would take considerable proof to convince an arbitrator that an employee who had his job changed twice during his tour of duty worked two "shifts" as that term is used in an overtime article.

4. Same word, same meaning.

Earlier, I mentioned the problem of "layering" in writing contract language. Layering occurs when negotiators keep adding new contract clauses without changing existing ones. It is a problem because an arbitrator who sees the same word used in various articles in a contract will assume that the parties meant it to have the same meaning each time they used it. For example, where the contract provides funeral leave of "up to three days, including days off," it is clear that "days" means "calendar days." If another clause provides a time limit for appealing grievance decisions of "thirty days," an arbitrator will likely assume that too means calendar, not work, days.

5. Different words, different meanings.

The other side of the previous assumption is that where the parties have used different words, they intend to mean different things. This sometimes creates a problem because of what linguists call "elegant variation." That is, somewhere back in high school, a drafter learned that it is important to provide variety for your reader. Consequently, the drafter refers first to a lunch break, then just says break, then says rest period, all in the same contract. The arbitrator may easily be convinced that three different kinds of breaks were intended by that language.

Assumptions About Drafters' Intentions

Arbitrators often make certain assumptions about drafters' intentions. These assumptions have their origins in the so-called "canons of construction." Carl Llewellyn wrote a celebrated article entitled *Remarks on the Theory of Appellate Decision and the Rules or Canons About How Statutes are to be Construed*, 3 Vanderbilt L. Rev. 395 (1950). In this article, Llewellyn lined up twenty-eight canons of construction that had been cited in different cases. Alongside each, he lined up its exact opposite, which other cases had cited. Llewellyn's point was that, although there are certainly rules for construction of statutes, they are really just guidelines to be used in interpreting what the drafters had in mind. Indeed, at times canons of construction are simply formal language that courts (or arbitrators) use to dress up their own views of what language means.

With that caution in mind, let us look at some of the canons of construction that arbitrators may apply in determining the intention of the parties.

1. Expressio unius est exclusio alterius.

This canon of construction means that a specific example or examples may be intended to indicate that the parties wanted to exclude all other potential members of the class of things involved. In the example, "The rule of strict seniority shall govern vacation picks, transfers, and shift assignments," *expressio unius* would work to suggest that the parties did not intend to have seniority govern other matters, such as promotions, days off, or overtime assignments.

2. Ejusdem generis.

This canon of construction suggests that parties intend lists to include all items of the same general character, for instance: "The rule of strict seniority shall govern allocation of job benefits and permanent vacancies, such as vacation picks, transfers, and shift assignments." Under this language it is more likely that an arbitrator could find the parties intended to have the "rule of strict seniority" cover promotions, days off, or overtime assignment. Although they are not specifically enumerated, they fall into the category of "job benefits."

3. If the meaning of a word is doubtful, the context will be relied upon.

In the collective bargaining agreement, context is often provided by such things as headings, titles of articles, and titles of clauses. Suppose a section read, "Bereavement Leave. Employees who suffer a death in their immediate family shall be entitled to three days' leave." If the section came under an article entitled "Miscellaneous," it might be questionable whether the parties meant a paid or unpaid leave. If that same section appeared in an article entitled "Leaves Without Pay," the context would suggest that the parties did not intend "bereavement leave" to be a paid leave.

4. Specific language controls general language.

In many instances, parties to a collective bargaining agreement use grandiose abstract language to describe their overall intentions. For instance, the contract may contain language such as this: "The employer agrees to continue its longstanding commitment to workplace safety. It recognizes that the health and welfare of its employees are among the most important objectives of the enterprise." Suppose, too, that a subsequent clause reads as follows: "The employer shall continue to provide safety equipment as it has in the past." If the employer has not traditionally provided steel-toed safety boots for workers, it is unlikely that an arbitrator would read the general language as requiring the employer to now provide such work boots. Rather, specific language of obligation (providing only safety items that had previously been provided) would control over the general hortatory language.

Assumptions About How Parties Draft Contracts

Where a contract addresses some specific aspect of the workplace relationship, the arbitrator is likely to assume that the parties intended to remedy some problems, regulate some procedures, or establish some rules. Thus, the arbitrator will read the language so as to accomplish one of those ends where a different interpretation will accomplish nothing.

Moreover, if the parties have incorporated a statement of intention into their agreement (or accompanying any particular article), the arbitrator will attempt to construe the specific language in accordance with the goals the parties have stated they want to reach.

There are three other implicit assumptions that arbitrators make in this area.

1. Construe all words of the section together.

An arbitrator is likely to reject an interpretation that requires him to ignore some portion of the parties' language in order to agree with one side's interpretation. Every word, phrase, and clause of the section must be consistent with the proposed interpretation.

2. Construe all parts of the contract together.

Where an offered interpretation of the contract would require the arbitrator to ignore other sections of the contract in order to agree with the offered interpretation, it is unlikely that he will do so. An arbitrator is also unlikely to accept an interpretation that makes other portions of the contract superfluous.

3. Avoid internal conflicts.

Any construction that puts the portion of the contract at issue into conflict with other portions of the contract is likely to be rejected. It is unlikely that the parties would have given something in one portion of the contract, while taking it away elsewhere. It is not impossible that they would have done this, but an arbitrator is unlikely to assume, as a rule of construction, that the parties so intended.

Assumptions About How Parties Normally Act

There are a number of things the arbitrator will assume the parties did not intend. These assumptions are based upon the way people ordinarily act. There is, however, a special madness associated with collective bargaining. Arbitrators are aware that at times parties negotiate inconsistent or just plain silly language, to gain an agreement rather than an impasse. An assumption, of course, can always be overcome by proof of a fact.

Here are some of the things that an arbitrator is likely to assume you did not intend.

1. Absurdity.

It is not likely that parties would intend an absurd result. Thus, for instance, if one party's argued interpretation would mean that an employee who works overtime on a holiday can get neither holiday pay nor overtime pay, the interpretation is likely to be rejected. It would simply be absurd to assume the parties intended an employee who not only worked, but worked overtime on the holiday, would get paid for all of his hours at straight time when either condition alone would entitle him to premium pay.

2. Injustice.

Similarly, it is unlikely that the parties intended an unjust result. For instance, if the interpretation offered by one party

would mean that an employee of twenty years' seniority loses all of his seniority for being late three times, it is unlikely that the parties intended this. This is not to say that the parties did *not* intend it. This rule of construction will not prevail if the language is absolutely clear, or the proponent proves through any direct methods, that this is what the parties intended. The arbitrator is unlikely, however, simply to assume that intention.
3. Ineffectiveness.

The arbitrator is equally unlikely to assume that an interpretation is correct that renders contract language ineffective to achieve its purpose. That is, if the proffered interpretation would result in simply eliminating an employee benefit the clause describes, it is unlikely that the arbitrator will assume the parties intended that result.

Actual Evidence of Intent

In talking about assumptions, I have been careful to note that no assumption need be applied where there is *direct evidence* of a fact. For example, bargaining history may provide direct evidence of facts that themselves establish, or from which the arbitrator may infer, the parties' intent. Bargaining history may include actual written proposals exchanged across the negotiating table, reports of what was said in negotiation by the parties who were present, or previous contracts that show what language existed prior to the current language. In each instance, the arbitrator is being asked to interpret a contract clause in light of how it was negotiated.

It is significant if one of the parties sought something in negotiations but was unsuccessful in achieving it. If either side made a proposal that never was incorporated in the contract, the difference between the proposed language and the actual contract language is significant in determining the parties' intent.

Finally, what the parties said across the table during negotiations is significant. Sometimes a negotiator has verbally committed himself to a particular meaning for an ambiguous word or phrase. The other side, based upon limiting the word or phrase to that meaning, accepts that proposed language. Thereafter, the accepting party is justified in relying upon what was said at the bargaining table. This is also true when one party has given assurances that particular language would not extend to cover certain situations. Having given that assurance in negotiations, the party cannot later successfully argue a contract interpretation at variance with it.

What parties have done since they negotiated the contract language at issue is also important. When the employer has long acted in a way it believes consistent with ambiguous contract language, and the union has knowingly accepted those actions, their joint behavior establishes the meaning of the language. This is not to say that an arbitrator will assume, if the employer "got away" with something due to lax enforcement of the contract, that the union is forever estopped from asserting its rights under the contract. Rather, when both sides knowingly acquiesced in a certain interpretation of ambiguous language in the contract, absent some new circumstances, that interpretation is likely to prevail.

The other side of that coin is when either side has acted in a manner inconsistent with its argued interpretation of the contract. That party will have a difficult time convincing an arbitrator that its new interpretation should prevail over its previous actions.

The Place of Past Practice

The basic rule is simplicity itself: "Past practice will not vary the explicit language of a contract." Applying this rule is more difficult. Arbitrators are frequently asked to operate between two extremes. On the management side, some believe that employers have absolutely unfettered discretion to do anything that is not specifically and exhaustively limited in a contract. On the union side, some assert that as soon as any management person has acquiesced in anything that is perceived as beneficial, negotiations are required to eliminate that "benefit." Obviously, both positions are incorrect.

As I noted earlier, a contract is sometimes silent about some matter because it seems too clear to the parties for them to bother putting it into the contract. For example, if the employees have always been paid weekly, negotiators may have felt it unnecessary to include that in their contract. If, however, the employer were to switch to a monthly payroll, the union might challenge that action based on "past practice." That is, the union would show that the action complained of is a significant one in the workplace relationship, that the previous action (i.e., paying weekly) existed for a long time, and that it had been known to and acquiesced in by the highest levels of management. If the union were able to show all of this, and if the parties' contract contained language preserving past practices, this would be a legitimate contract grievance. A naked assertion that something was "past practice," does not suffice to make it an enforceable part of the contract.

If, on the other hand, there were specific language permitting the employer to determine the payroll period, the union's argument would fail. Finally, if there was no specific, "past-practices-preserved" language, the union would have to tie this weekly pay practice to some other express contractual guarantee. It might be the workweek, or scheduling, or vacation pay; but the union would need to find some textual foundation to establish that the parties had agreed to a weekly pay schedule when they negotiated the contract.

Past practice plays an important part in your investigation and analysis of a case. You must ascertain the actual facts of any alleged past practice. After you find out the content of the alleged past practice, you must use the essential elements of a legitimate past practice as part of your evaluation matrix. You would first ask whether the alleged past practice was being asserted to vary a specific contractual obligation. Next, you would ask if there were a past practices clause in the agreement. Then, you would ask if the practice was widespread, long standing, known to and acquiesced in by higher management, and of significance to the employees. Finally, you would ask if agreement to this alleged past practice could be inferred from any specific language in the agreement.

Just Cause

"Just cause" is a shorthand phrase that incorporates the concepts of fair play that parties agree will govern discipline. What they adopt when they put "just cause" language in the contract, is a procedure by which disciplinary action must survive the critical review of an impartial third party. In a way, "just cause" in any particular case means whatever the arbitrator says it means. Scholars have written an enormous amount about what "just cause" means in disciplinary grievance arbitration. I do not intend to duplicate those works or provide hundreds of arbitration citations to support each assertion about the meaning of just cause. Rather, I will describe the major theories about the just cause obligation so that you can use them as essential elements in analyzing and preparing disciplinary arbitrations.

In general, there are three areas of employee behavior that fall within the just cause obligation: work performance, on-the-job behavior, and off-the-job conduct. First, there are certain aspects of employee behavior that are directly related to work performance.

1. Failure to perform the job.

An employee may be disciplined for failing to do the job he or she has been hired to do. In this category are failures to meet standards of production and general competence. As to both, the employer is generally thought to have an obligation to articulate the reasonable standards that the employee must meet. In addition, employers generally must provide a reasonable opportunity for employees to meet production obligations, whether by training or counseling. Furthermore, the employer has an obligation, in accordance with the concept of progressive discipline, to alert employees who are failing to meet their production obligations, to advise them how to achieve those obligations, and to warn them of the consequences if they fail to improve.

If you represent the employer, you must show the employee (a) was made aware of his or her obligation, (b) was warned of the consequences of failing to improve, (c) was given a reasonable opportunity to improve, (d) failed to meet that obligation, or (e) resisted the employer's efforts to assist the employee in meeting that obligation. To establish the obligation's reasonableness, the employer need only show that the standard applied to this employee was applied to all employees. That is generally sufficient to raise a presumption that the work requirement, either as to quality or quantity, is a reasonable one. That presumption can, of course, be overcome.

2. Neglect of duty.

Where an employee either extends breaks, goofs off, sleeps on the job, or simply disappears from the workplace for periods of time, there is just cause for discipline. The obligation imposed on the employer is simply to show that the employee was made aware of the proper periods for breaks, rest periods, or lunches, warned of the consequences of extending breaks, and failed to adhere to the time limitations. While a single failure is unlikely to result in discharge, repeated failures, in conjunction with progressive discipline, will give adequate cause for discharge.

A theory that has gained some minor currency is that an employee who takes excessive breaks is guilty of committing "theft of time," because the employee is using company time for his own purposes. This theory is used with contracts that provide an exception to progressive discipline for theft. Probably a similar argument could be made about an employee who occupies space at the workplace, but does an inadequate job. That employee, it might be asserted, is "stealing" space from the employer that might be better used by a productive employee. Thus, the employee is guilty of "theft of space," and the employer need not show progressive discipline. In either event, the "theft" theory seems a thin one that does not provide an adequate reason for terminating an employee for one instance of abuse.

3. Tardiness and absenteeism.

It is often said that an employee must not only come to work, but he must also do so on time and regularly. While each instance of tardiness or absenteeism is not, in itself, necessarily significant, the employee's overall record at the time of the discipline is. The more persistent the failures have been, the more severe the penalty is likely to be. Excessive tardiness and absenteeism may be indicia of other problems, such as drug or alcohol involvement. Many employers now have employee assistance programs for those whose problems are related to substance abuse. It is not, however, the obligation of the employer to force an employee into such a program.

Where absenteeism is caused by health problems, the just cause obligation is somewhat changed. The employer's sick leave policy—or that negotiated by the parties—measures how much illness will be tolerated. That is, an employee who uses most or all of his or her available sick leave for *legitimate* illness has not necessarily given the employer cause to discipline that employee. Moreover, arbitrators are likely to be quite sympathetic to employees who are recovering from on-the-job, or traumatic illnesses or injuries.

At some point, however, the employer is entitled to expect reasonable dependability; the employee must either show up for work regularly or find some other job. The number of absences beyond the contractual sick leave limit that will permit termination in these circumstances will vary from arbitrator to arbitrator. Relevant circumstances include the number of absences, the period of time over which they occurred, the cause of the absences, and the likelihood the employee's condition will improve within a reasonable time.

4. Work rule violations.

Many contracts permit the employer to make reasonable work rules. Where the discipline is based upon an employee's violation of a work rule, there are several factors that arbitrators look for. First, was the rule known generally, or by this employee? Alternatively, should the employee reasonably have known about the rule? Counselings by supervisors are often used as evidence that an employee was made aware of the existence of a rule. Second, was the rule itself reasonable? This is not a question of whether the arbitrator would make that same rule. Rather, it is a matter of whether the rule is so unreasonable as to offend the arbitrator's sense of propriety. Third, has the rule been consistently enforced? If the rule has only been selectively enforced, it is suspect. So, too, if it has just begun to be enforced after a period of dormancy. While it may be argued that the employer's failure to enforce a rule does not limit its right to do so in the future, most arbitrators believe that the just cause obligation requires the employer to at least warn employees of forthcoming strict enforcement where prior enforcement has been lax or nonexistent.

5. Insubordination.

The general rule is that employees must carry out the legitimate orders of their supervisors. If they are unhappy with those orders, they can "work now, grieve later." A major exception to this rule occurs when the order given represents an immediate threat to the employee's health or safety, or is patently illegal. Many contracts now have mechanisms for handling the former type of complaint. These procedures generally involve an expedited determination of whether a hazard exists.

The latter, illegality, is more problematic, for it is controversial to assert that the supervisor had no right to give a certain order. Smooth functioning of the workplace depends upon employees following apparently proper orders rather than engaging in debates with their supervisors. Thus, there is a strong tendency by management to find that an employee decided an order is illegal at his or her own peril. If the arbitrator later determines that there is no manifest illegality involved, a discharge based upon that refusal is likely to be sustained.

In general, insubordination requires (1) knowledge on the part of the employee that an order was given; (2) an order of sufficient clarity and possibility so that the employee could both understand and do what was required; and (3) refusal to carry out the order. On the one hand, arbitrators are not generally sympathetic with an employee who asserts that an order must be preceded by the phrase "This is a direct order." On the other hand, in most workplace settings, the employer is not entitled to expect the kind of immediate response that Marine drill instructors strive for. Grumbling is not necessarily insubordination.

A second general category of employee behavior that is cause for discipline or discharge involves gross failures to act in a manner consistent with the responsibilities of the workplace. These are acts or failures that are (or should be) so plain that no employee needs specific instructions in them. These fall under the classification of what a friend called the "string bean rule." This friend, a personnel director for a large organization, had the unpleasant task of counseling an employee whose lack of personal hygiene had caused disruptions in her office ranging from complaints by all of the other employees to several employees' taking matters into their own hands. They brought fans that they directed at the errant employee so as to insure that the flow of air was away from their own desks. Since the pungent employee regularly interviewed members of the public, management thought that both the aroma created by a lack of bathing and the tornado created by her fellow employees disrupted the atmosphere in the workplace.

The employee was called in for this most unpleasant counseling. The personnel director's nose immediately confirmed that the allegations about aroma were correct. He was somewhat surprised, however, when the employee insisted that he point to the rule in the personnel manual that required employees to bathe—ever. He replied, "It's not there. In fact, there is also no rule saying you can't run string beans up your nose while interviewing clients. We think you have enough common sense not to do it." Thus, the string bean rule—employers can expect that employees will exercise some common sense. It covers many areas beyond personal hygiene.

1. Fighting on the job.

Employees are expected to know that it is impermissible to have fistfights on the job. Arbitrators encounter difficulty when the employer takes different disciplinary action against the participants in the fight. There is some feeling, which we all probably share, that there is a difference in culpability between the person who provokes a fight and the person who simply defends himself or herself. This difference may well translate into a difference in penalties. Distinctions are often difficult to make, however, for there will often be credibility conflicts on such issues as who was the aggressor and whether the defender had a reasonable opportunity to withdraw from the confrontation. Consequently, employers who impose different penalties on participants in a fight will be obliged to show the difference in culpability that led to different penalties.

2. Stealing.

Many contracts contain clauses that provide for immediate termination of employees caught stealing. Even if the contract has no such clause, most arbitrators recognize the employer's need to protect its property. Difficulty arises when there are differences as to whether the action engaged in was actually stealing. For example, some employers permit taking scrap, defective product, or waste material home. In most food operations, be they processing or retail, employees are permitted to eat some of the product they work with. If they are not, they need to be told what is forbidden.

Beyond that, the theft area is fairly straightforward. Most arbitrators will not weigh the precise value of the item stolen, unless it is absolutely de minimis (a paper clip, a ballpoint pen, a rubber band). Rather, most arbitrators will uphold a termination based upon proven theft of any item of value.

3. Destruction of property.

Closely related to theft is deliberate destruction of the employer's property. The economic effect on the employer is the same, although the employee benefits only psychologically from destroying the employer's property. The critical distinction here is between the deliberate destruction of the employer's property and the inadvertent destruction of property through incompetence. Intent is key, and the employer must prove facts from which the arbitrator can infer that grievant either acted deliberately or in a way he should have known would destroy property.

A third general category of just cause involves employee conduct that occurs away from the workplace but affects the employer's interest. Employees may be charged with, or convicted of, crimes ranging from misdemeanors to felonies, which result in incarceration. The employer is left with the question of whether the employee is suited to work.

There are three general conditions relevant to determining whether the employer's just cause obligation permits discharging an employee for his or her behavior off the job. First, an employer needs to be able to point to some interest of its own that is affected. For instance, an employee who has been convicted of child molesting may still be perfectly capable of driving a forklift. If the employer has not received any notoriety because of this employee, it may be that there is no reason to discharge him.

There is a second consideration, however, which might obtain in this situation. Sometimes the crime for which an employee is convicted may be so violent or so heinous as to cause other employees to refuse to work with this employee. This is an extremely difficult area, since the employer must discriminate between realistic fears of the employees and simple distaste.

Third, the just cause obligation may require an employer to consider whether the particular crime for which an employee has been convicted renders him unfit to do his job. For instance, if the job requires an employee to be bonded, and conviction makes it impossible to be bonded, the conviction renders the employee unfit to do the job. An employer with a child care center could not allow anyone convicted of child molestation to continue working. Nor would any accounting department keep a convicted embezzler. The employer's basic obligation is to show the relationship between the employee's off-the-job behavior and the workplace.

Many more specific examples of the obligation imposed by a just cause clause, complete with case citations, could be enumerated. If you want further refinements in this area, you will find many other books that have that as their major goal.

Conclusion

In the first chapter I suggested the evaluation matrix as a tool for investigating and analyzing a potential grievance. That chapter focused on the importance of finding and proving facts. In this chapter I have concentrated on untangling contract language to find the essential elements necessary to prove your case. I have also pointed out some of the assumptions that arbitrators may use in deciding your case. By knowing the elements of the applicable contract language, the theories available to you, and the assumptions that the arbitrator may apply, you will be in the best possible position to both investigate and analyze your case. Then you can decide whether to try to settle the case at this stage, or go ahead and continue preparing for arbitration. If you decide to go forward with an arbitration, your next step is preparing your proofs.

3

Preparing the Proofs

Introduction

My purpose in this chapter is to help you select and prepare the most effective and persuasive evidence available for your case. With this evidence you will prove those facts that make up the essential elements of your case. Proper preparation requires: (1) culling the best proofs disclosed by your evaluation matrix, (2) ensuring that they will be provable at the hearing, (3) organizing their presentation in a logical order, and (4) preparing your witnesses so that the evidence you intend is the evidence you adduce.

We will first consider preparing witnesses whose oral testimony—under oath and subject to cross-examination—is evidence of the facts they claim to know. Next we will consider preparing real evidence—documents and things that prove themselves or their contents.

Preparing Testimony

Preparing testimony covers three broad topics: selecting witnesses (including expert witnesses), preparing witnesses, and the "care and feeding" of witnesses.

Witness Selection

The purpose of witness selection is to identify the people whose testimony will most likely be accepted by the arbitrator as proof of the necessary facts to establish the essential elements of your case. These witnesses must be believable, competent (in the legal sense of having firsthand knowledge of relevant facts), and available. To find them, you must refer again to your evaluation matrix to see what has to be proved so you can identify the witnesses most capable of proving it.

I will use grievant's evaluation matrix from Chapter 1 to illustrate how you select two witnesses and organize their testimony. If you have not yet read Chapter 1, a brief summary of the illustrative case may be helpful. Smedlap is grieving the company's failure to pay him overtime for coming in early to clean up an oil spill near his work area. The company has taken the position that Smedlap either did not come in to do the work, or that his overtime was not previously authorized by his supervisor. So that you don't have to keep turning pages, that matrix is repeated here, with the results of our "past practice" feedback loop on the authorization issue included.

CHART D
GRIEVANT'S EVALUATION MATRIX

Contract Obligation: _____ Overtime payment _____

Essential Elements	Necessary Facts	Source of Proof	Probative Value	Persuasive Impact
(a) Work	Cleaning oil spill on June 16	Smedlap's testimony	Direct	Credibility problems: interest, pugnacity
(b) Authorization	Greensleeves's words	Smedlap's testimony	Direct	Credibility problems: reasonable understanding, interest, pugnacity
		Co-worker's testimony	Direct	Credible
		Greensleeves's cross	Direct	Credibility problems: reasonable understanding
		Stipulation	Direct	Conclusive (eliminates cross)
(c) Before 8 A.M. or after 4 P.M.	7 A.M. to 8 A.M.	Smedlap's testimony	Direct	Same as (a)
		Co-worker's testimony	Indirect	Weak Inference
		Wife's testimony	Indirect	Credibility problem
		Smedlap's time card	Direct	Conclusive of presence
(d) Payment	No payment	Smedlap's testimony	Direct	Credible
		Smedlap's pay stub	Direct	Conclusive
		Stipulation?	Direct	Conclusive
(e) At time and one-half	Nothing	Same proofs as (d)	Same as (d)	Same as (d)

CHART G
GRIEVANT'S EVALUATION MATRIX

Contract Obligation: Overtime Authorization Issue

Essential Elements	Necessary Facts	Source of Proof	Probative Value	Persuasive Impact
Authorization	Greensleeves's words	Smedlap's testimony	Direct	Credibility problems: reasonable understanding? interest, pugnacity
		Co-worker's testimony	Direct	Credible
		Greensleeves's cross	Direct	Credibility problems: reasonable expectations, interest,
		Stipulation?	Direct	Conclusive (eliminates cross)
	Past practice loose with OT paid on less explicit instructions	Smedlap's testimony	Direct	Credibility problems: interest, pugnacity
		Co-worker's testimony	Direct	Credible
		Greensleeves's cross	Direct	Credibility problems: interest, defensiveness

Assume you represent grievant. To establish the essential elements of Smedlap's claim you will have to prove all of the facts you listed in column two of charts D and G. In column three you listed the sources of proof for each relevant fact. Presumably, you have examined all grievant's probative resources. You must now choose which of these sources to use, based on the assessments of probative value and persuasive impact you noted in columns four and five of the matrices. For each fact to be proved by testimony, you must select the most credible, most persuasive witness you have available.

Frequently your comments on probative value and persuasive impact make clear immediately whom you should use and whom to avoid. Sometimes circumstances require that you use a witness whose credibility and persuasive impact are less than ideal. For example, you have identified Smedlap's interest and pugnacity as potential credibility problems. He is, however, the only direct witness to the fact of his work and to its timing. In addition, because he is the grievant, you may feel as a matter of strategy that he must testify, under oath and subject to cross-examination, to demonstrate the good faith of his claim.

Because Smedlap has some credibility problems (as an interested witness), you should use feedback loops to identify surrounding circumstances that provide consistent support for the facts he alleges. Your feedback loop for supporting circumstances identifies his wife, his co-worker, his time card, and his pay stub as supporting sources of proof to confirm aspects of Smedlap's testimony. Each source of proof provides some additional evidence that Smedlap is telling an honest and accurate story. Your comments on probative value and persuasive impact will guide your choice of which of those resources to use.

In Smedlap's case, you might well decide that his wife's testimony about when he left for work is cumulative, trivial, and interested. Smedlap can testify as to when he worked. The time he left home does not prove when he got to work, and it would not be unheard of for a spouse to shade the truth to bring a bit more money into the family account. In short, Mrs. Smedlap is an additional witness with only marginal value. Moreover, on cross-examination she may provide harmful information (perhaps Smedlap has a history of leaving early for work because he is an alcoholic who stops for a drink on the way). When the marginal value of an additional witness is not worth the time it will take to present the witness and the exposure to potentially harmful cross-examination, don't use that witness.[1]

In cases where your matrix discloses a number of witnesses to the same necessary fact, you would of course choose those few whose testimony would be the most direct and most persuasive. The more witnesses you have, the less likely will be any dispute of the fact at issue. You must, of course, be sensitive to the point at which repetitious testimony becomes cumulative and alienates, rather than convinces, the arbitrator. The fourth witness on the same trivial point may not destroy the last shred of the arbitrator's doubts, but the last trace of the arbitrator's patience.

---

1. It is sometimes necessary, for tactical reasons, to have the witness present at the hearing. In some instances, the presence of a particular potential witness will worry some of your opponent's witnesses. They will be more inclined to tell the whole truth when they see that a person who can contradict their version of events is at the hearing. If witnesses are not excluded, you can instruct that witness to write you notes while your opponent's witness is testifying. It does not matter what the notes say. If witnesses are excluded, you can announce that you will be seeking a short recess after the direct testimony of your opponent's witness, so that you can consult with your "expert."

Expert Witnesses

In some cases, your evaluation matrix will disclose the need for expert testimony. There are two major uses for expert testimony: first, to express an opinion or draw a conclusion from facts; and second, to educate the arbitrator about a technical area that is important to your case. Experts differ from ordinary witnesses. With rare exceptions, ordinary witnesses testify to *facts* of which they have personal knowledge. They can testify to matters of opinion, or make inferences from those facts, only on questions of common experience requiring no special training or expertise. Examples include questions of a person's anger, a person's intoxication, a room's temperature, and the like. Experts, on the other hand, because of their specialized training or experience in a field, are entitled to testify as to their opinions based upon actual or hypothetical facts. In addition, if your case requires that the arbitrator learn specialized facts or standards by which to evaluate evidence, you will need an expert witness.

Beside his expertise, there is little to distinguish an expert witness from any other witness. Experts have to meet the same tests of credibility as any other witness. Their advanced degrees and learned articles do not guarantee their truthfulness. Nor does the fact that they are being paid for their time suggest they will perjure themselves. They must be able to communicate what they know clearly, effectively, and candidly. As with any other testimony, the arbitrator will evaluate expert testimony in terms of its clarity, its consistency with surrounding circumstances, and its consistency with common sense. This last factor is particularly important. Even an "expert" with a Ph.D. in cartography is unlikely to shake the arbitrator's belief that the world is round. Thus, you may be wasting your time if you search for an "expert" witness whose credentials will be offered as the sole support of an otherwise preposterous proposition.

Regardless of his credentials, an expert will not be an effective witness if he cannot communicate his expertise in a way that is likely to be accepted by the arbitrator. Obviously, a journeyman practitioner whose clarity, forthrightness, and candid competence inspire the listeners' confidence will be a much more effective expert witness than some over credentialed pedant whose condescending intolerance of listeners' ignorance invites resentment.

There are three things to look for and three things to avoid in an expert witness. You should look for, first, a person with years of experience in like or similar work, or who has other relevant research background or experience. For example, if you need someone to testify to whether a substance is cocaine, you do not need the world's greatest academic authority on cocaine. A toxicologist with a few years of clinical experience in testing substances will be quite adequate. The toxicologist will also be cheaper. Second, you should engage an expert who is able to make *you* understand the material about which he will be testifying. If you do not understand the expert's explanation, it is unlikely the arbitrator will. Beware of the expert who says the material is simply too difficult for *any* layperson to understand. That is a good indication that the expert wants his opinions accepted as a matter of "faith." Many arbitrators will resent being told they must accept opinions whose basis they can not understand. Third, you want to select an expert who has a straightforward style. There are experts who are so enamored of their fields that they just love to explain them to others. They make great witnesses.

The three things to avoid in experts have more to do with style than substance. First, you generally want to avoid an abstract theoretician in the field. For instance, you do not want the world's greatest authority on cocaine to testify at length to the pros and cons of the classification system that underlies the presumptive and confirming tests that are commonly used for identifying cocaine. You want someone who can say with authority: "Yup, the tests show positively that this substance is cocaine." Second, you want to use an expert who can offer opinions with a degree of certainty. Some experts are so accustomed to qualifying everything they say that it is difficult to understand precisely what, if anything, they are testifying to. You can often spot these experts by their dedication to the phrase, "On the other hand." Stick to "one-handed" experts, who understand contrary opinion but have a firm, well-validated, intellectual commitment to their own views. Third, avoid expert witnesses who are condescending, impatient with questions, or intolerant of anyone who questions their authority. An expert witness is going to have his authority questioned and may be bombarded with questions that demonstrate a lack of basic knowledge in his field. The expert should be able to deal with such questions in a way that educates the questioner without insulting him.

Selecting the right expert requires tailoring the degree of expertise to the needs of the case. The most common error is overreaching. It is impossible to state a general rule, but an example may help.

A case I am familiar with involved alcohol and drug abuse. Both sides' psychiatrists had already testified on the nature of addictive disabilities, each invoking the authority of the same, widely published professor of psychiatry at a major university hospital in the area. On the fifth day of hearing, in walked the professor, whose scholarly appearance and seriousness of purpose were enhanced by the unexpected fact that he was dressed in the beaver hat and black coat appropriate to his other profession: Chasidic rabbi.

After all had conceded his expertise, the employer's attorney asked, "Doctor, assume a cross-abuser of drugs and alcohol over seventeen years who had five unsuccessful detoxifications in the prior three years. Assume he had a sixth detoxification and completed a twenty-eight-day rehabilitation program. Assume that person was picked up from the program by his old drinking buddy and, three hours later, returned to his home where he reeked of alcohol, spoke with slurred speech, and walked so unsteadily that he kept bumping into walls and furniture. In your professional opinion, was that rehabilitation program successful?" After a pregnant pause, he answered, "For this you need a Board-certified psychiatrist?"

Witness Preparation

Witness Education

Proper preparation requires that you educate your witness about the essential elements of your case, the details of the testimony you want to adduce, and the general requirements of behavior for effective testimony. Your witness should have a solid understanding of where his testimony fits in your theory of the case.

The first important step of witness preparation is to prepare a general outline, by essential elements, of your entire case. The source of this outline is, of course, your evaluation matrix, which tells you what major points must be made, and by whom. You organize this material into an outline that will enable the arbitrator to readily follow your case. Every friendly witness should be shown a copy of the outline, and you should explain it before you begin preparing his specific testimony. A witness who knows the entire picture of a case and understands where his testimony fits will be more likely to limit his testimony to what is necessary, and to deal intelligently with surprise questions.

Using our evaluation matrix of Smedlap's case, you might prepare the following general outline:

GENERAL OUTLINE OF SMEDLAP'S CASE

To win, we must prove the following essential facts:

1. Smedlap cleaned up an oil spill near his lathe on June 16.

2. Greensleeves authorized him to do the work by threatening Smedlap with unspeakable consequences if the spill wasn't cleaned up the next morning.

3. Overtime authorizations have frequently been less formal and less explicit than Greensleeves's words were, and the company has paid overtime for such work.

4. Smedlap did the cleanup work between 7:00 A.M. and 8:00 A.M. on June 16.

5. Smedlap did not receive any pay—even at straight time rates—for that work.

The second step of witness education is to prepare for each witness an outline of his testimony. It should set forth separately numbered facts about which he must testify in order to cover those essential elements of your case he is there to address. I must emphasize that your purpose is *not* to put words in a witness's mouth or to manufacture facts. In this preparation process you (or your colleagues) have already interviewed the witness at least once before generating your evaluation matrix. All facts are, therefore, the *witness's*; your preparation just focuses his attention on those facts that are necessary to your case. Do not underestimate the intelligence of your witnesses. Give them an opportunity to use their intellect to understand your case, and your case will be stronger for the respect you have shown.

A word here about outlines. I prefer outlines because they are generally more effective than verbatim scripts. Outlines permit witnesses to use their own words, yet cover the essential material. Outlines help a witness know the "lay of the land" well enough to jump around on cross-examination without losing orientation. They also help a witness remember that he has a specific number of aspects of what he saw that you want him to mention. Thus, the outline can be a memory aid for the witness, so that he tells the arbitrator exactly what he told you when you interviewed him.

Scripts, on the other hand, invite rote memorization. Memorized testimony frequently sounds like it came from a lawyer's pen rather than the witness's mouth, and that sound invites skepticism from the arbitrator. Memorized testimony requires accurate reproduction and a certain amount of acting ability not universally shared. Finally, a witness with a script is at the mercy of a capable cross-examiner, who can drive him all over the lot and dramatize the rote character of his testimony.

Let's take two examples of testimony outlines from Smedlap's hypothetical case. Assume that you are grievant's attorney and that you have decided to use Smedlap and his co-worker, Ralph Rackstraw, as witnesses. With the assistance of your evaluation matrix, you might generate the following outlines for each witness.

OUTLINE OF WALDO SMEDLAP'S TESTIMONY

1. Identification.
   a. Name—Waldo Smedlap.
   b. Employment—Lathe Operator at Widget Co.
   c. Experience—Five years.

2. Location and Description of Work Area.
   a. Machine area.
   b. Walkways.
   c. Lubricating oil can.
   d. Trash barrels.
   e. Safety poster—"Safety First—Clean Up Your Spills!"

3. <u>Normal Cleanup Responsibilities.</u>
   a. Work area—each lathe operator.
   b. Walkways—cleanup crew.
   c. Experience: Cleanup crew sweeps *only* the walkways and leaves clean trail among steel shavings that had covered *both* walkways and machine areas.

4. <u>The June 15 Spill.</u>
   a. Time of day—3:30 P.M.
   b. Source—leaking oil can.
   c. Location—machine area *and* walkways.
   d. Extent—all the way to trash barrels.

5. <u>Greensleeves's Orders and your Response.</u>
   a. Greensleeves—"Clean it up."
   b. Smedlap—"I'll leave a note for the cleanup guys."
   c. Greensleeves—"Whatever—but this better not be here when I come in tomorrow."
   d. Greensleeves's usual arrival time—7:45 A.M.

6. <u>Overtime Work of June 16.</u>
   a. Work—cleaning spill from machine area and walkways.
   b. Arrival time—6:55 A.M.
   c. Procedure—time card entry.
   d. Identify and offer time card for week ending 6/17.
   e. Situation—oil in work area flowing into walkways but not to trash cans.
   f. Time of work—7:00 A.M. to 8:00 A.M.

7. <u>The Overtime Claim.</u>
   a. June 16 conversation with Greensleeves. Time—Lunch; Location—lunchroom.

Smedlap—"Be sure to put in an overtime slip for me. I came in like you told me at 7:00 and cleaned up the spill."
Greensleeves—"The hell I will. I never authorized any overtime."

b. June 16 entry on time card—"You owe me one hour OT for Friday, 7:00 A.M. to 8:00 A.M."
c. Time of entry—after conversation with Greensleeves.

8. Refusal to Pay.
   a. Next paycheck date—June 22.
   b. No overtime pay.
   c. Identify and offer pay stub dated 6/22 for week ending 6/19.

9. Past Overtime Authorization Experience.
   a. Date—March 15.
   b. Greensleeves's words—"This is a rush job; put it ahead of your other work."
   c. Time of work—March 15 from 4:00 P.M. to 6:30 P.M.
   d. Payment—time and one-half.

10. Why Did You Work the Overtime?
    a. Greensleeves threatened me; he had warned me last week about my "attitude" and I knew the cleanup guys don't usually clean the machine areas.

OUTLINE OF RALPH RACKSTRAW'S TESTIMONY

1. Identification.
   a. Name—Ralph Rackstraw.
   b. Employment—lathe operator at Widget Co.
   c. Experience—ten years.

2. Location and Description of Work Area.
   a. Machine area.
   b. Walkways.
   c. Lubricating oil can.
   d. Trash barrels.
   e. Safety poster—"Safety First—Clean Up Your Spills!"

3. Normal Cleanup Responsibilities.
   a. Work area—each lathe operator.
   b. Walkways—cleanup crew.
   c. Experience: Cleanup crew sweeps *only* the walkways and leaves clean trail among steel shavings that had covered *both* walkways and machine areas.

4. The June 15 Spill.
   a. Time of day—3:30 P.M.
   b. Source—leaking oil can.
   c. Location—machine area *and* walkways.
   d. Extent—all the way to trash barrels.

5. Greensleeves's Order and Smedlap's Response.
   a. Greensleeves—"Clean it up."
   b. Smedlap—"I'll leave a note for the cleanup guys."
   c. Greensleeves—"Whatever—but this better not be here when I come in tomorrow."
   d. Greensleeves's usual arrival time—7:45 A.M.

6. Smedlap's June 16 Work.
   a. Your arrival—7:50 A.M.
   b. What you saw—oil spill gone. Smedlap sitting by lathe dunking doughnut.

7. Past Overtime Authorization Experience.
   a. Date—February 10, 4:00 P.M. to 6:00 P.M. and February 11, 7:00 A.M. to 8:00 A.M.
   b. Words of authorization—"This is an important job, and it better be done by February 12 or you're in big trouble."
   c. Payment—Time and one-half.

Review these outlines with your witness as many times as necessary to assure yourself that the witness understands what factual information you want to elicit and confirms that those facts are indeed true. Obviously, you must change any aspect of the outline that is not consistent with the recollection of the witness.

The third important aspect of witness preparation is general. You must advise your witness what to expect in terms of procedures at the hearing, and you must make absolutely sure he is aware of several basic principles that will contribute to the credibility of his testimony. The first thing you should say to your witness is, "Tell the truth." There are two reasons for this: it is ethically correct and it is effective. The ethical point is obvious. The purpose of witness preparation is not to tell your witnesses what to say. Not so obvious, however, is the efficacy of the advice. First, your witness will be more comfortable if he knows that his only obligation is to tell the truth. Second, if your opponent asks, "Did you speak with your advocate before testifying here today?" and your witness replies, "Yes," your witness will be prepared for the next question. Inexperienced advocates frequently follow up by asking: "What did he say?" to which your witness can honestly reply, "He told me to tell the truth."

As a former advocate, I developed a document to give to witnesses when preparing them. I told the witnesses to read the document. We then discussed it, and they took it with them.

The document itself is a collection of good advice I was given, or read, or learned by painful error. Since it does not purport to be the last word, feel free to add the things you have learned in your own practice.

How to be a Good Witness

1. Your job is to give the facts as you know them. My job is to argue the case. Our mutual job is to convince the arbitrator you are truthful. If you put on a phony act and try to use vocabulary you are not comfortable with your words won't ring true. Dress and speak as you do in your everyday dealings with the world at large.

2. Give only information you have firmly in mind. If you do not *know* the answer to a question you have been asked, say "I do not know." If you do not *remember*, say "I do not remember." Do *not* attempt to be obliging when you do not know an answer or have forgotten it. Do *not* say "I assume so," or "probably," or "possibly." Stick to what you know.

3. Pause briefly before answering each question. Gather your thoughts carefully before answering and do not permit yourself to be hurried. Once you have given an answer it always looks odd when you later change it. Accuracy is far more important than speed.

4. If you don't understand, or if you can't answer the question as asked, say so. If you do not understand, say "I do not understand the question." Do not ask, "Do you mean. . . ?" It is not your job to discover what our opponent's advocate meant. It is his job to ask a clear question.

5. Be candid. Answer *all* questions truthfully, even though there may be unflattering or damaging material. Do not volunteer any information. Your willingness to admit unflattering details may convince the arbitrator of the truth of the important facts.

6. If the answer to a question is "Yes," say so. If the answer to a question is "No," say so. Do not say "I think so," or "I don't

believe so," or "In my opinion." Your answers should be direct, so the arbitrator does not think you are trying to conceal something.

7. If I say, "Objection," stop talking immediately. Do not say anything further until the arbitrator tells you to go ahead and answer the question or the other advocate asks a new question. Listen to what I say in my objection. It may help you to understand what portion of the question was not appropriate.

8. If I ask you a question and you can not remember the answer, say "I don't remember at this time." That will allow me to try to refresh your memory.

9. Never attempt to justify your answers. If you apologize or attempt to justify facts it appears as if you doubt the accuracy or authenticity of your own testimony.

10. Be sure of the facts you supply in answer to a question. If you must estimate something (for example, the distance between two people), the time to do it is before you testify. Discuss with me the way you arrived at your estimate. Once you feel comfortable that you have made the most accurate estimate you can, stick with it.

11. Don't agree with anything just to be agreeable. If our opponent's advocate says: "Wouldn't you agree that X is the case?" do not say "Yes" unless you really agree.

12. Control yourself. Listen to the questions carefully, and answer *ONLY* what was asked. Don't volunteer information, and don't try to show how smart you are. If you don't know an answer, admit that you don't know. Don't be angry, argumentative, or sarcastic with the other advocate; the arbitrator will not be impressed. Remain calm, and trust me to ask all the questions that must be asked.

13. Sometimes an advocate will ask the arbitrator to "exclude witnesses." If this is done, you will have to wait outside the hearing room until it is your turn to testify. It is a good idea to bring something to do or read, since the wait can be a long one.

Once you have discussed this advice with your witnesses, they will have a good idea of the general considerations that will make them able to do the best possible job as witnesses.

Witness Rehearsals

After completing this educational process, rehearse your witnesses. Do at least two "dry runs." Conduct your direct examination just as you would at the hearing, *without* leading. Let the testimony come from your witness in his own words. Let him use his outline the first time through. The second time through, take away the outline and vary the order of your questions to make sure your witness is answering and responding substantively with complete understanding of the case. If your witness seems nervous or unsure, do it again.

After your dry runs satisfy you that your witness understands his direct testimony, then cross-examine him *exactly* as you expect your opponent to do it. For this effort, use the evaluation matrix that you prepared for your opponent's case to focus on the issues that will be of greatest concern. It is far better to learn your case's weaknesses during preparation than at the hearing before the arbitrator. It is also important that your witness take the stand at the arbitration with a realistic expectation of what will happen. If your dry run on cross-examination produces damaging but not critical new information, consider eliciting that material candidly on your direct case, to avoid your opponent's bringing it out on cross-examination and accusing you of hiding something. After your dry run of cross-examination, also do the sort of redirect that you would at the hearing so that your witness knows from experience that you can correct misimpressions that may have arisen on cross-examination.

An important part of your preparation will be to anticipate and address any potential problems of *demeanor* evidence. Demeanor evidence includes anything about your witness's appearance or behavior at the hearing that the arbitrator may observe and consider relevant to his conclusion on any issue. The best known—and probably the least significant—example of demeanor evidence is the classic "shifty" eyes and nervous handwringing that supposedly suggest dishonesty. I have seen witnesses with amblyopia (a muscular dysfunction producing shifting eyes) and genuine anxiety about testifying that produced trembling of their entire bodies. In none of those cases was there any conflict of fact—just shifty eyes and handwringing. I have seen sweating witnesses who bolt for the bathroom immediately after their testimony. I have seen composed, calm liars who can tell you the earth is flat and state with conviction that they have seen the edges. As a result, I find those matters of demeanor of no use to resolve questions of credibility.

There are, however, some tendencies of witnesses that destroy either the witnesses's credibility or the arbitrator's patience. Five types of witnesses leap to mind: the Long-winded, the Short-winded, the Antagonist, the Qualifier, and the Good Buddy.

The Long-winded witness feels a need to explain gravity before he can say whether he saw the wrench drop to the floor. He often prefaces his answers with: "You have to understand. . . ." This preface usually leads into an explanation of matters that have little or no bearing on his testimony. Sometimes this witness begins an answer cogently, but then gets lost in his own thought processes because everything he says reminds him of something else. He then tells you about that "something else." And keeps telling you. At some time—it usually seems eons later—he asks, "Have I answered your question?"

A subspecies of the Long-winded witness is the speaker of pure Bureaucrat. It is a language with no active verbs. A torrent of words is loosed upon the listener, in the hope that he will be too concerned with drowning to worry about understanding what was said. The witness who speaks Bureaucrat will never say, "I decided," but only "It was decided that." The latter phrase, according to the linguistic conventions of Bureaucrat, absolves the speaker of all responsibility for bad decisions. By spouting noun strings, the speaker of Bureaucrat can obfuscate almost any answer. For instance, if asked: "Did you make a decision at that meeting?" the witness will reply, "At that point in time we were actively engaged in a decision-making type mode." This answer, of course, leaves the witness free to later decide whether it would be more advantageous to say yes or no.

Long-winded witnesses and speakers of Bureaucrat exist both in business and government. Your job as an advocate is to pursue your witness until you get to the core of the matter you need him to testify to. Then practice interrupting the witness every time he tries to take a running start on an answer, speak Bureaucrat, or go on indefinitely. It is a form of aversion therapy, since this witness hates being interrupted. If you can convince the witness you will have to interrupt him for the arbitrator's benefit, he may be able to temporarily change his behavior. Be aware, however, that under the stress of actually testifying the witness may revert to Long-windedness.

The Short-winded witness is the exact opposite. He has been impressed, usually at an early age, with cowboy movies in which the hero says only "Yup" or "Nope." When interviewing him you have to drag answers from him. The problem he causes as a witness is that he forces you to ask leading questions. Not only are leading questions technically improper on direct, but even where an arbitrator allows them he winds up hearing your testimony, and not the witness's. His testimony then becomes nothing more than confirmation of what you are saying. Since you did not witness the events to which he is testifying, your testimony is utterly unpersuasive to an arbitrator. The best thing to do with this witness is to drag answers out of him, in his own words, when preparing him. Write them down. When you ask him a question, remind him of what he previously said, so he does not need to search for words. Do, however, insist that he give a full answer each time. Tell him that the time for mono-syllabic answers is on cross-examination.

The Antagonist is hostile to the process, the grievant, the advocates, the arbitrator, or all of the above. This hostility makes him a poor witness because it supplies an apparent motive for him to lie. It also causes problems in the hearing when he tries to assert himself by arguing inappropriately with the advocate or the arbitrator. It is important to determine why this person is hostile, and to what. In many instances, manage-ment officials feel the arbitration process is a direct affront to their authority as managers. They do not want some arbitrator sitting in judgment of what they have done. It is sometimes possible to get the Antagonist to put aside his hostility for the purpose of winning the arbitration. If your opponent is aware of this tendency, however, you should expect a stringent cross-examination designed to goad the witness into an outburst. Your best course of action is to let the Antagonist know that you understand the source of his anger, but that winning the case may depend entirely upon his keeping it under control.

The Qualifier is incapable of making a statement. To the Qualifier, the world is so complex a place that no simple state-ments can be true. In one sense, he is right. But when a witness qualifies every statement it appears that he is hedging, and perhaps shading the truth. For instance, when asked if he saw

Ben hit Dan, the Qualifier will reply, "Of course, I could be mistaken, but I am pretty sure that I saw something like Ben hitting Dan, although I have to say it was some time ago and my memory is far from perfect." In fact, the Qualifier was standing only ten feet away and volunteered that he had seen it during your investigation. You must convince the Qualifier that everyone involved understands the innate frailties of human perception. You must warn him that arbitrators are likely to be convinced, however, that an over-qualified answer is unreliable.

The Good Buddy wants to be everyone's friend. When asked a question he tries to give the answer he thinks the questioner wants. He does a great job on direct examination, responding with precisely the answers that you want. He is devastating on cross-examination when the opposing advocate asks him to speculate about what might be possible. He speculates in ways that completely undercut his direct examination. He is dangerous to you both as a witness, and as a participant in your investigation of the events. During the investigation you must avoid giving him clues about what you would like to hear. In preparing him to testify, you must show him how his answers on mock cross-examination undercut his testimony on direct.

While each of these witness types present demeanor problems, the problems are all secondary. They do not provide direct demeanor evidence undercutting their testimony. Rather, their demeanor problems lead to a loss in credibility or effectiveness and render them less persuasive witnesses. Much more significant are those matters of conduct that are relevant to the case at hand.

For example, in a discharge case, grievant denied three alleged acts of picket-line violence: knocking a supervisor down, smashing a co-worker's attaché case against a concrete floor, and spitting on two other co-workers. During the hearing grievant sat quietly while a parade of witnesses described his aggressive, explosive rage. As five o'clock approached, the arbitrator observed that another day's hearing would probably be necessary. With no more cause than that, grievant suddenly blew up, smashing the table and screaming that everyone was jerking him around and that the hearing better finish that day. The hearing did go late, ending at 7:00 P.M. Grievant got his answer sooner, but the arbitrator got conclusive demeanor evidence on grievant's true nature. Other examples of relevant demeanor evidence include grievant's arriving an hour and a half late for a hearing on tardiness charges, or being hostile and uncooperative in a case involving allegations of discourtesy to customers.

Arbitrators observe how witnesses behave. If that behavior is relevant to a matter at issue, it will be persuasive demeanor evidence. In cases where demeanor could be dispositive, you should advise your witnesses and warn them. If you see a witness misbehaving in a relevant way during a dry run, you ought to ask yourself whether to reevaluate his credibility and the appropriateness of settlement.

The "Care and Feeding" of Witnesses

Preparing testimony also includes seeing to the mechanical trivia and not-so-trivial details of the environment in which your witnesses will testify. Your purpose is to facilitate testimony and to ensure circumstances that will maximize the likelihood your witnesses will testify as you plan. Here are some basic examples of things you might consider to accomplish that purpose.

Transportation: Give your witnesses written instructions and directions including the time, date, and place of hearing as well as how to get there. Depending on the sophistication of your witnesses, or their familiarity with the city where the hearing is being held, consider giving each a timetable of when he should leave home or hotel to arrive on time at the hearing. Be sure to get telephone numbers where the witnesses can be reached during the daytime and in the evenings, in case the hearing is postponed or canceled. A witness who has made an unnecessary trip to a canceled hearing will probably be resentful and uncooperative on the adjourned date. A witness who has gotten lost and barely made it to the hearing may be so upset that he forgets half his testimony.

Subpoenas: In some cases, a witness may be willing to testify but uncomfortable about *appearing* to have been willing. Address that discomfort with a timely subpoena that he can show to others at the workplace to establish that he has no choice in the matter. Even if his concern is unfounded, the witness's peace of mind will contribute to the effectiveness of his testimony. Rather than trying to convince the witness that no one will think badly of him for volunteering to testify, obtain the subpoena.

Special Needs: Inquire about special needs of your witnesses, such as schedule conflicts, child care obligations, transportation or dietary requirements. Address those problems beforehand so that they are *off* your witness's mind. A witness whose attention is distracted by real but irrelevant concerns is more likely to make mistakes. Avoid that possibility if you can by simple consideration.

Sequestration: Prepare your witnesses to expect sequestration, especially if you intend to ask for that yourself. (Of course, you may have already given a copy of "How to Be a Good Witness" to your witnesses, in which case you have prepared them.) Tell them that they are not being excluded because someone thinks they will lie if they hear what the other side says, but because hearing someone else's testimony may subconsciously alter their own. Advise them to bring books, knitting, cards, or a board game to help while away their boring hours outside the hearing room. This is especially important for

97

a nervous witness to keep his mind off his anxiety. Make sure that your hearing location has comfortable accommodations for sequestered witnesses.

Preparing Real Evidence

Documents and other real evidence are *things* that prove a fact in issue or establish the basis to infer a fact in issue. Witnesses testify; real evidence *is*. Like testimony, real evidence must be competent (authentic) and material (proving a relevant fact). Here are some examples of real evidence:

- In a theft case, grievant's gym bag containing thirty bottles of company product that he was trying to sneak out of the plant.
- In an absenteeism case, warning letters and letters imposing prior progressive discipline.
- In a contract interpretation case, a written bargaining demand that the union or employer failed to achieve in earlier negotiations.
- In a seniority case, the employer's posting of the vacant position.

Photographs, ruined product, broken tools, diagrams, payroll reports, business records—all are real evidence whose existence and contents tend to establish relevant facts.

Selecting appropriate real evidence is like selecting witnesses. Your evaluation matrix, column 3, lists your sources of proof for each necessary fact. As you did with witnesses, compare the probative value and persuasive impact of each document or thing listed in column 3. Choose the one that most directly and conclusively establishes the fact in issue.

In the Smedlap case, for example, chart F, the employer's evaluation matrix on the authorization issue, discloses written memoranda expressly authorizing specific overtime. They are a direct and conclusive probative resource. As employer representative, you should select an assortment of such memoranda to establish the consistent past practice of written, express authorization for all overtime. Indeed, you should hope to find specific memoranda to grievant himself that would show he was on notice that written authorization was required.

Having selected real evidence, you must immediately begin the process of locating and securing it for use in your case. Do *not*, under any circumstances, take your client's word that the evidence exists and will be made available at the hearing. Start the search *immediately*, and insist on having the evidence as soon as it is located. This is not to suggest that your client may intentionally deceive you. Memories may be faulty, filing systems are often imperfect, files in storage frequently defy location, and prior obligations delay searches. Imagine your frustration if, on the day of hearing, you learn that no one could locate an essential piece of real evidence on which you had built your case.

What if the real evidence is in the hands of your adversary or of some third party? Securing evidence or information from the other side for preparation in labor arbitration has a statutory assist. Section 8(a)(5) of the National Labor Relations Act as amended ("NLRA") imposes on private sector employers an obligation to bargain in good faith. Good faith bargaining includes the obligation to provide the union with information necessary to fulfill its representation duty, both in negotiating and in administering grievances. Many states' public sector collective bargaining laws include a similar obligation.

If you must secure real evidence from a third party for production at an arbitration hearing (or if your employer adversary is recalcitrant), the answer is a subpoena *duces tecum*. (The Latin means, literally, "under pain, bring with you.") State arbitration laws modeled on the Uniform Arbitration Act[2] give arbitrators subpoena power; that is, power to compel witnesses' attendance at hearings and production of evidence. In some states, the parties' attorney can issue subpoenas in arbitration proceedings.

If you want to resist an arbitral subpoena, you must move at the hearing to quash it by showing the evidence sought is immaterial or incompetent. A quashed subpoena is a nullity and has no compulsive effect. If the arbitrator denies your motion to quash, the subpoena remains effective and subject to enforcement. Chapter 8 on ancillary litigation details the typical methods of enforcement by a civil court of competent jurisdiction. As noted there, if your opponent refuses to obey a subpoena you can ask the arbitrator to draw an adverse inference from the refusal. That is, ask him to assume that the document your opponent refused to provide would show the favorable matter you allege it contains. Or, that a witness who is under the control of your opponent who is not produced would have testified favorably to your position.

Having located and secured real evidence, you must inspect it yourself. *You* must see the original, not a copy. I have seen numerous cases in which the original of a disputed document contains different color inks that establish certain entries were not simultaneous. That possibly relevant fact would not be disclosed by a monochrome photocopy. Examine the original to ensure that no such discrepancies exist.

Having approved the document, you must select, ensure the availability of, and prepare a witness who can qualify the document or thing for admission into evidence. That process of qualification, which involves establishing the exhibit's authenticity and materiality, is covered in detail in Chapter 5.

---

2. *See* Appendix 1.

Finally, if the evidence is a document, prepare sufficient *legible* copies for distribution at the hearing. At a minimum, there should be four: one for the arbitrator, one for your opponent, one for you, and one for the witness whom you will interrogate concerning the document. Lacking that last copy, the witness must look on with the arbitrator, possibly distracting both. The alternative is giving the witness your own copy, which leaves you to interrogate blindly. Neither is worth the price of an extra copy.

Once you have assembled your documents, with copies, it is useful to put them into separate files or a notebook. If there are voluminous documents, or a large number of documents, a three hole binder containing the documents is an excellent idea. If you prepare four binders, with numbered tabs for the exhibits, the arbitrator will have an easy time following your arguments as you move from document to document. What you want to avoid, at all costs, is having a huge pile of documents in front of you at the hearing. You look ill-prepared if you fumble through this mass of papers each time you try to introduce or refer to an exhibit. It is also useful to have a separate paper or set of papers on which you have listed exhibit numbers and descriptions of exhibits, together with a space for indicating whether they have been accepted into evidence.

Conclusion

Preparing your proofs can involve a lot of drudgery. It is, nevertheless, essential. The dividends you will earn in smooth presentation of your case will make the effort well worth your while. Moreover, the arbitrator will be impressed by and appreciate your professionalism. And that can't hurt.

4

Selecting the Arbitrator

Introduction

Choosing an arbitrator is an important part of case preparation. It is not, however, quite as important as many advocates think. While you would do your client a disservice if you failed to match the arbitrator to your case needs, choosing the "right" arbitrator will not guarantee a favorable outcome. Indeed, there will usually be a number of arbitrators who are suited to your case and the real problem will be in finding someone your opponent will accept.

In this chapter I will be discussing the mechanisms available for choosing arbitrators, and scheduling hearings. I will describe where arbitrator's awards are published, how to read those awards to glean useful information about arbitrators, and what to ask your colleagues about an arbitrator. I will also describe other resources available for learning about arbitrators and the problem of availability.

Contractual Procedures for Choosing an Arbitrator

There are three different ways in which you can provide for arbitrator selection in the collective bargaining agreement. First, you can designate a specific arbitrator, or panel of arbitrators, to hear all disputes that arise under the contract's arbitration clause. Second, you can incorporate by reference the rules of a specific neutral agency that has a mechanism for providing lists of arbitrators. Third, you can omit any reference to specific arbitrators or neutral agencies, and decide upon how an arbitrator will be selected every time there is a case that is ready for arbitration. Each method has its advantages and disadvantages.

Designating an Arbitrator or Panel

The first method, designating an arbitrator or panel, has significant advantages for parties with a continuing relationship and a fair number of cases. All of the haggling over who is acceptable occurs only once, when you first name a person or panel. Thereafter, when you have to arrange an arbitration hearing your choice of arbitrators is limited to the named neutral or a panel.

Panels

You can designate two types of panels: rotating and pool. It is advantageous to use a rotating panel, one in which arbitrators are selected for a particular case when they are the next name on the panel, as opposed to a pool of arbitrators, from which a name will be picked for each case. With the rotating panel the parties can set a time limit for availability. If an arbitrator is not available to hear the case within the time limit, the next arbitrator on the list is chosen. With a rotating panel there is never a question of which panel arbitrator will hear a particular case. The only question is whether the next arbitrator in the rotation is available within the time agreed upon by the parties. In addition, if you need rapid hearings in a high volume of cases, you can simply schedule hearings on certain days of the month. You fill those days with whichever cases are ready to go to arbitration. If you are not able to fill a day, you pay the arbitrator's cancellation fee. This method has worked well for very large bargaining units with a high volume of disciplinary grievances, and it has only rarely resulted in paying a late cancellation fee.

If the panel is a pool, then the parties must agree, among limited choices, on the arbitrator for a particular case. The disadvantage of this option is that it may be time consuming to agree on an arbitrator in each case. It is, of course, less time consuming than using a neutral agency's panel lists. The advantage is that you still maintain the control necessary to feel assured that you are choosing the arbitrator who is right for a particular case.

Single Arbitrator

Naming a single arbitrator, the alternative to a panel, is most useful in two situations: when the volume of cases is low, or when you want to promote mediation at the final step of your procedure. If you only expect a couple of cases a year, naming a single arbitrator is satisfactory. By having the arbitrator agree to any unique requirements you have beforehand, you can be assured that your chosen arbitrator will not turn you down when you have your first case. Since the volume of cases is low, the arbitrator is unlikely to use up his acceptability during the contract's term. You should, however, keep this possibility in mind.

In many collective bargaining relationships there comes a time when you have a difficult "political" case that will result in the arbitrator losing his acceptability, no matter which way he decides. There are two ways of handling this. You can make the named arbitrator the "default" choice in your contract, or you can provide for replacing the arbitrator if one party becomes unhappy during the term of the contract. Under the "default" option the parties contractually agree to choose arbitrators ad hoc but to use Smith if they do not agree on an arbitrator. Ordinarily, they will simply use Smith. In a political case they can choose a more expendable arbitrator. Alternatively, the parties can provide for an annual review during which either side can reject the named arbitrator, obliging the parties to reach agreement on a new person to be named. You may recognize that a certain decision was correct, even though it upheld the position of your opponent. You may, however, be obliged to get rid of the arbitrator because your side has to blame the outcome of a particularly sensitive arbitration on the failings of the arbitrator. Thus, the anual review gives you the opportunity to strike a particular arbitrator, without having to defend the benefits of arbitration to unhappy partisans on your side.

Imposing Conditions on the Designated Arbitrator or Panel

If you decide to use a panel, you will have the opportunity to determine the terms under which arbitrators will be asked to serve on the panel. Regardless of whether you have a rotating panel, a pool, or a single arbitrator, if you have some conditions you wish to impose on the arbitration process, such as requiring an expedited hearing or bench decision, you can ascertain beforehand whether an arbitrator is willing to accept the conditions. You can, if you choose, also impose a format for the award (for ease of reference and cross-indexing) and uniform billing practices.

The conditions you impose on the arbitrator or panel will determine the willingness of experienced arbitrators to serve on your panel. One possibility is to impose no terms, simply accepting the policies each arbitrator employs. This will make it most likely that arbitrators you choose will be willing to serve on the panel. If you only require a particular format for awards, or procedure for billing, it is unlikely that any arbitrator will be reluctant to serve because of those terms.

There are three terms, however, that are most likely to affect experienced arbitrators' willingness to serve: expedited scheduling of hearings, short time limits for preparing the award, and low rates of pay. The combination of all three terms is most likely to cause an experienced arbitrator to decline your offer to be named in the contract. All of these terms may be quite acceptable to newer arbitrators. Each needs further discussion.

If you have cases you want heard quickly, you will want to require expedited scheduling, say within thirty days of contacting the arbitrator.[1] If so, you may have to have the cases heard by someone other than the best known arbitrator in your area. The better known an arbitrator, the farther ahead he is likely to schedule. In one case, a California court decided that a union did not breach its duty of fair representation by waiting eighteen months to get a particular arbitrator. Ordinarily, acceptable arbitrators are not booking cases that far in advance. They may not, however, be able to promise dates within thirty days of contact.

The time you give an arbitrator to decide a case, after the hearing is closed, will often determine whether the arbitrator will accept a panel appointment. Some contracts call for a written award within three days of the close of the hearing. In a complicated contract interpretation case, this is too short a period for reflection and writing, particularly if there are briefs. What ordinarily occurs is that at the end of the hearing the parties offer to give the arbitrator whatever time is necessary to decide the case. If the arbitrator asks for additional time, one party will always acquiesce and the other party is put in the position of agreeing or looking churlish. While this is an unusually brief period, it highlights the problem with requiring awards too quickly: arbitrators will not accept your designation, or the requirement gets ignored. On the other hand, a

---

1. A complete set of procedures for expedited cases can be found in AAA's Expedited Arbitration Rules. *See* Appendix 7.

reasonable requirement, such as thirty days after the arbitrator receives briefs or the hearing is over, will not put many arbitrators off and will usually be adhered to.

The third term that may limit the arbitrators who will accept a designation is pay that is substantially below the median rate in your area. Arbitrator's median per diem rates vary from region to region. The median rate in your area can usually be obtained by checking with the Regional Director of the American Arbitration Association. If you have a high volume of cases, and if the rate you are willing to pay is the median rate in your area, many arbitrators who ordinarily charge a higher rate will accept an appointment to your panel. The volume of cases your panel produces will determine whether the arbitrator will accept. A high volume panel, which allows the arbitrator to get to know new parties or a new industry, is quite attractive.

If the best known arbitrators in your area will not serve on your panel, you have a very attractive alternative. There are many competent new arbitrators who are anxious for work. They may not be widely known, but that is not a reflection on their competence. As part of their apprenticeship, highly qualified new arbitrators are looking for panel appointments. You can pay a lower rate and employ an efficient process, without sacrificing quality. For instance, if you have a high volume of cases involving disciplinary infractions with penalties less than discharge, you may want to use a rotating panel with some newer arbitrators. You will be able to schedule the cases quickly and get a decision soon after the hearing. Since newer arbitrators are less likely to have a backlog of cases, they can adhere to one or two week award requirements for straightforward disciplinary cases. As a side benefit, you will learn who you find acceptable among the new people, and will be able to add to your personal list of arbitrators.

Using Written Side Letters for Uniform Panels

One last word on panels. If you use panels you can further control the arbitration process through written agreements that set forth the parties' understandings on various procedural and substantive issues. For instance, you may decide that the standard of proof in all of your cases is "a preponderance of the credible evidence," or that no offers of settlement or compromise will be admitted, or that there will be no closing briefs, or that there will be no stenographic record of the proceedings. You can agree that you will not pay more than one day of study time for each day of hearing in a disciplinary case. You can limit the number of pages in the written award. You can agree on any number of things. If you incorporate these agreements into a letter of understanding and make agreement to that letter of understanding a condition for serving on the panel, you can insure that the arbitration process will be both uniform and precisely tailored to your needs.

Designating Arbitrators by Adopting the Rules of a Neutral Agency

Instead of selecting an arbitrator you may wish to agree only on the method for selecting an arbitrator. There are three choices: you can say nothing about how you will select an arbitrator, you can agree to a specific method for selecting an arbitrator, or you can agree to use the services of a neutral agency. If you say nothing about how you will select an arbitrator, you will have to agree to a method in the midst of your substantive dispute. If you are unable to agree upon an arbitrator, arbitration statutes generally provide for a court to appoint one. If the method you agreed upon for selecting an arbitrator —at the time you negotiated the collective bargaining agreement—works, you will then be able to proceed to arbitration. If it does not, the arbitration statutes generally permit a court to appoint an arbitrator. This leaves the third method, using a neutral agency.

If you use the services of a neutral agency to choose an arbitrator you may, in some instances, have the option of using that agency to administer the case. Since case administration is a separate matter, it will be taken up in the next section. There are a number of different neutral agencies whose services can be used for choosing an arbitrator: the Federal Mediation and Conciliation Service, state boards (such as the California Mediation/Conciliation Service, or the New York State Mediation Board), state public sector agencies (such as the New York or California Public Employment Relations Board), and the American Arbitration Association. Each neutral agency has its own procedures for assisting the parties to choose an arbitrator. A brief comparison of the procedures can give you some idea of what you can expect if you use each of the agencies. You should, however, ask the neutral agency for its procedures before agreeing to use it.

Federal Mediation and Conciliation Service (FMCS)

The FMCS maintains lists of arbitrators that are made available on request. The request can either be joint or separate, and it is made on FMCS's form R-43. Upon receipt of the request FMCS sends each side a list of seven arbitrators together with their biographies and fee requirements. The parties can request a panel that has arbitrators with certain experience (for instance, in the canning industry or the public sector), or certain background (for instance, a lawyer with experience in pension matters). FMCS has the ability to provide such specialized lists. If there is no special request, the lists are regional so that the arbitrators will be available from an area that is relatively close to the location of the dispute.

After the lists are sent the parties can proceed in a number of ways. They can use any method of selection contained in their collective bargaining agreement, or they can choose by alternate striking, or they can strike and number names on the list. The usual procedure for alternate striking is to flip a coin to determine who will strike the first name. Since there is an odd number of arbitrators on the list, the person who does not strike first gets to choose between the last two arbitrators on the list. If you agree to strike and number the arbitrators, each party has the opportunity to eliminate any arbitrator it finds totally unacceptable. First, each party strikes any unacceptable arbitrator. Then, each party numbers the remaining choices, with the first choice numbered one. The lists are sent to FMCS, which determines who has the lowest aggregate number. That is the arbitrator designated to hear the case. FMCS sends that arbitrator a notice of designation that contains the addresses and telephone numbers of the parties. It is up to the arbitrator to set a date for the hearing with the parties.

If the parties are unable to agree to any names on the list, FMCS will send a second list. If the parties still can not agree, FMCS has no power to designate an arbitrator, unless that power is contained in the collective bargaining agreement. Presumably, that could also be done by a subsequent written agreement. If FMCS is not explicitly given the power to designate an arbitrator, you will have to rely upon a court to make the designation.[2]

California State Mediation/Conciliation Service (CSMCS)

CSMCS will respond to a request for a list of arbitrators that is submitted jointly or singly. It has no special form upon which

---

2. The rules of the FMCS are codified at 29 C.F.R. 1404. *See* Appendix 11. Since these rules may change, you should check the current rules before relying upon what is contained in this section.

the request must be submitted. Ordinarily, the list contains five names, although the parties can request a larger list. The CSMCS sends the biographies of the listed arbitrators, but not their fee schedules. It is up to the parties to decide upon how they will select an arbitrator from the list. If they can not agree on an arbitrator, they can jointly request a further list. CSMCS will not, even if there is a joint request from the parties, appoint an arbitrator.

After sending the list CSMCS does not have any further part in the selection of the arbitrator or administration of the process. Its letter transmitting the list indicates a willingness to act as a conduit for communication between the parties, should they need help in setting the place and time of the hearing. CSMCS does not have the capacity to provide special purpose lists, or arbitrators with specific qualifications.

New York Public Employment Relations Board (PERB)

The New York PERB is typical of state public sector labor relations agencies. It has established, by regulation, its Voluntary Arbitration Rules of Procedure. These rules require subjecting the dispute to the procedures contained in them. They do not permit the parties to simply use the services of PERB to choose an arbitrator. PERB's procedure for helping the parties choose an arbitrator is as follows.

After receiving a demand for arbitration or a submission agreement, PERB sends the parties identical lists of five arbitrators selected from its panel. You get a biographical sketch provided by the arbitrator, as well as a fee schedule. If you have not chosen a method for picking the arbitrator, the rules provide a method.

If more than three names on a list are acceptable, the parties rank them in order of preference, striking any unacceptable names. If two or more names are unacceptable, the parties can ask for a second list. Each party has the right to ask for one additional list. After that, the Director of Conciliation takes "whatever steps necessary to designate an arbitrator." He is forbidden, however, from designating an arbitrator who was stricken by either party. After an arbitrator is designated, he is notified by PERB. It is then his responsibility to communicate with the parties to arrange the time and place of the hearing.

American Arbitration Association (AAA)

AAA is a not-for-profit private corporation that maintains lists of labor arbitrators who are available under its various labor arbitration rules. By writing AAA into the collective bargaining agreement you also are deemed to have agreed to its labor arbitration rules. (*See* Appendix 3.) The rules provide for initiating an arbitration by a demand for arbitration or a submission agreement. AAA sends the parties identical lists of names from its national panel of arbitrators. These are accompanied by biographies and information on fees. The number of names sent varies among AAA's regional offices, with some sending nine and others eleven. Within seven days the parties must strike the name of any arbitrator who is unacceptable and number the rest of the arbitrators in order of preference, with one being the most preferred. If both parties have ranked the same arbitrator one, that is the arbitrator chosen. Otherwise, AAA determines which arbitrator has the lowest score and the closest ranking. For instance, if arbitrator X was ranked four by one side and one by the other, while arbitrator Y was ranked two by one side and three by the other, arbitrator Y would be designated. After designating the arbitrator AAA handles all of the arrangements for the date and location of the hearing. It charges an administrative fee for this work.

Initiating and Administering a Case

Whether you use the services of a neutral agency or act on your own, certain issues may come up before the hearing. If you have not agreed on how to handle them, or if you have not agreed to the rules of a neutral agency, these issues may result in litigation before the arbitration. There are four major issues. First, what happens if you are unable to choose an arbitrator? Second, what happens if you can not agree on where or when the arbitration will take place? Third, who pays if the arbitrator has a late cancellation fee and the other side makes an untimely request for an adjournment? Fourth, what happens if the other side says it has no intention of showing up at the scheduled hearing? Each of these pre-hearing problems can be anticipated through specific language in your collective bargaining agreement, or you can adopt the rules of a neutral agency in your collective bargaining agreement.

The first problem, who chooses an arbitrator if the parties can not, is handled most simply under the rules of neutral agencies. As previously noted, modern arbitration statutes provide for court appointment of an arbitrator if the parties' method of selection fails. It is unnecessary to litigate, however, if a neutral agency is used. FMCS requires that the collective bargaining agreement authorize it to designate an arbitrator. For public sector disputes, the PERBs generally have rules of procedure that permit them to designate an arbitrator if the parties have agreed to be bound by their rules. Finally, AAA's rules authorize it to designate an arbitrator if the parties are unable to select one. Even if you agree to submit the matter to AAA after the dispute occurs, you can still incorporate its rules, thereby insuring a method of selection if you can not agree on an arbitrator.

The second problem, agreeing upon the location and date for a hearing, is most readily solved by adopting the rules of administration of a neutral agency. It is simple enough to designate a location for hearings in a collective bargaining agreement. Designating the dates of hearings in cases that do not yet exist is much more difficult. If you have recurring disciplinary matters, you can designate a certain day, such as the second Tuesday of every month, for the hearings. It is much more difficult to schedule contract interpretation cases in the agreement. Consequently, it is easiest to use a neutral agency. AAA's Voluntary Labor Arbitration Rules (*see* Appendix 3) provide that it can decide where a hearing will be held. Since the rules give it the power to appoint an arbitrator, and since the arbitrator has the power to fix the date of the hearing, if you agree to be bound by the rules, you will be assured that a time and place for the hearing will be set.

The third problem, paying for late cancellations, is likely to be covered in the collective bargaining agreement. Most agreements call for splitting the arbitrator's fees and expenses. The rules of neutral agencies generally do the same. The New York PERB has a novel method. It provides that the party responsible for an adjournment pays the late cancellation fee, unless there is an agreement to do otherwise.

The fourth problem, what to do if one side insists it is not showing up at the hearing, is handled well by the rules of neutral agencies. You can, of course, agree in your collective bargaining agreement that the arbitrator will have the power to hold an ex parte hearing. Or, in states whose statutes permit it (or in federal court) move to compel arbitration. It is much easier, however, to operate under the rules of an agency, such as AAA, which permits the arbitrator to hold a hearing when a party who was duly notified fails to attend. The problems of arbitrability, which may be related to a party's refusal to attend the hearing, will be discussed in Chapter 8.

Finding and Reading Arbitrators' Awards

Introduction

Most experienced advocates have developed a list of acceptable arbitrators or a method for choosing arbitrators. Some of these lists and methods, however, are suspect. The list may simply be arbitrators with whom the advocate has won cases. The method may be a variation on reading tea leaves, or pseudo-scientific research, or relying on how colleagues feel about a particular arbitrator. There is no method for choosing arbitrators that will guarantee you will win your case. In fact, no method can even guarantee that you will always get the right arbitrator for your case. But that is the goal. You want to match the arbitrator to the needs of your case or (when you are selecting a panel) cases. There are a number of resources you can use. The arbitrator's published awards, colleagues who have appeared before the arbitrator, and commercial services. I shall examine the method best suited for getting the most out of each of these tools.

Published Awards

There are a number of places where arbitrators' awards are published. The Bureau of National Affairs (BNA) publishes *Labor Arbitration Reports*; the Commerce Clearing House (CCH) publishes a similar set of volumes called *Labor Arbitration Awards*. Both contain full texts of awards. The AAA has three different publications that deal with arbitration awards: *Summary of Labor Arbitration Awards, Labor Arbitration in Government*, and *Arbitration in the Schools*. None of these AAA publications contains the complete text of arbitration awards. Rather, they contain headings that describe the major points of the award, and a synopsis of the award that includes quotations. At the end of each award is an indication of the length of the original. These can be ordered from AAA at a nominal price. These services are all indexed by subject matter and arbitrator. I will describe these resources in fuller detail in the section on Resources for Evaluating Arbitrators.

How to Read an Arbitrator's Awards

Reading an arbitrator's awards is both an art and a science. It is an art, because a reader who is a competent literary critic can extract a great deal of information about the arbitrator from the written award. It is a science, because anyone can learn a method for looking at the award that will be helpful in deciding whether to use a particular arbitrator. I will leave the art for those who are fortunate enough to have it, and concentrate upon the science.

There are five aspects of an award you should concentrate on: directness, economy, sensitivity, remedy, and the intellectual predilections of the arbitrator. I will examine each.

Directness: An award should be direct. The facts and issues should be clearly stated and the arguments of the parties directly addressed. Be suspicious of an award that recites the stipulated issue and then goes on to narrate all of the testimony in excruciating detail. The issues should focus the testimony so that only relevant facts are included in the award. There should be a clear statement of the reasons for the decision. The arbitrator must demonstrate the mental processes he went through in deciding the issue as he did. If it is impossible to extract from the decision the arbitrator's reason or reasons for deciding the case as he did, you can suspect the clarity of the arbitrator's mental processes. An arbitrator who raises a series of equal "considerations" and then reaches a conclusion without indicating the link, has not provided a direct award. You should also be suspicious if there is absolutely no statement of the reasons for a decision. The arbitrator who states the issue, the facts, the arguments of the parties, and then a conclusion has failed to share his mental processes with you. There may be a good reason for the failure. The case may have been decided viscerally, rather than on the basis of a rational theory.

Economy: The second characteristic to look for is economy. The facts and the arguments should be stated concisely. A long recitation that combines relevant and irrelevant facts may indicate an inability to distinguish between the two. A synopsis of the testimony of each witness simply shows you that the arbitrator was awake or read the transcript, not that he understood the significance of that testimony. Simply quoting the arguments of the parties, at great length, may indicate that the arbitrator failed to assimilate those arguments. A succinct paraphrase shows that the arbitrator understood the arguments.

Another aspect of economy is the arbitrator's ability to support the conclusion simply, with a minimum of wasted words. Arbitral statements that are unnecessary to support a conclusion are potentially mischievous. General statements tend to take on a life of their own, and may lead from this grievance directly into a new one. In addition, a multiplicity of reasons for arriving at a single conclusion may leave you guessing as to precisely why the arbitrator decided the way he did. What aspect of your client's behavior needs to be changed in order to get the result you seek? If it is not possible to tell from the award, then it will have limited value for guiding the future relationship between the parties.

Sensitivity: The third aspect of an award is the arbitrator's sensitivity to the continuing relationship of the parties. Sometimes it is necessary to call a liar precisely that. At other times it may be more politic to speak of a lack of credibility. Most good arbitrators know when to do which. If the arbitrator uses emotionally toned language, it may be a clue about the conduct of the hearing or the arbitrator's ability to maintain his distance. In some instances it is a reflection of a hearing that was acrimonious and out of control. In other instances, it is an indication that the arbitrator was not successful in separating his feelings from the issues in the case. When one side has acted in bad faith or in violation of the contract, it is possible to describe the actions without impugning the actors. If the arbitrator does not do so, it may indicate that he decided the case viscerally.

Remedies: The fourth aspect to note in reading an award is the way the arbitrator deals with remedies. For most parties, the remedy is the key part of the award. It describes how much they won or lost. Arbitrators vary in the amount of attention they give to the remedy. Some seem satisfied to have decided the issues in the case and give almost no explanation for the remedy, other than characterizing it as "appropriate." Others simply announce a remedy, and leave it to the reader to determine how they got from the conclusion to the remedy. Still others apply a standard for determining the remedy that they enunciate in the award itself. The specificity with which the arbitrator describes the remedy, the breadth of the remedy, and whether the arbitrator "retains jurisdiction," are all important to the finality of the award. A carefully specified remedy is most likely to be capable of simple execution. A broad remedy may involve the parties in protracted wrangles over what is owed. By "retaining jurisdiction," the arbitrator makes himself available to hear disputes over the way in which the remedy is calculated.

There is some disagreement among arbitrators about the propriety of "retaining jurisdiction." As a general matter, once the arbitrator has issued his award he has no further powers, except those given him by contract or statute. State statutes often provide for the clarification of an award by an arbitrator when there is an evident miscalculation or error that appears on the face of the award. But there are no statutory provisions for retaining jurisdiction. Retained jurisdiction is an arbitral invention. Many arbitrators question whether an arbitrator can simply announce that he has "retained jurisdiction," unless the parties have agreed that he will do so. While it certainly may provide a quick mechanism for enforcing an award, it can also be an imposition on an unwilling party. An arbitrator who retains jurisdiction in every case may be indulging in a habit that you will be obliged to break by requesting that he refrain. You must decide whether you want to take on that obligation.

Intellectual Predilections: Certain intellectual predilections of the arbitrator can be determined from the award. The most common conception of arbitrators is that they always endeavor to "split the baby." As a general proposition this is not true. It is, however, true for some arbitrators. Their awards make it clear that they are unable to decide cleanly, but always attempt to give something to each side. They forget that Solomon never did "split the baby"—nor did he intend to.

Another type of arbitrator is the "strict constructionist." Every opinion ventured by this arbitrator is grounded in contract language. His view, as shown in the awards, is that the contract contains all of the rights of the parties. If a benefit is not in the contract, this arbitrator believes that it is beyond his power to grant it. This arbitrator is unlikely to be convinced that within the penumbra of the recognition clause lurks a guarantee of continuing employment for all bargaining unit members.

A particularly important intellectual predilection to look for is the arbitrator's view of "past practice." Some arbitrators view past practice as an independent source of quasi-contractual obligations. Others view "past practice" as simply a means of ascertaining how parties have previously interpreted ambiguous language. Some arbitrators will find a "past practice" after very few instances of a benefit being granted. Others will require a level of agreement just short of a written document.

Similarly, arbitrators differ significantly in their views of discharge cases. Some arbitrators view discharge as the industrial equivalent of capital punishment. These arbitrators may require stricter adherence to rules of evidence and proof of facts "beyond a reasonable doubt." They may also require extensive evidence of progressive discipline before they will permit a termination. Other arbitrators view discharge as simply another form of discipline. While they recognize the importance of a discharge case, they also take the view that the analogy to criminal law is flawed.

Arbitrators also differ over the weight to be given to management decisions. Most view the arbitration as a "trial de novo," ignoring what has gone before and looking only to whether an employer action is justified in light of the circumstances presented at the hearing. Others see their function as reviewing an action already taken, imposing their own notions of "reasonability." Finally, some arbitrators make it clear in their awards that they view themselves as chancellors in equity. Their task, as they see it, is to right wrongs.

Using What You Have Read

In discussing the varieties of information you can glean from reading an award, I have not made any suggestions on how to use that information. The reason is simple: the information is neutral. As I said at the beginning, you must match the arbitrator to your case or cases. If you have a case that is complex and theoretically difficult, for example, you would do better before an arbitrator who has demonstrated an ability to fully understand theoretical issues and handle complex matters comfortably.

Questions to Ask Your Colleagues

While you can glean a great deal of information about an arbitrator from published decisions, a colleague who has used the arbitrator is an invaluable resource. The award of an experienced arbitrator will always reflect a view of the facts that is consistent with the decision. It will reveal nothing about the way in which the hearing was conducted. Nor will it tell you anything about the arbitrator's ability to grasp new concepts and apply them sensibly. For all this important information you need a colleague who has used the arbitrator. In addition, you need to know the right questions to ask your colleague.

The first question to ask your colleague is whether he has won or lost cases with a particular arbitrator. It is amazing how intelligent, evenhanded, and capable the arbitrator looks to the advocate who won the case. That same arbitrator may look like an ignorant, biased, bumbler to the loser.

The second question should be how many times your colleague has used the arbitrator. After that, there are two general areas you need to question your colleague about: the conduct of the hearing and the arbitrator's posthearing conduct.

Does the Arbitrator Make Evidentiary Rulings?

As I noted in Chapter 5 on the hearing, the purpose of the hearing is, usually, to produce a record upon which the arbitrator can make a reasoned decision.[3] The conduct of the hearing relies upon the interaction between the advocates and the arbitrator. Some arbitrators take the view that the case belongs to

---

3. I say this is "usually" the purpose because there are times when your case is both impossibly weak and incapable of being settled. On those rare occasions your strategy may be to produce as much confusion as possible at the hearing, so that you have a chance of winning through a happy accident.

the parties but the hearing belongs to the arbitrator. You should ask your colleague if the arbitrator runs a tight hearing, one in which he controls the conduct of the advocates, rather than reacting to it. Does the arbitrator permit yelling, screaming, and advanced histrionics? Or, does he insist that the hearing be conducted civilly? Does the arbitrator make evidentiary rulings that impose discipline on the record? Some arbitrators are in the habit of taking any proffered evidence, "for what it is worth." If your opponent has offered some odd bit of evidence, such as a love note on a banana peel, you are left wondering what the arbitrator thinks it is worth, what it says about the arbitrator's view of the issues in the case, and how much time you need to spend refuting the evidence. Other arbitrators rule on evidentiary matters, excluding evidence that has too little probative value to assist in determining any material issue. At times, an arbitrator will admit a piece of evidence about which there is protracted wrangling, and advise the parties of the probative value he attaches to that piece of evidence. One arbitrator sometimes tells the parties that weight of the proffered piece of evidence is, in the words of the metaphysical poet John Donne, "like gold to aery thinness beat." Even the most nonliterary advocate should recognize this as a signal that the evidence should not be relied upon by its proponent and need not be rebutted by its opponent.

Does the Arbitrator Participate in the Hearing?

A critical area of arbitral behavior at the hearing is the degree to which the arbitrator intrudes inappropriately into the case. There is nothing more frustrating to an advocate than to have an arbitrator conduct the case the way he would have presented it, rather than letting you do it the way you decided was best. There are two extremes in arbitral behavior, each posing its own dangers. At one extreme is the arbitrator who resembles an idol from Easter Island. During the entire hearing he sits, unmoving, as evidence comes in. It is difficult to know if the arbitrator understands the testimony, the documents, or the points you are making. At the other extreme is the arbitrator who takes such complete control of the case that neither side gets to present its evidence the way it had planned. Sometimes, it appears that this type of arbitrator decided the theory of the case in the first few minutes and is directing the presentation to conform with that theory. Both of these extremes are dangerous to you as an advocate. Your colleagues can help you avoid both.

Is the Arbitrator Educable?

It is critical that you know whether the arbitrator is educable. Find out from your colleagues if the arbitrator asks intelligent questions during the hearing so as to clarify things that puzzle him or to understand new ideas. The most dangerous arbitrator is the one who does not understand the technical aspects of your case and is afraid to ask questions that will expose his ignorance. Fortunately, most arbitrators are sufficiently self-assured that they are not afraid to ask questions to educate themselves.

Closely related to asking questions is the willingness of an arbitrator to grapple with difficult concepts or technical data. Some arbitrators are not comfortable with scientific or technical data, or with highly complex cases. Their tendency is to oversimplify, rather than struggle to understand the complexity. If an arbitrator is unwilling to expose his lack of understanding at a time when you can remedy it, or unwilling to struggle with complexity, you need to know these facts in order to decide whether the arbitrator is appropriate for your case. The best way to learn this is from a colleague who has used the arbitrator before.

124

Posthearing Conduct

The second major area for questioning your colleagues is posthearing conduct. You can ask three questions about the decision, the answers to which will not be apparent from the face of the award. First, was the decision timely—i.e., was it mailed within the period provided by the contract or the administering agency? As a general guideline, FMCS requires decisions be mailed within sixty days from the close of the hearing.[4] Second, did the arbitrator's statement of the facts fairly reflect the evidence introduced at the hearing? In asking this, you must, of course, consider the arbitrator's stated judgments as to credibility and relevance. The key is not whether the arbitrator believed a particular witness or document, but whether the arbitrator simply ignored evidence that was inconsistent with his view of the case. Third, ask whether the award completely resolved the controversy and was sensitive to the continuing relationship of the parties. To an outsider reading an arbitration award, a remedy may seem perfectly appropriate. The parties, however, may be aware of difficulties that were explained to the arbitrator but inadequately handled in the remedy. Even more important, the way in which the arbitrator reached a certain conclusion may help or hurt the continuing relationship of the parties. Only someone who is keenly aware of that relationship can assess whether the arbitrator helped or unnecessarily hindered the continuing relationship.

There is one more important piece of information that can only be learned from a colleague. Was the arbitrator's bill fair? Did it reflect a ratio or study time to hearing days that was

---

4. A hearing is usually considered closed at the end of the actual hearing if there is no transcript and no briefs. It is considered closed after the transcript and last brief (or reply brief if any were permitted) has been received by the arbitrator.

appropriate to the complexity of the case? If there were any problems with the bill, a colleague can tell you how the arbitrator handled those problems.

There are two final questions to ask a colleague. First, would you use this arbitrator again? If not, why not? If so, for what kind of case? Second, is this arbitrator someone who is willing to make tough decisions? There are some cases in which one party clearly wins or loses. No compromise is possible. If you have that kind of case, it is likely that the loser will be unhappy with the arbitrator. Can this arbitrator take the heat? If not, you will want to use a different arbitrator for the tough case. You should, however, still keep this arbitrator in mind for less demanding cases.

Using Other Resources to Evaluate the Arbitrator

Introduction

There are three basic tools available for researching arbitrators. There are publications that contain arbitrators' awards, services that "evaluate" arbitrators, and user networks. The last, user networks, may exist in only a few areas. For instance, the New York-New Jersey Arbitration Group consists of industrial relations officers and lawyers who meet occasionally to discuss arbitrators. The group has an annual session to which it invites some new arbitrators so the group members and arbitrators can meet one another. Since the other two resources are available around the country, they will be dealt with at greater length.

Publications

In researching arbitration awards through the various publications you should keep in mind that many arbitration awards are never published. There is no requirement that an award be published. To the contrary, the only requirement is that arbitrators get permission of the parties, in a noncoercive way, before submitting an award for publication. Some arbitrators never submit an award for publication. The only way one of their awards would be published is if a party submitted it, or it was an AAA case and neither party objected to the award being published. While at one time FMCS required arbritators to send it the award in cases where the arbitrator was picked from its panel, that is no longer done. Similarly, in the federal sector, the Office of Management and Budget (OMB), which operates the federal LAIRS system, once required that all agency arbitration awards be sent to it. Because of budgetary constraints, it no longer requires that. Consequently, agencies may choose which, if any, awards to send OMB.

All of this should make clear to you that an arbitrator's published awards may not be representative of his work. Moreover, any statistical analysis of how many times an arbitrator decides for management, or the union, or splits the case, is inherently suspect because of the sample involved.

Bureau of National Affairs (BNA)

BNA is a well known publisher of labor relations materials. As part of its labor relations service it publishes *Labor Arbitration Reports*. This series contains the full text of arbitration awards, together with headnotes, and numbered references to the BNA classification system. The series contains both public and private sector awards, although private sector awards predominate. The awards are sent in by arbitrators, with the permission of the parties. Awards that are sent in by anyone else are not published unless both parties agree to the publication.

Each volume is indexed by subject matter and contains a table of cases and directory of arbitrators. There are cumulative indices for the series, which appear every five years. When an arbitrator's award first appears in the series, bibliographical information for that arbitrator is included in the back of that volume. In addition, the cumulative indices contain biographical data for all the arbitrators who appeared during the previous five years. The biographical data are from the FMCS panel cards. The data are supplemented, according to BNA, by questionnaires. They can also be corrected by the arbitrators.

In addition to publishing the full text of awards, BNA publishes the *Directory of U.S. Arbitrators*. This volume lists biographical data for arbitrators, as well as the industries and types of disputes in which they are experienced. It is published every two years.

It is also possible to do computer searches in the "Labor Law" database of BNA on the Human Resource Information Network or Dialog. The databases do not contain full texts of arbitration awards. Rather, they have the digest note of the case and the reference to the BNA classification system. Arbitrators' biographies are available only on the Human Resource Information Network.

Commerce Clearing House (CCH)

CCH publishes a series of labor relations services similar to those published by BNA. For arbitration awards CCH publishes *Labor Arbitration Awards*, which contains the full text of awards, with headnotes. Each volume has tables of awards by party and arbitrator, as well as tables of parties and a topical index. There are cumulative topical indices to assist in research.

American Arbitration Association (AAA)

The AAA has three publications: *Arbitration in the Schools*, *Labor Arbitration in Government*, and *Summary of Labor Arbitration Awards*. None of these publications contains the full text of awards. Rather, they contain headnotes that summarize the award, together with carefully edited synopses of the awards. Each award has a number and an indication of how many pages it contains. The full text of any award can be ordered from AAA. In addition to the awards, there are semiannual subject matter and arbitrator indices. The awards are limited to selected cases administered by AAA, in which neither party has objected to publication.

LRP Publications (LRP)

LRP has the most extensive database of arbitration awards. In its monthly publication, *Labor Arbitration Information System* (LAIS), it indexes all the cases from the public sector (including the federal sector) and the private sector that it has obtained through its own resources, or that appear in BNA or CCH publications. The monthly LAIS has tables of cases by employer, union, subject, and arbitrator. The entry contains the caption information, together with an indication of who prevailed. The monthly volumes are bound each year. The bound volume also contains a master listing of key classification numbers and a subject index.

LRP also offers database searches by arbitrator name, international union, local union, employer, subject, or any combination of these. The database extends back to 1970, and contains, according to LRP, over 70,000 cases. You can use a search to investigate an arbitrator, as well. The search gives a list of the arbitrator's awards with a synopsis of each, who won, and a citation to available summaries or full text of the award. In addition, it provides the most recent biographical data of the arbitrator (taken from FMCS and AAA panel cards) and a statistical analysis of the arbitrator's awards. This analysis separates discipline and contract interpretation cases and indicates what percentage of cases in the database were won by which side. Since LRP indexes cases for private parties (unions and employers), these cases are included in the database, although the full text is not available.

For federal sector arbitrations LRP publishes the *Federal Labor Relations Reporter*. This contains summaries of cases, with the cases classified according to a key number classification system, and a headline that gives the significance and outcome of the case. It has tables by arbitrator, by union, and by employer. For each case the LAIRS number is provided, so that a full text can be obtained. The service also tracks cases that have been appealed to the Federal Labor Relations Authority (FLRA) or courts, and provides cross-references so that they can be followed. This database is available for computer searches by subject, as well as for statistical analyses of arbitrators' records of awarding for management, or the union, or for splitting a decision.

Private Services

In addition to the services that are available through traditional publishers, there is a company called R.C. Simpson. It describes itself as preparing and releasing, "a nationwide, confidential Arbitrators' Qualifications Reports Service to management representatives on a conditionally-privileged basis." Simpson sends questionnaires to arbitrators, asking for their qualifications. In addition, it collects comments from management representatives and provides these, with its biographical sketches, to its subscribers. A typical form gives a biographical sketch that includes the arbitrator's education, experience, and publications. It also contains a list of "Subjects Treated" divided according to whether an award went to the employer or the union. Following that it has a "Management Reaction" section. This contains indications of management approval or disapproval, including the type of cases for which the arbitrator would be approved or disapproved by the unidentified rater. The section also contains comments such as: "Conducts orderly hearing.... Gave weight to pertinent citations.... Must be restricted to avoid displeasing results." These comments are followed by a "consensus" section. On one arbitrator the consensus was "Qualified for clear cut cases." The section also contains fees and may contain a "Special Report." The latter may make some judgment, such as, "A restrictive submission agreement, a transcript, and posthearing briefs are generally recommended."

The value of a report such as this may be limited. On the one hand, it contains information that is not available through the other published sources. On the other hand, the sources of the information are not identified and some of the comments are cryptic. For instance, it would be difficult to know what to do with the comment: "Must be restricted to avoid displeasing results."

You may do as well asking your own colleagues the questions we listed earlier. Their responses, together with a careful reading of the arbitrator's recent awards, are most likely to enable you to make an informed judgment about using an arbitrator.

Is the Arbitrator You Want Available?

There are two important factors to consider when looking at arbitrator availability. First, is this case one in which a quick determination is the most important factor? Second, is this a complex case that requires an arbitrator with a technical background or many years of experience? Each will affect your choices.

In some cases it is more important to resolve the matter quickly than "correctly." For instance, employers who use progressive discipline for time and attendance problems may need a quick adjudication of whether an employee has broken the attendance rules. In order for progressive discipline to succeed, the arbitration needs to occur quickly, before further infractions occur or existing infractions become stale. In that situation, you may want to use newer arbitrators who tend to have greater availability. In addition, you may want to require that decisions be made within two weeks after the close of the hearing. If you tell the arbitrator of this requirement before he accepts the case, you can be reasonably well assured the decision will be timely.

There are other cases that need to be settled quickly. Disciplinary cases that involve a penalty less than discharge need to be decided quickly for a progressive discipline system to effectively correct employee behavior. You may want available, rather than well-known, arbitrators. So, too, with discharge cases where potential back pay may be more important than the reason for which discharge was imposed. You would not, of course, want to use an arbitrator you were not familiar with for a discharge case where the behavior was notorious, or the employer was breaking new ground in its disciplinary procedures. For instance, if an employee was fired in 1986 for refusing to give a urine sample for drug testing, it would be quite important to have an experienced arbitrator decide whether this was proper. This is a situation where the precedential value of the decision is as important to the parties as the actual outcome of the discharge decision.

Second, there are some cases that are extremely complex— legally, factually, or contractually. These cases may require an arbitrator with special experience. For instance, in a case where the NLRB has deferred to arbitration, you may want as an arbitrator a lawyer formerly employed by the Board. You could be reasonably well-assured as to that arbitrator's familiarity with Board made law. While you may not be able to predict the precise outcome of the case because you do not know how the arbitrator will view the evidence, you will have an idea of the range of outcomes. So, too, with a technical case. In some instances the industry is highly technical and you may want an arbitrator who is familiar with that industry, so that you do not have to educate him about the basics. Alternatively, there may be technical evidence that must be introduced, and you want an arbitrator with a technical background so that he can be easily educated. Finally, there may be cases that have a highly complex factual basis. You know from experience that certain arbitrators have the ability to both grasp many details and see the overall picture simultaneously. Other arbitrators are less comfortable with detail and take a "view" of a case based upon an early acquaintance with the overall facts. In any of these cases, arbitrator availability should be a secondary consideration. It is far better to wait for the right arbitrator, than to get a quick decision from an "almost right" arbitrator.

The right arbitrator is not always the busiest or best known arbitrator in your area. It is a mistake to confuse widespread name recognition with competence for every type of case. When you have a complex or especially difficult case, you should ask your colleagues the questions suggested earlier— even if you are going to use a well-known and highly respected arbitrator. You must match the needs of your case to the abilities of the arbitrator. That is the only sure way to get a "good" decision—regardless of who wins.

Conclusion

Arbitrator selection is not a science, nor is it a mystical process in which only the initiated have a hope of success.

Because gaps in knowledge are inevitable and human thinking is never totally predictable, you will sometimes be disappointed in your choice of an arbitrator. If you follow the suggestions in this chapter, however, you will be employing a rational process in choosing an arbitrator. That is the best you can hope for.

5

The Hearing

Introduction

The purpose of the hearing is to produce the factual record on which the arbitrator will decide the case. It is also an opportunity for you to make arguments that shape the arbitrator's understanding of the facts you prove and that convince him of the legal significance of those facts to sustain or defeat the claim at issue. Hearings are most efficient when the arbitrator manages the enterprise and enforces principles of order, relevance, and competence.

In order to insure an efficient hearing, there are certain decisions and arrangements that must be made before the hearing convenes. The arbitrator must make appropriate disclosures; the parties must agree on scheduling, location, and use of a reporter. In a highly complex case, the parties may agree to a series of scheduled stipulations, disclosures, and pre-hearing memoranda that permit the arbitrator to be a "hot bench."

At the hearing itself there may be initial disclosure problems, as well as preliminary motions to quash subpoenas or exclude witnesses. The parties will need to define the issue for the arbitrator before getting into their cases. After that the case will proceed from opening statements, through the examination of witnesses and the presentation of documents and other evidence, to rebuttal and surrebuttal, and ultimately to closing statements. In some instances there may be settlements at the hearing itself, or consent awards.

I will first examine the pre-hearing arrangements, and then move to an examination of the hearing itself.

Pre-hearing Arrangements

After you have informed the arbitrator of his selection, he will have his first opportunity to make any necessary disclosures. Arbitrators are required to disclose any potential conflicts of interest, or relationships that may affect the appearance of impartiality. In the labor-management relations arena, where attorneys and arbitrators frequently enjoy close personal and professional relationships, and repeatedly encounter one another in hearing rooms, it would be futile to attempt to disclose all prior professional relationships. Where the relationship goes beyond the hearing room into committee work, or teaching, it may be appropriate for the arbitrator to disclose the relationship, even though it raises no questions about the arbitrator's ability to decide the case impartially. Disclosure clears the air, enables parties to raise further questions to satisfy themselves that the arbitrator suffers no disability from acting, and allows the arbitrator himself to field those questions and allay the parties' concerns.

If you get a disclosure from the arbitrator you have chosen, do not simply dismiss that arbitrator and look for someone else. Evaluate what has been disclosed and ask yourself whether the relationship or interest is one that is likely to interfere with the arbitrator's ability to decide the case fairly. Remember that the arbitrator is compelled by ethical considerations to disclose even matters that he may not think are terribly significant, rather than risk a disgruntled losing party later attempting to vacate the award on the grounds of bias.

In cases involving nurses, an arbitrator might disclose that his wife is an RN, even though she has not practiced in years. Or in a case where the arbitrator knew an advocate simply because they went to the same law school, an arbitrator might disclose this. In both cases there is no reason to believe that the arbitrator could not decide the case fairly. Rather, the arbitrator is simply protecting the process from a later charge, by an unhappy loser, that the award is tainted by bias. Do not hesitate to request a conference call if you are concerned about anything in the disclosure. Furthermore, most arbitrators will not be offended if you are uncomfortable with the matter disclosed and want a different arbitrator. A polite statement about how it bothers your client is all that it takes to get a sophisticated arbitrator to withdraw when his disclosure has created the possibility of the appearance of impropriety.

Scheduling the Hearing

There are three important factors to consider in scheduling hearings: the type of case, the complexity of the case, and the availability of witnesses. It is not always wise to schedule a hearing at the arbitrator's earliest available date. Some cases need to ripen before they can be heard, others may disappear because the political forces that are driving them to arbitration may slacken. Since arbitration awards involve a winner and a loser, avoiding arbitration may be a useful strategy, even when you are at the stage of setting a date.

Type of Case

The type of case will be an important consideration in deciding how quickly to schedule a hearing. Generally, you want to schedule discharge cases quickly to avoid extensive back pay and to limit grievants' period of involuntary unemployment. On the other hand, you may view contract interpretation cases as less pressing. In both instances, your major concern is your client's potential exposure to liability. The liability is obvious in discharge cases where it translates as potential back pay or extended periods without income. It is less obvious in discipline and contract cases where exposure involves the impact of the underlying issue on the parties' continuing relationship. Strikes in alleged violation of no-strike clauses and claimed improper changes in working conditions are high exposure cases, with potential for physical harm and property damage. More subtle cases involve the political considerations of living with the disruptive impact of an unresolved issue. Questions of work load or safety that arise every day, can have devastating effects on morale and productivity. In all of these high exposure cases it is best to schedule hearings quickly, even if special arrangements must be made to use evenings and weekends.

Complexity

When scheduling complex cases you need to consider two things: preparation time and the possibility of multiple hearings. First, if you anticipate extended preparation, a far-off hearing date will allow you to prepare effectively and give you a useful opportunity to settle the matter based on a knowledgeable assessment of your case's strengths and weaknesses. Second, complex cases usually involve multiple hearings. At the outset, consider scheduling consecutive hearing dates to avoid between-hearing delays. If your arbitrator is popular and the advocates busy, delays between hearings can be as much as four to six months. A ten-hearing case might take eighteen months to litigate. This means you have to do extensive preparation before each hearing date, so that you are "up to speed" when you begin the new hearing date. Witnesses may become unavailable and the arbitrator may forget details and impressions. The explosive impact of your brilliant cross-examination may be reduced to a shadowy recollection.

Consecutive hearing dates preserve continuity, keep recollections fresh, and pay off in efficient preparation and limited exposure to arbitral error. The only disadvantage is the risk of late cancellation fees if you wind up not using all of the dates you have scheduled. Since arbitrator's fees are usually the least expensive aspect of an arbitration, they are a small price to pay for the many benefits of consecutive hearing dates.

Availability of Witnesses

Before committing to dates that the arbitrator and both advocates can make, be sure your witnesses will be available. Besides checking vacation schedules, you should be aware of less obvious competition. For example, some Christian sects celebrate Christmas twelve days after December 25. Some Orthodox Jews begin Sabbath observance on Fridays at sundown; during winter months they must end work at mid-afternoon to finish traveling by sundown. Moslems, Hindus, and Orientals celebrate holidays many Americans do not know exist. And, in some industries, March 17 and 18 are days of extraordinary absenteeism and low productivity. If you know that a particular witness will be unavailable on the day when his testimony would logically be given, consider asking the arbitrator if that witness could be taken out of order so that hearing time could be used efficiently. Or, check to see if your opponent is willing to stipulate a needed fact so that the witness will be unnecessary.

Procedures for Setting the Hearing Date

The American Arbitration Association performs the administrative functions of contacting the parties and the arbitrator to schedule hearing dates. If no agency is administering your case, the arbitrator will have to contact the parties after receiving a notice of appointment. Depending upon the arbitrator's resources and efficiency, that process of scheduling will be more or less speedy. In some areas it is traditional for the arbitrator to write the parties, offering available dates. They then contact the arbitrator to inform him of which date is acceptable. Then the arbitrator writes a confirming letter. If the arbitrator has been told where the case will be heard, the letter will contain the time, place, and date of the hearing. Otherwise, there will be further letters setting forth the location of the hearing. In other areas, the entire scheduling process is handled by telephone, with the arbitrator's office sending a confirming letter to the parties and the stenographer—if the parties have decided to use one.

If you want fast resolution of an arbitration issue, you can begin your scheduling efforts before even sending the arbitrator his notice of appointment. By far the most efficient method is a telephone conference call among the arbitrator and both advocates. When the parties can simultaneously consult their calendars, you can eliminate expensive and exhausting "shuttle diplomacy" by the arbitrator.

Location of the Hearing

Two factors are important in deciding on the location of the hearing: convenience and neutrality. Convenience usually means the least travel for the greatest number of people. If you expect numerous witnesses from the workplace, holding the hearing at the plant site makes sense. Witnesses can be found quickly and used with minimal disruption of productivity. Where you intend to exclude witnesses, a site at, or close to, the workplace becomes even more critical. Since witnesses will only be sitting outside the hearing room while waiting to be called, it is better for both parties if they are permitted to work but be "on call." This will also permit the least disruption of production.

The second concern about location is the appearance of neutrality. If you feel your witnesses might be intimidated or the arbitrator overawed by holding the arbitration on the other side's "turf," by all means insist on a neutral location such as a conference room at the American Arbitration Association's regional office, a state mediation board, or a local hotel. If the parties' agreement requires splitting the cost of arbitration, then the cost of the hearing room is also split.

The Hearing Room

The two most significant considerations in choosing the hearing room are: accommodations and amenities. The room must be large enough to accommodate all the necessary attendees, and the tables should be wide enough to enable the parties to spread out and keep track of their notes and exhibits without being able to read each others' documents upside down. A cramped hearing room shortens tempers and may distract the arbitrator.

In one instance, a hearing was being held in a small conference room in a prison, and a seventeen-year-old felon was being cross-examined about the actions of a guard whom he alleged had taken money from him. An in camera inspection of the young man's record showed that he had committed two violent murders, one before he was fifteen. The record also revealed that he had an explosive temper and the verbal skills of a third grader. The hearing room was so small, the felon sat jammed against the arbitrator, while counsel was seated some eight feet away, across a large table. As the cross-examination became more intense, the witness became more agitated and less able to answer questions. The arbitrator called a halt to the proceedings and suggested that the witness was having difficulty answering because he could not hear the questions. He moved counsel next to the witness and took counsel's place across the table. The cross-examination became less acrimonious and soon ended. The problem could have been avoided, however, if the room had been large enough to provide a comfortable distance between the witness and the arbitrator.

If the case is a significant one to which the parties have invited numerous spectators, make sure there is sufficient room for them away from the table. That arrangement emphasizes their spectator status and eases the arbitrator's burden of maintaining an orderly proceeding. It is preferable if the spectators are in a position where they can be seen by the arbitrator. This will make them less likely to inadvertently use facial expressions and body language to help the witnesses with their testimony. Should any lapses occur, the arbitrator will see them and be able to quietly confer with counsel about the impropriety so that no one is embarrassed.

You should also consider the arrangement of the tables. It may seem a trivial matter, but since international peace talks have almost foundered on this issue, it is worth a few words. A U-shaped table with the arbitrator at the foot of the "U" keeps the parties well separated and gives the arbitrator room to spread out. It becomes inconvenient, however, when the parties must pass copies of exhibits across the gap to one another. You can either narrow the "U" (which limits the arbitrator's room), or place the witness chair inside the gap facing the arbitrator (which allows the witnesses to be the go-between for passing documents), or open the corners of the "U" so advocates can easily cross the gap to exchange documents. Many arbitrators prefer a "wide I" table configuration. That allows easy passage of documents, plenty of room for the arbitrator's records, and effective separation of the parties without creating the appearance of an unbridgeable gulf.

The hearing room should also provide the basic amenities for a comfortable and efficient proceeding. There should be nearby bathrooms, telephones, facilities for a lunch break, and accommodations for sequestered witnesses. If you expect smokers, make sure the room has adequate ventilation.

Stenographic Transcripts

To Transcribe or Not to Transcribe

Whether you order a stenographic transcript of proceedings should depend on a rational purpose. Automatically ordering transcripts in all cases incurs needless expense and will unnecessarily increase the time it takes to finish a case. Conventions differ significantly, between the East and West Coasts. In the East a transcript is a rarity; in the West it is the norm. According to AAA statistics, 22 percent of the labor cases it administers have transcripts.

There are appropriate occasions for ordering transcripts. If, for example, you have reason to anticipate judicial proceedings to enforce, vacate, or modify an award based on what happened at the hearing, a stenographic transcript will be conclusive evidence of what went on. As we will see later, certain statutory arbitrations—like multi-employer pension plan amendments withdrawal liability cases—must be reviewed in all cases. A second appropriate reason to order a transcript involves the nature of expected evidence. If your case is factually complex or involves extensive technical or numerical proof, you may want a transcript to provide an accurate memorialization for the arbitrator's easy reference. If you anticipate a multi-day hearing, transcripts are extremely useful to insure that no testimony gets lost because the arbitrator has forgotten it. Transcripts may also provide useful evidence of effective and fair representation where parties anticipate further litigation by a grievant hostile to his union. Finally, transcripts do make the arbitrator's job easier, permitting him to devote more attention to witness demeanor than would be possible if he were struggling to take notes on witness testimony.

Sharing Transcript Costs

Transcripts are expensive and you ought to know the ground rules for allocating their cost before ordering one. Under the American Arbitration Association's Voluntary Labor Arbitration Rules (*see* Appendix 3), both parties share the expense of a transcript ordered jointly or by the arbitrator. Where a single party orders the transcript, that party pays the entire expense and must provide a copy for "inspection" by the other side. Some parties anticipate transcripts and their expense in collective bargaining, placing contractual limitations on the number of cases in which either may order a transcript, or requiring payment by the party ordering the transcript.

When one party unilaterally requests that a record be made, and the other party insists that it does not want to go to the expense of a record, the arbitrator has to make a difficult ruling. You should ask the arbitrator if he wants a transcript made. If so, the opposing party can gracefully agree to the inevitable. If not, it is likely that the arbitrator will rule in accordance with the AAA rules, because they provide a sensible solution.

Arbitrators are often faced with unilateral requests to tape record the proceedings. Most arbitrators will deny those requests. Tape recordings are inaccurate because people talk over one another, or speak faintly. Furthermore, they are terribly subject to tampering. Finally, they are horrendously time-consuming to use, since they require as much time to listen to them as it took to record them.

Impact of Transcripts

Transcripts increase the time and expense of arbitration proceedings. Without paying a premium for an expedited copy, parties can expect to wait two or three weeks before receiving transcripts. Analysis of transcripts lengthens preparation and the size of briefs. The parties' advocates must also be paid for their time analyzing the record and preparing their briefs. Long briefs lengthen the time the arbitrator will need to review the record and produce his opinion and award. Transcripts and briefs usually increase the arbitrator's study time charges, and that, too, adds to the parties' expense. Since having a transcript involves considerations of both time and money, some thought should be given as to whether the transcript is necessary.

Certain cases are usually inappropriate for a transcript. If you want a bench decision, a transcript will not be helpful. If you have an expedited case, a transcript will slow the process. If you have nontermination disciplinary matters, the cost of a transcript may be an impediment to progressive discipline, because it makes hearings more costly. The important thing to remember is that if you need to control costs, or expedite the hearing, ordering a transcript should not be an automatic process.

There are some that argue that transcripts have a persuasive impact as a signal to the arbitrator that the parties take their case seriously and want his full and careful attention. If that is your only reason for ordering a transcript, save your money. No arbitrator worth his salt requires such a message. Cases are our professional stock-in-trade, and we take them *all* seriously.

Time Arrangements

Hearings, by custom, start at 10:00 A.M. and run until 5:00 P.M. That is a normal hearing day. Sometimes the parties prefer beginning earlier or ending later. Most arbitrators will agree to start earlier or go later when that will avoid the need for a second hearing day, provided you ask them about this when you are arranging the hearing. In some areas, traffic considerations may make it extremely difficult to start at an earlier hour. These same traffic problems may make the arbitrator quite willing to extend the hearing past 5:00 P.M. At some point in the early evening, many arbitrators will charge for a second day of hearing. Arbitrators who do this will indicate the practice in their pre-hearing billing disclosures. If you are using an administering agency, you should inquire specifically about this.

At times it is useful to plan an extra long hearing. If the parties have gone to great travel expense to get to the hearing location, it makes better sense to stay late than to convene a second day of hearing. If this is your intention, be sure to tell the arbitrator and the reporter. Sometimes, a case that you had not anticipated taking more than a normal hearing day will begin to go longer. If you see this happening, you should assess whether skipping lunch would enable you to finish that day. Most arbitrators will willingly eliminate or shorten the lunch break if that will enable the parties to finish in one day. What arbitrators find frustrating, however, is skipping lunch, extending the day, and having to come back for three hours on a subsequent date. To avoid this frustrating situation, try to be realistic, not optimistic, in your estimates of how long your case will take.

The hearing moves at a more productive pace when lunch is kept to an hour and breaks are regular but short. The parties must exercise some self-discipline, since the arbitrator will not want to break into conversations held outside his hearing, since they may involve matters he should not hear. Inattention to time reflects itself everywhere. Ten-minute breaks become twenty-five; one hour lunch breaks take ninety minutes, and six-hour cases require two hearing days. Attention to time insures an effective hearing process.

Pre-hearing Activities in Complex Cases

Complex cases involve complicated issues, burdensome documentation, masses of factual details, or all three. Examples of such cases include multi-employer pension plan withdrawal liability claims, public sector interest arbitrations, and disciplinary proceedings involving malpractice of professional employees. In such cases, pre-hearing activities can substantially simplify and shorten the hearing process and ensure more effective service from the arbitrator. While pre-hearing activities are a nontraditional approach to arbitration, it is worth your while to participate.

Here is an example of pre-hearing activity. On January 3 the parties to MPPAA withdrawal liability claim chose their arbitrator and set three consecutive hearing dates beginning April 15. In a January 10 conference call, the parties' attorneys, with the arbitrator, agreed to the following timetable, expressly preserving their opportunity to deviate from it if common sense required:

   a. By January 31, the parties would mark and exchange the documents that they intended to offer in evidence, together with a covering list.
   b. By February 14, the parties would exchange each other's document lists marked to show those to which they had no objection and those to which they will raise objections of relevance or authenticity.

c. In a February 21 conference call, the parties would argue and the arbitrator would decide evidentiary disputes. The parties would mark—for identification only—those exhibits as to which there would have to be qualifying testimony at the hearing.

d. By February 28, the parties would exchange lists of proposed stipulations of fact.

e. By March 7, the parties would exchange each other's proposed stipulations, marked to show those accepted and rejected. The next day they would combine their accepted stipulations, if any, in a single joint exhibit.

f. By March 21, the parties would exchange pre-hearing briefs with attached exhibits detailing the facts they will prove, how they intend to prove them, and the legal significance of those facts.

g. By April 7, the parties would exchange and send the arbitrator their answering memoranda, together with the pre-hearing briefs and exhibits.

On April 15, the arbitrator would arrive at the hearing as a "hot court," with a complete understanding of what issues would arise and a sound background on which to evaluate testimony, decide objections, and ask intelligent questions. As important, the parties would arrive with a history of responsible cooperation that facilitates an efficient hearing.

At the Hearing

The hearing is the heart of the arbitration. It is your sole opportunity to adduce evidence upon which the arbitrator will make his decision. In this section I will follow the order of a typical hearing, step-by-step. Since pre-hearing activity is usually confined to special cases, I will assume that there has been none.

Preliminary Problems

When the arbitrator walks into the hearing room, he frequently encounters unanticipated problems that may threaten the efficient conduct of the hearing. Poorly configured tables can be moved, unnecessary people can be banished to the hallway, and stipulations can eliminate the need for absent witnesses. Substantive problems involve greater challenges. For example, what happens when the arbitrator arrives to discover for the first time that one party's attorney was his college classmate? Where the arbitrator feels the late-discovered relationship may, in fact, impair his impartiality or his appearance of impartiality, he has no alternative but to disqualify himself and withdraw from the case.

Another example of a substantive problem the arbitrator may encounter upon arrival at the hearing is an angry witness brandishing a subpoena that he protests he never should have received. In many jurisdictions, state law allows attorneys to issue subpoenas in arbitration proceedings, and witnesses must attend and challenge the subpoena at the hearing. Most frequently, a motion to quash presents the issue to the arbitrator. Arbitrators evaluate motions to quash just as they do objections to evidence. The ultimate question is whether the witness sought is likely to produce relevant, competent evidence which will help him decide the case. Particularly if the witness sought is hostile to your client's interests, you should consider asking that he be excluded from the room while the parties argue the motion to quash. That avoids "educating" the witness concerning precisely what you hope to elicit from him.

Stipulation of Joint Exhibits and Facts

In almost every labor arbitration, there will be at least one joint exhibit: the collective bargaining agreement under which the proceeding arises. Usually, it establishes the arbitrator's jurisdiction and powers, and provides the standards that he must apply. You should mark that Joint Exhibit I and direct the arbitrator's attention to the language at issue and any relevant limits on his power. Give the arbitrator a moment to familiarize himself with the language before proceeding.

Some advocates include as Joint Exhibits the original grievance, determinations at the grievance procedure's earlier steps, and the appeal to arbitration. These constitute the "pleadings" in the arbitration. If there is some issue of timeliness or the appropriateness of earlier proceedings, it can be resolved through these documents, or by a stipulation that the matter is properly before the arbitrator for final determination. Arbitrators usually must decide the question at issue de novo, and the earlier statements of the parties' contentions do not add any weight to evidence produced at the hearing. Of course, if there is some contention that a party is surprised by the position of its opponent at the hearing, this may be disproved through the pleadings. At times, the documents provide a concise statement of the positions of the parties. If you want the arbitrator to have a quick education in the case, you can give him time to read the pleadings.

You may also have a strategic reason for wanting the pleadings in the record. There may be a fact that is no longer capable of being proved, but which was accepted at the lower levels of the procedure. Introducing the pleadings may make it easier to get a stipulation on that fact from your opponent. Offering the pleadings as a joint exhibit may lend an appearance of probity to them, and it is unlikely your opponent will be successful in keeping them out.

Efforts to stipulate facts at the hearing will not always be successful. Where attorneys are involved, the parties' adversary posture often guides their thinking. Even when there is no essential factual dispute, disputes over wording and punctuation often make it faster to get the evidence by testimony rather than stipulation. I do not mean to suggest that you should never try to arrive at stipulations in appropriate cases. Rather, you should recognize when both you and your opponent are attempting to argue the case through stipulations.

Defining the Issue

Here is a frequently encountered, frustrating, and entirely unnecessary scene at some arbitration hearings:

> **Arbitrator**: Well, folks, what's the issue?
> **Union Attorney**: We think it should be "Did the company violate the contract when it unjustly refused to allow grievant the vacation to which he was entitled? If so, what shall the remedy be?"
> **Employer Attorney**: No, no. It should be "Did the employer abuse its absolute discretion under Article No. VII.a.2. when it refused to grant grievant's unreasonable request for time off to which he had no contractual right? If so, what shall be the remedy?"
> **Union Attorney**: "No, no. That's much too narrow. How about this...."
> [Two hours later] **Employer Attorney**: "No, no. That's much too broad. I can't possibly agree to submit that issue."

Of course, making clear what has been submitted to arbitration is of critical importance, for it defines the arbitrator's jurisdiction and limits the damage he can do to the parties' interests. That colloquy is unnecessary, however, for two reasons. First, there may already exist a submission agreement that defines the arbitrator's power. It usually appears in the collective bargaining agreement's arbitration clause, which defines what a moving party can submit to arbitration. Here are two examples of such language:

> Step 4. The Union may appeal to arbitration any grievance that remains unresolved after completion of Step 3.

> Step 4. The Union may appeal to arbitration any Step 3 decision with which it is not satisfied.

In the first case, the parties have agreed to submit to arbitration unresolved grievances. That means, absent an agreement on the wording of a more precisely stated issue, the question for the arbitrator is, "Does the Union's grievance have merit? If so, what shall be the remedy?" In the second example, the parties have agreed to arbitrate the Union's appeals of Step 3 decisions it does not like. As before, absent agreement on more specific language, this is the issue to which the parties have *already* agreed: "Was the Step 3 decision correct? If not, what shall be the remedy?"

The second reason that colloquy is unnecessary is that the difference between the parties' proposed issues often comes down to the characterization of some behavior. That is, they agree on the contract article in issue and that certain behavior is alleged to have occurred, but they disagree about what to call that behavior. Beyond that, each side wants to achieve a litigating advantage through a statement of the issue that requires its opponent to concede a critical point.

If the answer is so simple, why do parties and arbitrators waste time arguing over an issue they have already established? I think there are two principal reasons. First, the adversarial instinct pervades some advocates' very tissues. They cannot pass up the opportunity to gain a litigating advantage by a favorable statement of the issue. The problem arises, of course, when an equally competent adversary seeks the same result. Each insists on his own wording, and neither will back off the confrontation.

A second contributing factor is the arbitrator who will not proceed without an agreed statement of the issue, and will not look to the contract if all else fails. Frequently one sees arbitrator's awards that begin with a recitation of both parties' proposed statements of the issues and their agreement that the arbitrator frame the issue in his opinion. I think it a mistake for parties to agree to such a procedure. The arbitrator should be extremely limited in his ability to frame the issue. You can allow him to frame the issue between the poles represented by the parties' statements of the issue, but you should not permit him to go beyond that. When the essential disagreement arises solely from the advocates' attempts to state the issue in a way that forces an opponent to concede a point, allowing the arbitrator to choose an issue that lies between the two stated by the parties is a face-saving way to get out of an unproductive confrontation.

In some cases, the parties may jointly wish to submit to the arbitrator a question that goes beyond their agreement's submission clause. In those cases, you must be sure to execute a new submission agreement that precisely describes the issues to be decided and provides standard of decision for all issues on which the contract itself is silent.

Sequestering Witnesses

Sequestering witnesses—excluding from the hearing room all potential witnesses who are not actually testifying—is important where you anticipate credibility questions. Sequestration serves two purposes. First, it insures that witnesses will not "go to school" on each other's testimony, varying their own testimony to match that which preceded it. Second, arbitrators deciding credibility questions often use three tests of consistency to evaluate testimony: (1) consistency of descriptions by witnesses to the same alleged incident, (2) consistency of testimony with surrounding circumstances and documents, and (3) consistency of testimony with what common sense suggests is the likely way things happened. As to all three tests, the arbitrator has much more to work with when each witness's testimony is "pure" and unaffected by someone else's words.

If sequestering witnesses will help your case, be sure to make that motion *before* the opening statements. It will defeat the sequestration's purpose if witnesses hear detailed statements of what each side intends to prove and how they intend to prove it. In credibility cases, the hearing is a laboratory; keep your samples uncontaminated.

Elements of the Hearing

Opening Statements

The purpose of opening statements is to provide a "road map" to orient the arbitrator through your case-in-chief. At a minimum, you should state the essential elements of your claim, how you intend to prove them, and the relief to which you are entitled. That will enable the arbitrator to understand your witnesses and how their testimony fits into your entire case. It permits intelligent questions, and it provides the arbitrator with a simple checklist for confirming that you have made your case. Most important, a clear statement of your probative intentions will give the arbitrator a firm basis to evaluate and overrule relevancy objections to the testimony you offer. Indeed, when responding to objections, you can refer back to the major points of your opening statement to show how the witnesses' testimony fits into your overall case. That will reinforce the firm impression of structure in the arbitrator's mind and may make him subliminally more receptive to it. An effective opening statement can establish the arbitrator's evaluation matrix. Like a paint-by-number canvass, it graphically illustrates what you have done and what you will do to complete your successful case.

So important are effective opening statements that I am convinced that only rare strategic concerns would support waiving openings when you bear the burden of going forward. One such situation, not particularly strategic, might be where you have submitted a pre-hearing brief that you *know* the arbitrator has recently read.

Some attorneys express a tactical intention to avoid "tipping their hand" by making an opening statement. This strategy is extremely shortsighted. By and large, when you waive an opening statement, you invite the arbitrator to a game of blindman's-buff: he will spend the hearing groping for significant threads of your theory of the case. If he catches the wrong one, blame yourself. In addition, it will be difficult for you to effectively argue on objections, since the arbitrator will not be clear on where your overall case is going.

Openings are equally important if you bear the responding burden. Show the arbitrator the holes in the moving parties' case so that he can listen to that evidence with a careful and critical ear. If those holes are so apparent that you intend to rest at the end of your opponent's case, let the arbitrator know so that he can prepare to make a bench decision, if that's what you want. If you intend to adduce your own responding evidence, tell the arbitrator what you will prove, how you will prove it, and why it is important. If you expect to drop a "bombshell" that you don't want to give away lest it be anticipated and neutralized, at least let the arbitrator know there will be a "bombshell" that you will not drop until the other side has established its relevance by adducing perjured or other bad-faith evidence.

As responding party, when should you defer your opening statement until the close of your opponent's case? One strategy supporting deferral is that, when you expect your opponent will fail to establish an essential element of his claim, you should defer opening so as not to signal that likelihood to your opponent and invite a special effort to correct the problem. If that is your strategy, be sure to tell the arbitrator you are following it. For example,

> Mr. Arbitrator, respondent is deferring its opening at this time because we are convinced that the grievant will not be able to establish one or more of the essential elements of his case. Rather than provide him a free legal education now, we will defer our opening statement until the close of grievant's case. We expect that, unless grievant manufactures evidence to fit his theory, we shall rest. Our opening statement will be our closing argument.

That statement alerts the arbitrator to your intention and also covers the potential for embarrassment if grievant does adduce some evidence on the weak element, and you are obliged to put on your case.

The disadvantage of deferring is that the arbitrator will have no contrary guidance with which to evaluate the moving parties' case as it comes in. Arbitrators, like other humans, are constantly evaluating data and forming and reforming working hypotheses as the record develops. Although they resist drawing fixed conclusions on incomplete records, their interim hypotheses are less likely to be favorable to you if you have given the arbitrator no opening statement on which to question grievant's proofs.

Here are some further tips on ensuring the effectiveness of your opening statements. First, avoid hyperbole and other argumentative "danger signals." Overstatements and use of such easy words as "clearly" and "grossly" tend to raise arbitrators' suspicions. Situations that are clear or gross tend to speak for themselves; they do not require dry characterization. Second, overstatements raise expectations that are disappointed when not fulfilled. Promise only what you can deliver, and anything more that comes in will simply underscore the essential validity of your position. Third, limit the damage that can be done by adverse facts that you know you will be unable to keep out. Give the arbitrator a framework within which to understand the fact from your point of view. For instance, if your chief witness to alleged drug use by employees is a supervisor who was himself involved in drugs, bring that fact out in your opening. Point out that he is expert in drug matters who has renounced drugs and turned in his friends in the hope of helping them, not hurting them. If you have a lemon, as the saying goes, make lemonade.

In addition, be specific about the remedy you seek. Let the arbitrator know beforehand what relief you want and why you are entitled to it. As described in Chapter 3, you must tailor your requested remedy to cure the contract breach you claim. When the arbitrator knows from the outset what you want and why you deserve it, he can keep a mental checklist to guide him in finding what you are entitled to.

Finally, keep in mind that the objective of opening statements is to *cover*, not smother, the issues. Avoid extended argument and counterargument. It is sufficient for each side to advise the decision maker what they intend to prove, how they intend to prove it, and why those facts are important. Protracted opening argument accomplishes little and wastes valuable hearing time. It is *proof*, not argument, that the arbitrator requires.

Examination and Cross-examination of Witnesses

The purpose of examination and cross-examination of witnesses is to adduce *facts*, not argument. It will be your job as advocate to argue the significance of facts adduced through testimony. Sometimes the fact you want is, in effect, a conclusion. For some conclusions, such as medical conditions and identification of controlled substances, you need an expert in the field. If the witness is an expert and you seek her opinion, you must lay a foundation of credentials and other facts to establish her expertise, her familiarity with the subject matter, the data that she considered in reaching her opinion, and the analytical process by which she reached it. Then she can testify to a conclusion.

For other conclusions, such as the apparent mental or physical state of an individual, lay people can testify if they provide the basis upon which their judgment was made. If your witness, not an expert, is to testify that her supervisor was furious and out of control, you should lay an adequate foundation of factual observations to support that conclusion. The examination might sound like this:

Q: Describe your supervisor's appearance and behavior that day.

A: She was running around the office screaming at the top of her lungs at everyone. Her face was flushed, and she was yelling so hard that spit was coming out of her mouth. At one point, she threw the papers she was holding down on my desk so hard that it scattered some other papers onto the floor.

Q: Is that her normal behavior?

A: No. She is normally very quiet, courteous, and in absolute control of herself.

Q: Based on what you saw, what, if anything, did you conclude about her anger and her state of control?

A: I thought she was furious and out of control.

As we will discuss in this chapter, that interrogation allowed your witness to testify completely as to the facts she observed and how she reached a conclusion based on those facts. It allows an arbitrator the fullest opportunity to favorably assess your witness's credibility and the dependability of her conclusions. And you have accomplished that purpose by asking a series of simple questions that allowed *her*, not you, to recite the necessary information. In the following pages I will examine various techniques for using direct and cross-examination of witnesses to make your case most effective.

Direct Examination: On direct examination you ask questions of your own witnesses that allow them to testify to the facts that support your case. In this section, I will address only the form and rationale for questions. I will assume that you have adequately prepared your case and your witnesses before the hearing.

Proper questioning on direct gives your witness the opportunity to testify. Your questions on direct should simply let the witness know what area of inquiry you want them to address; they should *not* themselves provide the factual content of the answer sought. To accomplish that most simply, you must focus your witness's attention on the subject matter and begin your inquiry with one of these words: "who, what, where, when, why, and how." If you follow that simple rule, you will never be accused of having asked a "leading question": for it will be your witness and not you who provides the substantive fact that your question seeks.

Leading questions, which you may not ordinarily ask on direct examination, seek nothing more from the witness than confirmation or denial of facts stated by the questioner. By asking leading questions you put words in your witnesses' mouths. If you do this on direct, you neutralize the persuasive impact of your witness's testimony. You present the arbitrator with your testimony, not the witness's. And, as a legal matter, you are incompetent.

Imagine yourself as an arbitrator evaluating the testimony of your witness concerning her supervisor's anger and lack of self-control. Recall the questions and answers when your witness described in lurid detail her supervisor's yelling and storming around the office scattering papers in her wake. Compare the impact of that testimony with the likely impact if the interrogation had proceeded like this:

Q: Did your supervisor raise her voice?
A: Yes.
Q: Was she shouting?
A: Yes.
Q: Was her face red?
A: Yes.
Q: Was she shouting so loud that she was spitting?
A: Yes.
Q: Did she knock papers onto the floor?
A: Yes.
Q: Is she normally like that?
A: No.
Q: Was she angry and out of control?
A: Yes.

Obviously, there is no comparison. The witness properly questioned gave a lively and compelling account of her observations. On a critical subject, she gave the arbitrator substance and drama that he would find impossible to ignore. The witness responding to leading questions, however, gave the arbitrator a series of monosyllabic grunts. The questions focused attention on the advocate, not the witness. Whatever drama or compulsion there was had to come from the advocate's questions, not the witness's responses. It would be easy for an arbitrator to ignore, discount, or simply forget such testimony on direct.

If your opponent had objected that your questions were leading, the objections would have been sustained. But a canny opponent will not make that objection. Rather, she will let you lead your witness through the testimony and undercut your own case. Indeed, she might do nothing more on cross-examination than ask the witness questions about how she was prepared and leave your testimony undisturbed. For instance, she might ask your witness: "Did you meet with Mr. Advocate before you took the stand today?" and "Did he tell you any of the questions he would be asking here today?" If your witness answers truthfully, the suggestion that she was coached is clear. If the witness lies and says she never met you before and knew nothing of what you were going to ask her, it appears that she was so unreliable you had to testify yourself. Either way, you have an uphill battle on redirect.

There may be times when leading questions are appropriate on direct. For example, if there are uncontested introductory facts necessary to set the stage for direct on operative facts, leading helps get them in efficiently. If you use that technique, however, you ought to show your "class" (as well as your knowledge of the difference between leading and proper questions) by asking your adversary and the arbitrator if they have no objection. For instance, if other witnesses have already identified your current witness as having been at a certain meeting, it is acceptable to say: "Now, you were at the meeting of November 5 with Jones, Smith, and Doe, at the hat factory, were you not?" Or, when a witness is known to everyone in the room, but his qualifications need to be put into the record it is acceptable to ask: "Now it is true, is it not, that you have been an employee of the Fedora Company since 1953, that you were the former chief shop steward, that you moved into management in 1965, first as a foreman, then supervisor, then Assistant Plant Manager, and in 1982 you began your current job as Plant Manager at the Elmira plant?" When you get to operative facts, however, stop leading no matter how great the temptation. Remember, there is *always* a proper way to ask a specific question without having to lead.

Here is a common situation that seems inevitably to invite leading questions. In an overtime case where the disputed issue is supervisory authorization of extra work, your witness told you at a pre-hearing conference that his supervisor had used these words, "I don't care when you do it, but it better be done by the time I get in tomorrow morning!" At the hearing your witness has testified to the supervisor's first words, that he didn't care when the work was done, but he has omitted the last part of that crucial sentence. Inartful examiners, eager to fill the void, ask, "Did he tell you that the work had better be done by the time he gets in the next morning?" The answer, a simple "yes," neutralizes the impact and terminates further inquiry.

How much more effective would be this approach:

Q: Did he give you an order?
A: Yes.
Q: What, if anything, did he say that sounded to you like an order?
A: He said, "It better be done by the time I get in tomorrow morning!"
Q: Why did that sound like an order?
A: Well, his tone of voice was threatening. And the last time he said that, three months ago, Jimmy Jones didn't finish the job because he went home on time, and he got a written warning for insubordination.

If you have prepared your witness by using outlines, not scripts, so that he knows where his testimony fits into the entire picture of your case, proper direct examination is a cinch. You have educated your witness so that he can testify with intelligence and independence, not as a performing monkey who repeats tricks by rote. Because of that approach, it does not take much of a nudge to have such a witness fill gaps in necessary testimony. For instance, if the witness has forgotten something he told you during his preparation, you should have instructed him that you might ask, "Can you remember anything else?" The proper response is: "Not at this time." This will give you an opportunity to refresh his recollection through a word, phrase, of piece of physical evidence. You are entitled to show your witness anything—from an artichoke to a zebra—to refresh his recollection. Moreover, the impression of independence and intelligence that testimony from refreshed recollection makes on the arbitrator is invaluable to your case.

Having covered how to ask questions, let us turn now to what to ask. Key your questions back to your evaluation matrix, and limit your inquiry to the necessary *facts* to establish your case's essential elements. Keep two checklists in your arbitration looseleaf. First, list the essential elements for your entire case; and, second, the essential facts that each witness must cover to establish those essential elements. As testimony progresses, check off each point on both lists. If any point remains open, you *must* adduce testimony or evidence to fill that hole or your case will fail. It may sound simplistic to suggest you keep lists, but there is an extremely good reason for it. A clever opponent may raise numerous objections in order to sidetrack your direct examination. These objections may lead into a long discussion that causes you to forget what you were after in the first place. If you check off each fact *after* there has been testimony on it, you will know exactly what to go back to.

Only prove what is necessary to establish your case. Surplus evidence can confuse the arbitrator and provides additional subject matter for your opponent to probe on cross-examination. Moreover, surplus invites rebuttal, which lengthens the hearing, complicates the case, and may open up new issues on which you must offer surrebuttal.

Occasionally, on direct examination your own witness will provide testimony that goes beyond the question you posed. If that happens, you do well to cut off your witness politely but firmly, reminding her to answer only the question asked. That is necessary to keep your witness on track, to establish a useful habit for her to follow on cross-examination, and to prevent her from blundering into an area where she may volunteer harmful information. Establish that pattern of cutting off early in your witness's testimony when the issue is unimportant. That way your interruption does not smell fishy when you do it when the subject is important.

Do not repeat your witness's answers. If you wish to emphasize something your witness has said, either ask her to repeat the answer (acting as if you had not heard clearly) or ask a slightly different question that will elicit precisely the same answer. Constantly parroting a witness's testimony—especially as a matter of habit—adds nothing to the case except time and boredom.

Finally, do not recast your witness's testimony to fit your theory of the case. Consider the following testimony:

> Q: What did you see when you came into the plant at 7:50 A.M. the next morning?
> A: I saw that there was no oil on the floor and Smedlap was sitting by his lathe eating a donut.
> Q: So, you say that, in fact, Smedlap had cleaned up the oil spill between 7:00 and 8:00?
> A: Objection. Leading. Speculation.

Leave drawing inferences or characterizing observations for closing argument, where it belongs. Restating your witness's words in different form is counterproductive in two ways. First, you cast doubt upon the accuracy of your witness's observations by suggesting they are insufficient to stand alone. Second, you demonstrate your own inadequacy as an advocate by asking an obviously leading question. Recall, if you will, the example in which you gave your witness the opportunity to supplement his testimony by asking him what, if anything, had sounded to him like an order. Your witness's response was a credible and convincing description of words and circumstances that added up to compulsion. In your closing statement you can repeat that testimony and dramatically characterize the compulsion as authorization to work overtime.

Notice how much of that effect you would have lost if you had followed up your witness's testimony with this question:

> Q: In other words, you felt your supervisor had authorized you to work overtime?
> A: Yes.

While in your own mind you may be saying "gotcha," you have mitigated the impact of your witness's testimony. You have focused the arbitrator's attention back on you and off the witness. And you have set your witness up for cross-examination on your words and conclusion, not his own.

Remember, the purpose of direct examination is to elicit the necessary facts to fulfill your case's essential elements. The more directly and simply your witness's testimony accomplishes that purpose, the more compelling your case will be and the less vulnerable it will be to attack on cross-examination.

There is one time when asking leading questions on direct examination is both appropriate and necessary. If you have a hostile witness, whom you have called because he has knowledge of the events, you need to lead him through his testimony so that he provides only the facts upon which you want to rely without adding a commentary. In some states, if you are calling such a witness in court, the rules of procedure require that you call the witness as a "hostile witness" and ask permission of the court to question the witness in accordance with the applicable section of the evidence code. In an arbitration it is sufficient to indicate to the arbitrator that the witness is a hostile one and that you are going to be proceeding accordingly. If, for example, the foreman hates your grievant, but saw the fight and had to have seen that the other party swung at grievant first, you might proceed as follows:

Q: Were you near the dough mixer at about 2:00 on November 15?
A: Yes.
Q: And you heard some shouting from Grievant and Joe?
A: Yes.
Q: And when you heard this shouting you were approximately ten or fifteen feet from them?
A: I couldn't say exactly how far away I was.
Q: Would ten to fifteen feet be a reasonable estimate?
A: Yes.
Q: Now, you have normal vision, do you not?
A: Yes.
Q: And you can see, for instance, if someone who is facing you at that distance is smoking a cigar, can't you?
A: Yes.
Q: And you don't suffer sudden blackouts, do you?
A: No.
Q: Now isn't it true that when you heard the shouting you turned and looked at Grievant and Joe?
A: Yes.
Q: And isn't it also true that the first person you saw take a swing was Joe?
A: Yes.

Q: And you saw Joe land that punch on Grievant's nose, didn't you?

A: Yes.

By leading the witness you have not given him any opportunity to offer his opinions about the confrontation, or who was correct in the underlying argument, or anything else that might be helpful to your opponent.

Cross-examination: On cross-examination you ask questions of opposing witnesses after their direct examination. Effective cross-examination has three purposes: first, to elicit facts omitted on direct examination; second, to correct facts misstated on direct examination; and third, to undercut the credibility and authority of the witness's direct testimony.

Before you begin to cross-examine, decide the specific purpose you want to achieve. Limit your inquiry to those purposes *only*. Use a written checklist to ensure that you cover all necessary points—then stop. If you cannot articulate a purpose for cross-examining a particular witness, do not cross-examine.

On cross-examination you should avoid simply reiterating the witness's direct testimony. That accomplishes nothing positive and may be counterproductive in three ways: first, repetition emphasizes the authority of the witness's direct testimony. Second, repetition may reinforce any positive impressions the witness made on direct. Third, repetition may bore and alienate the arbitrator because it wastes time and gives the impression that you are floundering or fishing.

On cross-examination there is no bar to asking leading questions. Because the witness is presumed hostile, you may appropriately lead in order to focus the inquiry and limit the witness's responses.

Here are two examples of appropriate cross-examination. The first demonstrates the witness's lack of authority. Assume

that the witness, grievant's co-worker, has testified that grievant cleaned up an oil spill before 8 A.M. on the day in question.
You know from the witness's time card that he did not punch in
until 8:02 A.M. Here is the cross-examination:

> Q: You testified on direct, didn't you, that grievant
> cleaned the oil spill before 8 A.M.?
> A: That's right.
> Q: But you didn't punch in that day until 8:02, correct?
> A: Correct.
> Q: So you didn't actually see grievant do that work
> before 8 A.M., did you?
> A: No, I didn't.
> Q: So you really have no personal knowledge about griev-
> ant's claim do you?
> A: No, I don't.

If, at any point in that cross-examination, the witness had
claimed personal knowledge, you could confront him with the
time card to undercut his credibility. As the cross-examination
unfolded, you have undercut the authority of his testimony on
direct and should move on to other productive questions.

By asking leading questions, you limit the witness's opportunity to volunteer potentially damaging information. Having
accomplished that purpose, do not open the door by allowing
explanations of earlier testimony that you cannot control. See
how our cross-examiner, who has just secured the witness's
admission of no personal knowledge, completely loses the
advantage of that concession by asking an additional, unnecessary question:

> Q: So how could you have testified with such certainty
> that grievant did the work?
> A: Because our supervisor told me later that he had come
> in at 7:30 A.M. and saw grievant cleaning up the spill.

That answer, arguably an admission against interest by the management representative, would be an exception to the hearsay rule that could be used to prove the fact alleged. It certainly can come in as a prior inconsistent statement of the supervisor who is likely to be one of your own witnesses.

Here is a second example of proper cross-examination designed to undercut the witness's credibility by showing prior inconsistent action. This actually happened in a case. On direct, grievant had testified most emphatically that on February 17—which had been the last day for him to return to work from an overextended medical leave—he had called the personnel director from home and received oral permission to delay his return one more week.

Q: You called the plant on February 17?
A: Yes.
Q: You were home in bed?
A: Yes.
Q: Are you absolutely sure?
A: Yes.
Q: You weren't in Florida?
A: No.
Q: During your leave you were still covered for medical treatment under our health plan, weren't you?
A: Yes.
Q: So you could have used your Blue Cross card for hospital treatment, right?
A: Right.
Q: Would you please tell the arbitrator what this document is? (Handing the witness Blue Cross hospital claim form from a Florida hospital for emergency room treatment grievant received February 17, a copy of which Blue Cross had automatically sent to the company's personnel department.)

You have trapped grievant in a lie. How dramatically you press is a matter of personal choice and style. Just remember to keep asking leading questions that limit his opportunity to explain the conflict or reverse the advantage. If the witness tries to volunteer information that goes beyond your question, cut him off early, even if the extra information is harmless. As on direct, you want to establish the pattern early of limiting answers to questions asked. This will make it look normal if you have to do it when it counts.

Redirect and Recross-examination: In both of these forms of examination, you ask the witness further questions based on his prior testimony. The purpose of redirect is to correct impressions established on cross by expanding facts, correcting facts, and reestablishing the witness's credibility and authority. You do this through eliciting explanations that your opponent may have cut off by his leading questions. Because it is a continuation of direct, you may not lead; you must use standard direct examination technique.

Similarly, on recross-examination your purpose is, as on cross, to undercut the authority and credibility of the redirect testimony. Again, you should not ask any questions that do not serve an appropriate purpose.

As a general rule, on direct or cross-examination you should avoid asking any question for which you do not know the answer. The problem with asking these questions is that they provide opportunities for the witness to foul up your case with harmful or irrelevant testimony. Left to their own devices, witnesses will invariably say the wrong thing. Don't let them.

I can think of just two exceptions to that general rule. First, when surrounding, verifiable circumstances lead you to infer the answer with a fair degree of certainty, your exposure to bad answers is minimal. If necessary, you can later correct the record by proving the surrounding circumstances. Second, and I hope rarely, your case may be in so much trouble that one more bad answer cannot do it further harm, and a potentially good answer may save it. In courtroom melodramas that last question, asked by a desperate lawyer, results in startling information that saves the case. Rarely does that happen in real life.

Presentation of Documents and Other Real Evidence

Documents and other real evidence, such as a half-full beer can, the broken tool, or the allegedly stolen product, are things that prove a fact in issue or establish the basis to infer a fact in issue. Like testimony, real evidence must be relevant. For uncontested documents such as the collective bargaining agreement, the parties will usually stipulate genuineness and relevance before offering it in evidence. For other pieces of real evidence, there are some simple steps to be gone through to introduce the document.

Here are the basic steps. First, ask the arbitrator (or reporter if there is one) to mark the exhibit for identification. Second, give a copy to your opponent. Third, hand a copy to the witness and ask questions that allow the witness to identify the document and establish that it is genuinely what it purports to be. Or, if the identification does not establish the document's source and genuineness, ask further questions to establish those facts. Fifth, move the document into evidence.

At that point, your opponent may raise objections or ask for voir dire. If there is an objection to the admission of the document, you will have to answer it, or meet it by asking additional questions to establish the exhibit's relevance and competence. I will discuss voir dire below.

Real evidence speaks for itself. It is the best evidence of what it is or what it says. If you want your witness to characterize real evidence, make sure you give her an opportunity to do so before the exhibit goes into evidence. Compare these two examples.

Example 1:

> Q: What happened next?
>
> A: Out of the blue, I got a letter wrongfully denying my promotion and unjustly criticizing my performance.
>
> Q: Here is a document the arbitrator marked for identification as Union Exhibit 2. Can you identify it?
>
> A: Yes, that's the letter I received from the company.
>
> COUNSEL: I offer Union 2 in evidence.
>
> OPPONENT: No objection.
>
> ARBITRATOR: In evidence.

Example 2:

> Q: I hand you the document the arbitrator marked for identification as Union Exhibit 2. Please identify it.
>
> A: It's the letter I received from the company on March 21st.
>
> Q: What does it say about your performance?
>
> OPPONENT: *Objection!* The document speaks for itself.
>
> ARBITRATOR: Sustained.

Note that in Example 1, you may get an "impact bonus" if your opponent objects to the characterization of the letter. You can then reiterate the characterization by introducing the letter through saying: "Mr. Arbitrator, we are confident that this letter wrongfully denying the promotion and unjustly criticizing grievant, speaks for itself. We would like to have it marked for identification." In Example 2, even if the arbitrator allows the witness to read the letter, he is unlikely to permit the witness to characterize it.

When your opponent offers real evidence that you have reason to doubt is authentic or relevant, you may conduct voir dire examination. Like cross-examination, the purpose of voir dire is to undercut the probative value of the proffered exhibit so that it is excluded from the record and therefore not considered by the arbitrator.

Here is an example of successful voir dire examination.

Q: Can you identify these two empty Budweiser beer cans that have been marked for identification as Employer's Exhibit 2?

A: Yes, those are the beer cans I found in grievant's lunch box on the day of the accident.

Q: Move Company 2 into evidence.

UNION COUNSEL: Voir dire, please.

VOIR DIRE EXAMINATION

Q: Have you kept those beer cans with you since the day of the accident?

A: No.

Q: When was the last time before today that you saw those cans?

A: The day of the accident.

Q: What did you do with them that day?

A: I gave them to my foreman.

Q: What did he do with them?

A: I don't know.

Q: And you haven't seen them from that day to this?

A: That's right.

Q: And who had them when you first saw them today?

A: The company's lawyer.

UNION ATTORNEY: Objection to Company 2; insufficient foundation.

ARBITRATOR: Sustained.

Based on that voir dire examination, the beer cans, which were a brand that is commonly sold in the area, did not come in. That would not be dispositive unless the beer cans were the sole evidence of grievant's alleged misconduct. The witness could still testify to his having found beer cans, and he and others could testify to facts they had observed from which the arbitrator could infer grievant's misconduct.

Rebuttal and Surrebuttal

At the end of your opponent's case, you have an opportunity on rebuttal or surrebuttal to answer new facts with additional evidence that supports your case's essential elements or undercuts your opponent's affirmative defenses. It is not proper rebuttal simply to duplicate testimony already given, even if the credibility of one of your witnesses has been seriously damaged. The time to plan for that is in your case-in-chief.

Here is an example of proper rebuttal and surrebuttal. Assume that on the union's case-in-chief grievant testified that his supervisor had orally authorized him to work overtime on June 15. Assume as well that on the employer's answering case the supervisor testified he never orally authorizes overtime and he always sends a written memorandum confirming the assignment to the individual, with a copy to the paymaster. Proper rebuttal for the union would be testimony by grievant and others as to specific occasions, supported by pay stubs or payroll records, on which they had received overtime pay for work done without written authorization. Proper surrebuttal by the company would be production by the paymaster of his copies of the supervisor's written memoranda covering the overtime dates alleged by the union's rebuttal witnesses. Again, it is not proper rebuttal after your opponent has contradicted your witness to put your witness back on to insist on the truth of his original testimony.

The Hearing

Closing Statements

The purpose of a closing statement is to summarize the evidence on the record and to show how it supports your case and undercuts your opponent's. Closing statements are delivered immediately upon the close of evidence while recollections and impressions are fresh. Unless you intend to submit a formal brief, you should insist on the opportunity to close. You will not have a better opportunity to persuade the arbitrator of the merits of your case.

Like opening statements, there is no magic formula for a successful closing statement. At a minimum, you should remind the arbitrator of the essential elements of your case and show how you have fulfilled, through credible evidence, what you had promised to prove on your opening. Show as well how your opponent has failed to establish the essential elements of its affirmative defense. Where there are conflicts of testimony, explain why the arbitrator should believe your witnesses and discredit your opponents.

In effect, your closing statement should sound like the opinion and award you hope the arbitrator will issue. You should be as precise in your remedial argument as you want the arbitrator's remedial award to be. State clearly what it is you want, give the arguments that provide a logical basis for that remedy, and provide the numbers or process for exact calculation of all sums due. If you want the arbitrator to retain jurisdiction of the case to evaluate remedial compliance, say so. And be prepared to give a good reason for that to happen. Frequently, your opponent will agree, since that simplifies resolution of any disputes over the remedy. If your opponent does not agree, however, you may have a problem.

Many arbitrators are loath to retain jurisdiction of a case without the parties' agreement that they do so. Those arbitrators feel they lack jurisdiction to give themselves jurisdiction and that their job is to decide the case cleanly the first time

175

through. That includes drafting a clear enough statement of their remedial intent so that the parties need no further guidance to implement it. Other arbitrators will retain jurisdiction on their own motion if they anticipate factual disputes concerning remedial elements such as interim earnings. Make clear in your own mind whether you would want the arbitrator or a judge in the award's enforcement proceeding to make such determinations. That way you can give a clear direction during your closing.

Finally, still other arbitrators retain jurisdiction on their own motions for a limited period of time when their award presents remedial possibilities that the parties themselves had not had an opportunity to address at the hearing with evidence or argument. Under such circumstances, those arbitrators will, in essence, remand the case to the parties for their own negotiations concerning remedy, giving either the option within a stated period of time following the award to invoke that retained jurisdiction for final determination. In those cases, the arbitrator is likely to label his first award, "Interim Award," so that he does not lose jurisdiction by having issued a final award.

Settlements and Consent Awards

At the outset I should make clear that arbitration and mediation are very different processes. Arbitrators have complete power to decide the issue that the parties have submitted to them. Mediators, on the other hand, have no power to decide anything and operate (through persuasion) to help the parties reach their own voluntary resolution. Successful arbitration and mediation involve very different skills. There is no guarantee that your arbitrator possesses both.

Is mediation by an arbitrator ever appropriate? Of course. When the parties request it. Before making that request, however, you should be aware of your exposure. During mediation, the arbitrator will hear statements that would not be appropriate testimony if offered on the record of an arbitration. Before inviting mediation, therefore, you should be confident of your arbitrator's professionalism that will enable him, if unsuccessful at mediation, to decide the arbitration case *on the record* and not on what he may have heard during mediation efforts.

Very occasionally an arbitrator may suggest the parties reconsider settlement and offer his mediation services. For example, the arbitrator may have heard substantial testimony that convinces him both sides have such significant exposure that they might not want to risk having a written award and opinion. Under those circumstances, the arbitrator is entitled to tentative opinions concerning the course of the case, expression of which is *not* misconduct and may provide the basis for a voluntary settlement by the parties. Alternatively, both sides may have watched their key witnesses crumble and, standing in the ruins of their "impenetrable" case, be anxious to avoid a debacle through negotiating a settlement.

How should you respond to such arbitral invitations? First and foremost, be honest. If you do not want the arbitrator to mediate, say so clearly and emphatically. You need not worry about hurting his feelings. He would not have chosen to be an arbitrator if he had a fragile ego. More practically, you can gracefully decline the offer by emphasizing the extent of your confidence in his skill as an arbitrator, which leads you to believe that arbitration poses no risk.

Even when the arbitrator does not offer to mediate, but only suggests that the parties might like to "talk about where the case is going from here," it may be wise to explore the possibility of settlement with your opponent. Settlements can be appealing in many cases. An agreed settlement replaces uncertain exposure with a certain outcome that the parties themselves chose. Since they must live with the settlement, they can shape it to reflect their relationship and avoid anticipated problems.

Many resolutions of arbitration issues are reached by the parties at the hearing itself. Some arbitrators enjoy thinking that the immediate prospect of disinterested justice they represent impels the parties to resolve their differences. Although such thoughts may be gratifying, I think there are two more likely reasons. First, having finally had the opportunity to complete investigation and preparation of their cases, the parties know their exposure and can more intelligently assess the appeal of settlement. Second, the uncertainty as to how an arbitrator might decide the case, and the immediate prospect of an arbitrary—not necessarily just—remedy, make a known outcome extremely attractive.

If you reach a settlement at the hearing, you have two choices for memorializing it. You can either reduce the agreement to a signed memorandum, or agree to have the arbitrator issue a consent award, incorporating the agreed terms. While the two choices are equivalent as to the terms of the agreement, there is an essential difference in enforcement.

Enforcement of a consent award occurs just as enforcement of any arbitration award. As I discuss in more detail in Chapter 8, judicial enforcement of arbitration awards is usually fairly simple. Either party can commence a summary proceeding to confirm the award as a court judgment, and judicial enforcement of that judgment proceeds as it would for enforcement of any other judgment.

Memorandum agreements, however, involve more complicated enforcement issues that you must address. If the memorandum amends a provision of the parties' collective bargaining agreement that is covered by the grievance procedure and arbitration clause, if there is a future breach, the memorandum would be enforced through the grievance procedure. Enforcement would proceed the same way if the memorandum expressly provides that claimed violations are subject to the contract's grievance and arbitration procedures.

In the absence of such express provisions, however, you may have problems with enforcement. That is not to say that the memorandum would be unenforceable; it is as enforceable as any other written contract. The problem lies in determining the appropriate forum for relief. For example, in the public sector, some states have created special courts for securing money damages against the state itself and special proceedings for equitable relief against governmental bodies. Making a claim against a public entity may be time consuming, expensive, and uncertain. In fact, that is probably why the parties chose arbitration in the first place. In the private sector there may be an even greater problem. If claimed breaches of the memorandum are not subject to the contract's arbitration clause, they will also not be subject to its express or implied no-strike clause. In deciding on whether to have a memorandum agreement or consent award you need to keep these considerations in mind. Either should be shaped with a view to future enforcement.

Limitations on consent awards are more practical than legal. As exclusive collective bargaining agent for the employees involved, the union has complete authority to resolve grievances, consistent with its duty of fair representation. Because of uncertainties concerning the substantive content of that duty, however, if you represent a union you would be wise to secure the individual grievant's consent to the agreed resolution. You can ask the arbitrator to assure himself that the consent is voluntarily given and to recite that voluntary agreement in his consent award.

A formal limitation on the arbitrator's participation in consent award appears in Article 2-I(1), Paragraph 65 ("Consent Awards") of the Code of Professional Responsibility for Arbitrators of Labor-Management Disputes (*see* Appendix 6), jointly promulgated by the National Academy of Arbitrators, American Arbitration Association, and Federal Mediation and Conciliation Service. That section provides:

> 1. Prior to issuance of an award, the parties may jointly request the arbitrator to include in the award certain agreements between them, concerning some or all of the issues. If the arbitrator believes that a suggested award is proper, fair, sound, and lawful, it is consistent with professional responsibility to adopt it.

Although the Code has no legal status, it does have significant practical weight. The three organizations that issue it are significant forces in the arbitration community; and two of them are significant sources of business for many arbitrators. As a result, most arbitrators pay careful attention to the Code's provisions which, in any event, reflect the prevailing ethic of most arbitrators.

No discussion of consent awards is complete without considering those cases in which the parties' consent is not disclosed in the award. At times the principals know what the outcome must be. For example, in contract interpretation cases the union representatives may concede the limits of what was negotiated, but they may feel compelled to bring a grievance and process it through arbitration for its political or cathartic effect. In such cases, the hearing often becomes an elaborate ritual to reach a predetermined end.

This is not to suggest that agreed outcomes (also known in the labor relations trade by the unfortunate term "rigged awards") are, in all cases, improper. Agreed outcomes in contract-interpretation cases have long been useful devices for blaming on arbitrators (who are paid to act as professional lightning rods) what either union or employer representatives, or both, felt politically unable to achieve directly.

There is, among arbitrators, a spectrum of willingness to serve such purposes in contract-interpretation cases. Those that accept the view that arbitration is a creation and extension of the collective bargaining process tend to participate; those who see themselves more as judges independent of the parties do not. I know of no one, however, who knowingly participates in agreed outcomes in disciplinary cases.

There is an essential difference between disciplinary and contract-interpretation grievances. The former usually arise under contract provisions limiting the employer's power to discipline bargaining unit personnel without "just cause." The parties typically do not negotiate the substantive content of "just cause;" to do so would require dozens of pages. Instead, they invoke just cause as shorthand for traditional concepts of fair play in industrial relations and submit the discipline to impartial review by a third party. In disciplinary cases, therefore, an individual grievant may have rights and remedies independent of what the parties agree is appropriate. In every disciplinary case, a grievant's particular factual circumstances will have more to do with the outcome than the parties' bargain. Thus, an agreed upon outcome may deprive an individual of substantial rights. For that reason most arbitrators do not participate in disciplinary cases with agreed outcomes.

In contract-interpretation cases, on the other hand, grievant has no contractual rights beyond those the parties *expressly* negotiated. The union is, therefore, a definitive initial source for evaluating grievant's contract claim. Moreover, in marginal cases involving ambiguous negotiations, the union may decide that it better serves the overall unit's interest to choose the most appealing factual cases for raising new claims. It may not want to pursue a less sexy case, just because it came up first.

Because of changes in the duty of fair representation, the appeal of agreed outcome awards to certify entirely appropriate outcomes has increased. In contract-interpretation cases where the union concedes it never won in negotiations what grievant seeks, and where careful investigation has revealed no factual basis for relief, parties may still opt for an agreed outcome proceeding. Obviously, you would do this to avoid the greater expense and trouble of a duty of fair representation litigation that you both can reasonably expect to win on the merits.

If you intend to have a hearing designed to support an undisclosed agreed outcome, be certain beforehand that your arbitrator is willing to participate. Although the Code of Professional Responsibility (*see* Appendix 6) is silent on the extent of disclosure of consent, it does address the arbitrator's obligation to know and understand the appropriateness of the agreed award's substance. Article 2-I(1) gives the following amplification of its general principles:

> a. *Before complying with such a request, an arbitrator must be certain that he or she understands the suggested settlement adequately in order to be able to appraise its terms. If it appears that pertinent facts or circumstances may not have been disclosed, the arbitrator should take the initiative to assure that all significant aspects of the case are fully understood. To this end, the arbitrator may request additional specific information and may question witnesses at a hearing.*

Finally, an essential element of undisclosed settlements is that they must remain undisclosed. Disclosure is embarrassing, and the image of union and employer representatives skulking about behind an individual grievant's back may suggest an impropriety to a reviewing court, despite the settlement's substantive terms. If you cannot be assured that an agreed upon outcome will remain undisclosed, don't even try it.

Conclusion

This completes our consideration of issues that will arise before and during the hearing of an arbitration case. All my advice and your efforts have as their goal a successful outcome. All are subject to the overriding rule of common sense. If your pragmatic judgment tells you that any suggestion will not help in your particular case, by all means reject or modify it. After all, your goal is to present your case in the way most likely to result in a successful outcome for your side, and you are the ultimate judge of what is best.

6

After the Hearing

Introduction

When the hearing is over, the advocate's job is far from complete. She may have to request that a hearing be reopened. She is likely to write a brief, evaluate the award, and assess the arbitrator's bill. The most important of these activities is writing the brief; therefore, I will discuss that critical endeavor first.

Writing the Arbitration Brief

What Is It?

An effective arbitration brief is a written argument that convinces the arbitrator to rule in your favor. It is concise, accurate, persuasive, and technically correct. It is concise because it does not include every argument that might have some relevance, but only those upon which the case turns. And those critical arguments are made in as few words as possible. It is accurate because you scrupulously adhere to the facts and evidence that came in at the hearing. It is persuasive because you select and order the facts and arguments so that your position is compelling while your opponent's is exposed in all its weakness. It is technically correct because you carefully edit and proofread the brief, so that the arbitrator feels comfortable in relying upon you. While in all these ways an arbitration brief is similar to briefs you are familiar with in other settings, in one critical way it differs from all other briefs you write.

There is no system of precedent in labor arbitration. There is no one set of rules developed by legislatures or judges that arbitrators must apply in all cases. Rather, there are a multitude of collective bargaining agreements, each of which sets up a series of rules by which the parties themselves agreed to live. And there are thousands of arbitrators, each of whom is called upon to interpret these agreements.

Arbitrators are not organized in a hierarchy of tribunals, each reviewing the level below. Nor do courts review arbitrators' decisions to establish a "common law" of arbitration. What one arbitrator said in a case not involving these same parties and this same contract is not precedent for your arbitrator. Another arbitrator's statement of a principle may seem sound to your arbitrator, but it does not bind her.

Thus, you cannot make the most commonly made legal argument: an appeal to authority. You can tell a federal district court judge that she is obliged to do something because the Supreme Court has ruled a certain way. You cite the Supreme Court case as your authority, and, if the principle is applicable, you can reasonably expect that the district court will follow it. But you cannot do that with an arbitrator, because she is not obliged to do what some other arbitrator did.

This point—that the appeal to authority has almost no place in arbitration—is frequently forgotten. As a result, arbitration advocates make statements about how a point in their case should be decided, follow these statements with string citations to published arbitration decisions, and believe that they have done all that needs to be done to persuade the arbitrator. Not so. Their citations to published arbitration awards have almost no persuasive value because no arbitrator is obliged to follow a principle, whether it has been used by ten or one hundred arbitrators ruling under different contracts. This is not to say that your arbitrator cannot be easily persuaded to follow a sound principle, but string citations are not the way to do it. I will discuss a better method later on in this Chapter.

Should You Write a Brief?

Some advocates automatically write a brief. In most arbitrations, however, no brief is necessary. And an unnecessary brief raises the cost to the parties by adding to the time the advocates spend arguing the case and the arbitrator spends deciding it. Instead of writing a brief as a reflex, in each case you should consider whether it is necessary.

The best reason for writing a brief is that you think it will help you win your case. There are four circumstances in which a brief is likely to be helpful. First, an arbitration may involve a complex factual or contractual issue. In such a case it is always worthwhile to write a brief. It gives you the opportunity to show the arbitrator how that complex situation can be understood in light of your position.

Second, it may be that the theory of the case you were originally prepared to argue is no longer useful because the evidence that you thought would come in at the hearing did not. Thus, you may want to write a brief in which you organize new and effective arguments around the evidence that actually came in at the hearing.

Third, the hearing may have become somewhat diffuse. As a result, you feel that the effectiveness of your arguments may have been lost among the many trivial things—such as an objection to a particular piece of evidence—that were argued at the hearing. A brief gives you the opportunity to make an organized argument that effectively states your case.

Finally, you may be obliged to write a brief because your client insists or because the union you represent fears a duty of fair representation suit. In those instances, you will write a brief because it is easier to persuade an arbitrator to rule in your favor than to persuade your client to change its position.

There are also four compelling reasons for *not* writing a brief. First, your client may insist that it no longer wishes to throw good money after bad. Having heard the quality of its evidence at the hearing, your client may decide that enough is enough. Second, you may want to save money on minor cases and have your awards more quickly. (Many parties do this for discipline cases involving penalties other than termination.) Third, certain cases turn exclusively on the credibility of a witness. Using a brief to say that Jones was "incredibly believable" will not help your case, and it may well hurt your image as a sophisticated user of the English language. On the other hand, there may be complex motives at work that affect the credibility of the crucial witness. If that is so, you may still want to write a brief to explain these to the arbitrator. Finally, there are short cases with straightforward evidence that are based on a simple theory. In those cases, a brief does no more than repeat what you already said at the hearing. Since the arbitrator probably decided that simple case on the ride home, a brief adds nothing but cost and time.

Since the purpose of a brief is to persuade the arbitrator, you should be mindful of what the arbitrator needs. Notice whether the arbitrator is focusing on the issues during the hearing or appears to be confused. If the arbitrator asks a question of a witness, it may indicate an area that is unclear in the arbitrator's mind. Or it may suggest a theory of the case that the arbitrator finds more germane than the one you are espousing. These cues suggest that you ought to write a brief to clarify the arbitrator's thinking.

If all else fails, ask. I have never been bothered by advocates asking whether I would find a brief helpful. Nor have I hesitated to say that I was so comfortable with the clarity of counsel's arguments that a brief was not necessary. On the other hand, do not expect an arbitrator to refuse your opponent the opportunity to submit a brief because both you and the arbitrator believe it is superfluous. In states that follow the Uniform Arbitration Act, and under the United States Arbitration Act, refusing to allow either side to make arguments on behalf of its position is a potential ground for vacatur. Thus an arbitrator may think a brief unnecessary, but she is unlikely to refuse it.

The Form of an Arbitration Brief

Unlike briefs to a court, whose form may be dictated by rules of the court, there are no "official rules" for what an arbitration brief should look like. What follows is a suggested format. Adapt it in any way you like.

Suggested Arbitration Brief Format

A. Title page
B. Statement of the Case (optional)
C. Issue
D. Facts
E. Argument
F. Conclusion

Title page

You should include certain identifying elements on a title page.

1. **The caption of the case.** Who are the parties to the arbitration? Identify them as you want the arbitrator to identify them in the award and opinion.

2. **Identifying numbers.** You should include the American Arbitration Association case number (or that of any other agency administering the case), the arbitrator's case number, as well as any case identifying number you and your opponent have used. In addition, it is useful to use a short title, such as "Overtime Pay Grievance," to jog the arbitrator's memory.

3. **Identity of the party submitting the brief.** You should identify the party (i.e., the name of the company or the name and local of the union) as well as the name of the person who wrote the brief. For instance, this section might say:

> Brief of IBEW, Local 83
> Submitted by John Jones, Chief Steward

> or

> Brief submitted on behalf of International
> Conglomerated Holding Company
> By Harvey Smith, Esq.
> John Doe, of Counsel.

4. **Date.** While this date will not necessarily establish that you submitted the brief on time, it will remind the arbitrator of when her award and opinion is due.

Statement of the Case

This section, which is optional, contains background information about when and where the case was heard, whether a transcript was made, and any understandings entered into by the parties at the end of the hearing. For instance, it might say: "The parties agreed that they would submit briefs on the arbitrability of this grievance, and that the arbitrator would render an interim award and opinion. If she decides that the matter is arbitrable, the parties have agreed to go forward on the merits." In addition to stating any understanding reached at the hearing, you should use this section to continue any objection to arbitrability or procedure that you made at the hearing.

Issue

If there was a stipulated issue, say so. Be sure you have it exactly right. For instance:

The parties stipulated the following issue:

Did the company violate Article III, Section C of the current collective bargaining agreement (J-1) when it refused to pay Grievant at the overtime rate for all of the hours he worked on Saturday, July 11, 1986?

If so, what shall be the remedy?

If you have not stipulated an issue, you will want to state the issue in a manner that is favorable to your position. In so doing, it is important that you do not state the issue so that it is *obviously* slanted. For instance, in a situation in which the collective bargaining agreement calls for premium pay on all holidays worked, and the dispute is over whether Good Friday is a holiday requiring premium pay, an obviously slanted issue would look like this:

Did the Company violate Article VI ("Holiday Pay") of the current collective bargaining agreement (J-1) when it failed to pay Grievants at the premium rate for work done on the Good Friday holiday, which occurred on Friday, April 20?

This is obviously slanted because it assumes the issue before the arbitrator. That is, it asserts that Good Friday is a holiday within the meaning of Article VI of the contract. A statement of the issue that is not obviously slanted would leave out the word "holiday":

Did the Company violate Article VI ("Holiday Pay") of the current collective bargaining agreement (J-1) when it failed to pay Grievants at the premium rate for work done on Good Friday, April 20?

Note that this still uses the phrase "Good Friday" which, from the union point of view, implies a holiday. A statement of the issue by management might look like this:

Did the Company violate Article VI of the current collective bargaining agreement (J-1) when it paid Grievants the hourly rate specified by Article II of the contract, for all work performed on April 20?

Notice the difference between the two "fair" issues. The management statement uses positive language ("it paid Grievants") where the union statement uses negative language ("it failed to pay Grievants"). Both sides use factually accurate language to imply support for their position in the arbitration. The union uses "Good Friday," capitalized, to suggest a holiday. Since Article VI is entitled "Holiday Pay," the union also includes the title in its statement of the issue so that the arbitrator will draw the connection between holiday pay and Good Friday. The employer uses only the number of the article, and the date upon which the work was done. In addition, the employer includes a piece of factually correct information that is probably not in dispute, that grievants were paid "the hourly rate specified by Article II of the contract," to imply its strict compliance with the contract. All of these methods are acceptable ways of stating an issue favorably without appearing to slant your statement of the issue.

Facts

In the same way that your phrasing of the issue can help persuade the arbitrator, your statement of the facts can direct the arbitrator's attention to facts that support your argument.

All too often, however, advocates think that by omitting facts that are harmful to their case or using emotionally toned characterizations (for example, "Grievant's *vicious* verbal attack on her supervisor") they are advancing their argument. That is simply untrue. Arbitrators can quickly recognize these omissions or characterizations and may well conclude that they are attempts to prop up a weak case.

Worse still, advocates are occasionally tempted to change a fact slightly in order to make it better fit their theory. Don't do it. There are grave risks if you are caught. Nothing so destroys an arbitrator's confidence in an advocate as seeing that he or she has changed the facts of the case in order to improve an argument. And this loss of confidence may not be limited to the case at hand.

You want to present the facts of your case in the light most favorable to your position. There are a number of different devices you can use to do this, including: selection/omission, ordering, repetition, and word choice.

Selection/Omission: These are, of course, two aspects of the same technique. The facts you include or exclude give a persuasive slant to your fact section. Of course, there are certain facts that you must include, since they are vital to your case or defense. Likewise, there are facts you must admit because they were both proved at the hearing and key to your opponent's position. Leaving out any of these latter facts lessens your credibility. You can, of course, show in your argument section how these inconvenient facts are really not the ones upon which the arbitrator should base a decision. Furthermore, you can increase the contrast between facts you want to emphasize and facts you must admit. Whenever possible, use quotes and references to pages in the transcript for facts you want to emphasize and paraphrase for facts you must admit.

There are other facts, however, which are neither critical to your argument nor necessary for your credibility. They should be included or excluded on the basis of whether they strengthen or weaken your argument. For instance, in the discussion on stating the issue, we used the example of a grievance over premium pay for Good Friday. If you were stating the facts from the union's point of view, you might simply assert, "It is undisputed that April 20 was Good Friday." From the employer's point of view, this assertion needs some qualification. Thus, the employer might say, "In the Christian religion, April 20 was the holy day known as 'Good Friday.'"

Stating it this way does two things. First, by adding the fact that this is a holy day in the Christian religion, you call attention to the fact that neither Moslems nor Jews nor Buddhists, nor any other religious group, believes that there is anything special about the day. Second, by setting it off with quotation marks you emphasize that "Good Friday" is a title of a Christian holy day, rather than the common name for April 20. Quotation marks should be used sparingly, and never sarcastically. When quotation marks are overused they lose their effectiveness, just as red ceases to be a warning when it colors everything. The sarcastic use of quotation marks may undermine your argument by highlighting your own failure to make the argument explicit. For instance, a management representative who writes grievant's "injury" is really writing, grievant's "so-called injury." This advocate's argument would be more effective if it made explicit the reason for questioning whether there really was an injury. Thus, it might be better to say, "Neither Dr. Jones nor Dr. Smith found anything wrong with Grievant. He had no injury. It would therefore be more appropriate to speak of Grievant's complaint." And after saying this, the advocate should substitute *complaint* for *injury* throughout the argument.

Another aspect of this selection/omission technique is to include marginally relevant facts. For instance, if grievant worked overtime on Good Friday, that is relevant to the remedy, or the total amount due him. The union might include it in the fact pattern in this way:

> Grievant began work at 8 A.M. on Good Friday and worked until 4 P.M. At that time, his foreman asked him if he would be willing to stay an extra two hours to finish the repairs. Grievant agreed to stay two extra hours or "as long as it took to finish the job." (Tr. at 31)

It is obvious that this does not bear directly on whether Good Friday is a holiday under the contract. It does, however, cast grievant in a favorable light and bears sufficiently on the remedy to be included. Small touches like this, if not overdone, can help in your overall attempt to persuade the arbitrator.

Ordering: The order in which you present the facts may advance or impede your argument. Your basic goal is to order the facts so that those that are critical to your position stand out, while those that are harmful to your position almost disappear. This ordering occurs in the overall statement of the facts, in each paragraph of facts, and within the individual sentences that make up the paragraphs.

The easiest way to write a statement of facts is to follow the chronology of the events. Thus, in an insubordination case, you might start with saying what time the grievant got to work, and follow him through the day up until the events occurred. Since the arbitrator is likely to have already heard the facts in that order at the hearing, this is not an effective way of presenting them. Nor is it effective to simply provide a synopsis of what each witness testified to at the hearing. A brief that goes through all of the testimony is usually more soporific than persuasive.

Instead, a management representative might begin by saying: "Grievant said to his supervisor 'buzz off, dragon breath,' in response to a direct order to clean the pipe wrenches. This

happened at 2 P.M. on August 20, in the maintenance shop."
The management representative would then go on to fill in the
relevant details of the events from the testimony at the hearing.

Notice three things about this initial statement. First, by
using grievant's exact words ("buzz off, dragon breath") and
specific details ("pipe wrenches"), it focuses the reader's attention on concrete facts rather than abstractions. It would be far
less powerful if the advocate simply said, "Grievant engaged in
insubordination."

Second, by giving the details of time and place *after* grievant's statement, it avoids distracting the reader with a series of
less important details to be remembered before getting to the
main point. Notice the effect of changing the sentence to read,
"On August 20, at 2 P.M., in the company maintenance shop,
Grievant said, 'buzz off, dragon breath,' in response to an order
to clean pipe wrenches." The latter sentence buries the reader
in detail.

Third, by beginning the entire fact section with grievant's
statement, the management representative colors the arbitrator's view of grievant as he reads through the rest of the facts.

The same sentence also illustrates the prominence that the
beginning of the paragraph gives to a statement. Linguistic
research shows that the beginning and end of a paragraph are
the two most important positions for information. People
remember what they read first and last. For our purposes, this
suggests two things. First, put what you want to have
remembered in the beginning of a paragraph, at the end of a
paragraph, or in both places. Second, if you have an inconvenient fact that you must include to preserve your credibility,
bury it in the middle of a paragraph, preferably as a
subordinate clause in a long and complex sentence. This leads
us to the next aspect of ordering.

The position of a word, phrase, or clause in a sentence helps
determine the ease with which a reader remembers it. Again,

readers remember best what is at the beginning or end of a sentence. If you want your reader to ignore a fact, bury it through "subordination." For instance, let us suppose that the grievant we were talking about in the last paragraph was being disciplined for insubordination for the third time. It would be impossible for the union to ignore this fact without appearing dishonest. Suppose, however, it appeared in the following sentence:

> Grievant is a twenty-year employee who, although having two prior insubordination disciplines, has an excellent work record for attendance, punctuality, and work quality.

While the prior disciplines do not completely disappear from sight, the structure of the sentence emphasizes grievant's good qualities. It does this by using an interrupting phrase between the subject (grievant) and verb ("has"), by using a subordinate clause ("although"), by listing three positive items, and putting those items at the end of the sentence where they are likely to be remembered.

Repetition: By repeating a fact you emphasize it. That much is obvious. Doing it subtly is a bit more difficult. Suppose, for example, you want to emphasize the fact that this is grievant's third discipline for insubordination. You could say:

> Grievant was disciplined for insubordination on August 21, 1980. Grievant was disciplined for insubordination on June 10, 1982. Grievant was disciplined for insubordination on February 5, 1983.

By stating each disciplinary incident in a separate sentence, and by putting all three sentences in the exact same form (parallel structure), you have driven home the information. If you wish to go one step further, you can *summarize* by saying, "Thus, this is Grievant's third discipline for insubordination." This allows you to repeat the point time after time, without ever saying the same thing twice.

Another way to summarize for emphasis is to make an implicit calculation explicit. For instance, if you say, "Grievant worked at the higher level job from 14 March 1983 to 16 May 1983," you are simply stating facts. If you add, "This amounts to sixty-one days, or over two months," you have emphasized the facts. Again, note that you do not do this by simply saying the same thing twice.

Word Choice: Mark Twain said it best: "The difference between the right word, and almost the right word, is the difference between lightning and a lightning bug." There is no rule that you can follow to be sure you use the right word since that is an art. You can, however, keep in mind the importance of using concrete rather than abstract words and recognize the different connotations of the words you use.

Concrete words describe something you can see or feel ("pickle"), as opposed to an abstract word that brings no immediate image to mind ("food"). The connotation of a word is the set of associations that usually go with it. For example, "yacht" connotes the sort of boat on which passengers wear blazers with crests on the breast pocket. Concrete words, because they convey immediate and specific images, are more useful than abstract words for persuading arbitrators.

On the other hand, abstractions hide uncomfortable facts. For instance, the employer advocate might say, "Grievant pushed his supervisor," while the employee advocate might say, "Grievant rebuffed his supervisor." It is easy to form a mental picture of one person "pushing" another; it is more difficult to picture one person "rebuffing" another. In fact, "rebuff" is sufficiently abstract to cover anything from physical shoves to cutting looks.

If you want to emphasize, use concrete words: "Grievant was forced to work in a sleet storm." If you want to downplay, use abstract words: "Grievant was forced to work in inclement weather."

Two aspects of connotation are important to consider in persuasive writing. First, some concrete words carry more vivid images than others. The "stench of rotting corpses" is more likely to offend the arbitrator's nose than the "odor of spoiling cadavers." The nuances of difference between factually accurate words may have a cumulative effect on the arbitrator.

Compare these two descriptions. First, "Grievant shouted an answer to his supervisor." Second, "Grievant shouted a retort to his supervisor." Shouting is speech that can indicate either the level of background noise that the speaker must overcome, or the mental state of the speaker. In the first example, when it is combined with the neutral "answer," the arbitrator has no reason to believe that the decibel level of grievant's speech is related to anything more than background noise. In the second example, when it is combined with "retort," which can be simply an answer or return of an argument or charge, the arbitrator is likely to conclude that grievant was acting in an angry way.

If you substituted "shrieked" for "shouted" in the second example, you would suggest grievant was almost hysterical. However, in so doing, you would also leave yourself open to the charge of characterizing grievant's speech rather than stating facts. If you characterize the fact, you lose credibility with the arbitrator because you suggest that the unvarnished facts are simply not sufficiently favorable to your point of view. It is not worth it. By playing the connotative values of words against one another, you can persuade the arbitrator without losing your credibility.

Argument

This section is the most critical portion of the brief. It is often poorly done. Brief writers sometimes devote so much energy to repeating everything that was said at the hearing that they have neither adequate time nor space for their argument. The theory seems to be that if the arbitrator believes everything the advocate included in the fact section, then he must inevitably decide in the advocate's favor. Unfortunately, the arbitrator is not given any reason for deciding. He is simply left to guess the reason for himself.

Alternatively, the brief writer fails to organize the argument section. He simply tosses alternative arguments at the arbitrator, hoping something will stick. All too often, what sticks is an impression that the advocate has a lousy case with no substantial support in the contract or the record. To avoid this losing impression, you need to organize both your overall argument and individual sections of it so as to effectively persuade the arbitrator.

One tool for organizing individual sections, which law students often learn, is IRAC (pronounced "eye-rack").[1] This is an acronym for Issue, Rule, Application, Conclusion. It is a tool for organizing data to order your arguments. For instance, in our Good Friday example there are two issues: Is Good Friday a holiday? and, Is it covered by the holiday pay article? Focusing on the issue of whether it is a holiday, you might want to argue by *definition*. The best definition, of course, is one contained in the collective bargaining agreement. If it defines Good Friday as a holiday, your grievance is probably won. Assuming it does not, however, you might look for another source of definitions, such as a dictionary. Webster's defines holiday as a "holy day." This provides you with a Rule, i.e., any "holy day" is a "holiday."

The next step is Application. You might reason that since Webster's defines holiday as a "holy day" and since, as you showed at the hearing, calendars list Good Friday as a "holy day," it fits the definition of "holiday."

---

1. See, BRAND & WHITE, LEGAL WRITING: THE STRATEGY OF PERSUASION, 53-74 (1976).

Therefore, your Conclusion is that Good Friday is a holiday. From this, you might go on to reason that, since the contract does not specify named holidays, and since Good Friday fits the definition of a holiday, it is covered by the contract. Finally, from this you argue that grievant is entitled to holiday pay.

The argument might look, in part, like this:

> Good Friday is a holiday. [Issue stated positively.] Since the contract does not define a holiday, we can look to the ordinary dictionary definition. Webster's defines a holiday as a "holy day." [Rule] All the calendars introduced at the hearing (U-3, 4, 5, 6, 7) showed April 20 as a "holy day," called Good Friday. [Application] Thus, by definition, Good Friday is a holiday. [Conclusion]

Notice that the Issue has not been stated as a question, since you do not want to give the arbitrator an opportunity to answer it the wrong way. It has been stated as a positive assertion. Furthermore, both the first and last sentence in this paragraph say the same thing. That increases the likelihood your point will be remembered.

While we have been using an argument by definition as an example, there are many other forms of argument that you might use. To the extent you find it helpful as an organizing tool, you can always use the Issue, Rule, Application, Conclusion format. For instance, you may be arguing that your interpretation of a contract section is more consistent with the meaning of the related contract sections than your opponent's interpretation. Your Issue is that your interpretation is most consistent with sections X, Y, and Z of the contract. Your Rule is that the interpretation of a particular section that is most consistent with related contract sections on the subject (or does the least violence to them) is most likely to be correct.[2] In the

---

2. The "Rule" is, in fact, simply the same principle of logical consistency that courts use when they construe statutes *in pari materia*. As a logical

Application section, you spell out how your interpretation fits with each of the other relevant contract sections. Your Conclusion, of course, is that the arbitrator must interpret the article as you have in order to be faithful to the contract as a whole.

Other types of arguments also effectively fit into the IRAC framework. For instance, we mentioned earlier that the mere citation of twenty cases after some point you have made is a waste of effort because there is no system of precedent in arbitration. When you want your arbitrator to adopt a Rule used by another arbitrator, however, you can use other cases for an argument by *analogy*.

To make an effective analogy, the cases compared must be similar in important respects; any differences between them must be explained as unimportant. For example, suppose you want to argue that the Rule to be applied in your case is that words said in jest do not constitute insubordination. Your grievant said, "buzz off, dragon breath" when his supervisor asked him to clean some pipe wrenches. You find another case where an arbitrator has stated that Rule and described the reasons for it in a convincing way. Your argument might look like this:

> Words said in jest do not constitute insubordination. [Issue stated positively.] Arbitrator Doe stated this principle succinctly when he said, "A humorous comment, when it is unaccompanied by a failure to perform the required task, is not, in itself, insubordination." 47 XZ2d 2131. [Rule] In the case before us Doe a fry cook in a fast food chicken franchise said,

---

matter courts assume that when the legislature acts on the same matter or subject in different statutes, it intends its acts to be harmonious rather than contradictory. In the same way, logic requires the assumption that when the parties to a collective bargaining agreement speak about the same subject in different sections of the agreement, they do not intend to have the sections conflict with each other. As with any logical principle, it is merely a rebuttable presumption. Evidence of bargaining history may rebut the presumption.

"Ain't nobody here but us chickens, you airhead." His supervisor had asked the fry cook, who was in the freezer at the time, to bring out certain boxes of frozen chicken. After some delay, the fry cook complied. In both that case and this, the response was not immediate compliance. There, as here, the job was eventually done. In both cases the employee's purpose was to get a laugh from fellow employees at the expense of the supervisor. As Doe noted, "Levity is the lubricant that makes work go smoothly. If every employee joke at the expense of a supervisor were considered insubordination, there would be nothing but somber workplaces with unhappy employees. It is work, not joking words, that counts." 47 XZ2d 2139. While Doe was talking about a fast food franchise, the principle is the same for a maintenance shop. Nor is there any significance to the fact that the fry cook's boss laughed and Supervisor Hortence failed to find Grievant funny. [Application.] Words said in jest, as long as they are not accompanied by an actual refusal to perform the requested work, do not constitute insubordination. [Conclusion]

In the argument by analogy you rely upon two things. First, the arbitrator you quote must have offered convincing reasons for the Rule propounded. If your arbitrator is not convinced that the Rule is sound, he or she will not adopt it.[3] Second, the application section of your analogy must persuade the arbitrator that your case is like the cited case in all of its essential points. If you are going to use the argument by analogy, you must carefully craft your issue and fact sections to highlight the similarities between your case and the one relied upon. If all three of these sections of your brief work together, you will increase your chance of persuading the arbitrator.

---

3. In some instances, of course, you are working with a Rule that is so well accepted (e.g., "work now, grieve later") that it is unlikely your arbitrator needs to be convinced of its soundness.

Another useful persuasive tool is the argument from "troublesome consequences." In this argument you attack your opponent's reasoning by saying, in effect, that because the argument leads to an unacceptable conclusion it cannot be correct.

Lawyers are accustomed to seeing this argument in judicial opinions. For example, in *Hynes v. New York Central Railroad Co.*,[4] Judge Cardozo rejected the argument that a boy diving from a plank projecting from the railroad's land into the Harlem River was a trespasser to whom no duty was owed. The railroad had argued that since he was a trespasser, they were not liable when their electric wires fell and electrocuted him. Cardozo wrote:

> Without wrong to them [bathers in the Harlem River], cross-arms might be left to rot; wires highly charged with electricity might sweep them from their stand, and bury them in the subjacent waters. In climbing on the board, they became trespassers and outlaws. The conclusion is defended with much subtlety of reasoning, with much insistence upon its inevitableness as a merely logical deduction. A majority of the Court are unable to accept this as the conclusion of the law. 231 N.Y. 229, 233.

Here is how the argument might look if you were to use our Good Friday example:

> Good Friday is not a holiday covered by Article VI (Holiday Pay). [Issue] The union has argued that all "holy days" are holidays under the contract. If all holy days were holidays for purposes of additional pay, the result would be absurd. [Rule] The Italian calendar introduced at the hearing (E-9) shows that every day of the year is a Catholic saint's day. The entire month of Ramadan is holy to Moslems. Jews regard all Saturdays as holy days. Thus, if the arbitrator were to accept the union's

---

4. 231 N.Y. 229 (1921).

position, every day of the year is a holiday for which Article VI provides premium pay. The parties cannot have intended that result. [Application] Good Friday is not a holiday covered by Article VI by virtue of being a holy day in the Christian religion. [Conclusion]

As you can see, the argument is most effective when the consequences of your opponent's argument can be made to appear truly absurd.

Obviously, this type of argument can be quite effective. There is, however, some danger in using it in arbitration briefs. Parties are under no obligation to avoid negotiating absurd clauses for their contract. Indeed, in some negotiations I have been involved in, both sides sought a way to put more money into the package without forcing the employer to back down from a stated wage position. They negotiated productivity formulae, differentials, and job titles that were absurd on their face, but that provided enough new money to settle the contract. Thus, you must carefully explore the relevant bargaining history before making this argument.

A final logical argument you might consider using is the *a fortiori* argument.[5] This argument is based on the assertion that if one thing is true, then another thing is even more likely to be true. For instance, a fruit is the edible reproductive body of a seed plant, especially one having a sweet pulp associated with the seed.[6] If a tomato is a fruit (and it is), even though it has no sweet pulp, then *a fortiori*, a pear—which has a sweet pulp—is a fruit.

---

5. This does not exhaust the possibilities in logical argument, only the room I have to discuss it. A recent and useful book on argument is *Logic for Argument* by Pitt and Leavenworth, which provides a relatively simple introduction to symbolic logic. A classic in the field of traditional logic is Bishop Whately's *Rhetoric*, first published in 1853.

6. WEBSTER'S SEVENTH NEW COLLEGIATE DICTIONARY, 1963.

The argument says, in effect, if one agrees that X is in the category being considered, then it is even more likely that Y is in the category, since Y has more of the properties associated with that category. Using a collective bargaining agreement example, your argument might run like this:

> Discharge is the proper penalty for Grievant's theft of company property. [Issue] He is less deserving of consideration than two other employees whose recent discharges for stealing have been upheld by arbitrators. [Rule] Lukas, a 12-year employee, stole $50 worth of scrap copper. Frothingham, a 10-year employee, stole $40 worth of paper clips. Both were fired, and their discharges upheld. Grievant, a three-year employee, stole $150 worth of mechanical drawing equipment. Since the discharge was proper for the other employees, it is even more appropriate for Grievant. [Application] The penalty of discharge must be upheld. [Conclusion]

The *a fortiori* argument, since it depends upon the common perception that two items belong to the same category, has some dangers. If the arbitrator does not agree that two items are in the same category, your argument will fail. For instance, an employer argued that many arbitrators have upheld the employer's right to require polygraph examinations of employees it suspects of theft. These exams were conducted by the employer's hired specialists, and the results were available to the employer, who used them in determining whether to discharge the employees. *A fortiori*, the employer argued, it has the right to require employees whom the police suspect of theft to take police-administered polygraph examinations whose results are not available to the employer.

This argument failed because the arbitrator thought that employer-administered polygraph exams fell into the category of job-related rights covered by the collective bargaining agreement and the employer's preserved managerial prerogatives.

On the other hand, police-administered polygraph examinations involved, the arbitrator felt, constitutional rights that were unaffected by the collective bargaining agreement. Thus, the *a fortiori* argument should only be used when you think there is a high probability that the arbitrator shares your perception of categories.

In addition to organizing your individual arguments effectively, you must carefully organize the argument section as a whole. Your argument section may be composed of a series of interrelated arguments or a number of independent arguments. In either case, it is useful to provide "point headings" to guide the arbitrator through your argument section. For instance, the point heading for the section on insubordination might be: "WORDS SAID IN JEST ARE NOT INSUBORDINATION."

Point headings are particularly useful when you have a complex argument based upon a series of reasoned conclusions. If you provide point headings, the arbitrator can simply look through them and follow your overall reasoning to arrive at the conclusion that you desire. If the arbitrator has an opportunity to grasp the structure of your argument before becoming bogged down in the details, she will have a context in which to fit each subsection of the argument as she reads.

Where the different arguments contained in your argument section are independent, point headings are still useful. They will make it clear to the arbitrator that there are, in your view, several separate reasons for reaching the conclusion you desire.

In general, it is best to begin with your strongest argument and end with your second strongest argument. Like sentences in a paragraph, first and last are the two positions in the argument section that are most likely to be remembered.

One argument that should always be included but is often omitted is the "proleptical" argument. This is the argument in which you directly address your opponent's argument to show why it should not be accepted. It is vitally important to show the arbitrator *both* that your argument should win and that your opponent's argument is so flawed it must lose. Remember, the arbitrator wants to be able to justify, in her own mind, the decision she reaches. If you can provide the arbitrator with good reasons for rejecting your opponent's arguments, you have done a great deal towards having your own arguments accepted.

There are three important points to remember about the proleptical argument. First, do *not* give your opponent's argument too much prominence by beginning with it or devoting as much space to refuting it as you do to making your own arguments.

Second, use the techniques of paragraph placement and subordination (which were discussed under Facts), to undercut your opponent's argument. For instance, you might say:

> We have shown that Good Friday is a holiday by any definition of the word. While the Company says it is not a holiday, it relies only on the absence of the phrase, "Good Friday" from the definition section of Article VI. But that cannot be controlling, since that definition section does not contain definitions for "premium pay," "overtime," or many other terms the parties have defined elsewhere or thought too clear to need any definition. Good Friday is so clearly a holiday the parties thought it unnecessary to specifically define it.

Notice how the quoted section begins and ends with the union position. The company position is contained in a subordinate clause, which is combined with a much longer independent clause. Both of these techniques help drain the force from the company's argument.

Third, do not feel bound to answer your opponent's arguments in its own terms. That is, if the union brought in forty calendars showing that April 20 was Good Friday, the employer should not feel obligated to reply that sixty calendars say nothing about Good Friday. Instead, the employer might say:

> Good Friday is not a holiday under Article VI. While the Union brought in many calendars that list Good Friday, as they list other holidays, that is irrelevant to the issue before the arbitrator. When the contract refers to "all holidays," it is referring only to those previously observed by the parties. Good Friday was not previously observed by the parties, and is not a holiday under Article VI.

Again, notice the techniques of paragraph placement and subordination that are being used to undercut the union's argument. Furthermore, notice that the employer is dismissing as irrelevant the union's argument while insisting that its own argument is critical.

You should be careful in taking this approach. Be certain that you are not dismissing your opponent's argument as irrelevant simply because you haven't been able to come up with an easy answer to it. The best proleptical arguments illustrate flaws rather than arguing irrelevancy.

Similarly, it is a poor idea to ignore any major weaknesses in your own case. An arbitrator wants to know how the weaknesses in your case can be reconciled with deciding in your favor. To the extent you give the arbitrator an adequate way of rationalizing those weaknesses, you improve your case. Sometimes, it is simply true that one element of the proof does not fit your theory of the case. Or, it may be that a credible witness testified to something that is harmful.

In those cases, the only thing to do is follow the adage that I mentioned earlier, "If you have a lemon, make lemonade." Admit the flaw, express your own puzzlement at it—if nothing else is possible—and go on. Do not dwell on the flaw, but don't overlook it. This at least gets you high marks for honesty and improves your credibility with the arbitrator. And that is much more than you will gain if you simply ignore an uncomfortable fact.

Conclusion

All too often, advocates waste their conclusion section by simply saying, "For all the foregoing reasons, the grievance must be denied." It may simply be that by the time you get to the conclusion section, you are exhausted. That is understandable. But with very little additional effort you can increase the overall force of your argument. Simply list the two or three compelling reasons why the arbitrator should, in your view, deny the grievance. This significantly reinforces the arguments you have previously made.

Furthermore, the conclusion section is the appropriate place for discussing the remedy. No arbitrator wishes to appear to be giving punitive damages, since that might be a ground for vacatur under most statutes. Thus, if you do not give adequate reasons for a proposed money remedy, the arbitrator may be reluctant to grant it. The arbitrator may also be unwilling to grant the remedy you seek if you have failed to make clear the calculations upon which it is based. Finally, the reasons for a particular remedy must be as convincing as the reasons for winning your case. Thus, you should avoid perfunctory treatment of remedy.

Language Considerations in the Brief

I discuss language in brief writing to promote eloquence and to ensure clarity. I will gladly sacrifice the former, however, to secure the latter.

Because arbitration has many characteristics in common with legal proceedings, advocates often look at legal writing as their model. That is a mistake. Lawyers' writing is and has been under considerable attack for its lack of clarity. It is not my intention to make that attack here. Lawyers have probably already heard it; lay advocates probably have no desire to get embroiled in the controversy.

What I will argue against is lay advocates attempting to sound like lawyers. There is nothing worse than an imitation of legal writing that makes all of the errors common to legal writing, while losing the force and good sense that frequently characterize lay advocates' writing. Just because you are writing a brief does not mean you should try to sound like a lawyer.

For many years, linguists and lawyers have been studying legal writing. Some of the results of their studies have been embodied in guidelines for writers.[7] I have selected six guidelines to emphasize, because I think they are the most important to brief writers.

Two introductory cautions: First, the comprehensibility and clarity of language is measurable and not simply a matter of personal preference or prejudice. Thus, I am not telling you to write a certain way because it sounds better. Rather, psycholinguistic research shows that certain techniques aid in comprehension and recall. Since both are essential to persuasion, it is useful to incorporate these techniques into your persuasive writing.

Second, you may notice that I have already advised you to do certain things that violate these guidelines. As a general rule, when you want to bury a weak point or undercut an opponent's argument, when you want to be obscure, weak, or ineffectual, do the opposite of what these guidelines tell you to do. Use these guidelines to make your writing clear and forceful where it needs to be.

---

7. *See,* Charrow & Erhardt, Clear and Effective Legal Writing, Little, Brown and Company, Boston and Toronto, 1986.

Write Short Sentences

There is no better way to lose your reader than to write a 300-word sentence. Nor is there a better way to lose your own train of thought. Long sentences can serve the dual purpose of confusing you and your reader. Why use them? Instead, separate your ideas into single thoughts and put each into its own sentence.

For instance, consider the following sentence:

> The purpose of this brief is to demonstrate the inaccuracy of the Grievant's claim to an entitlement, under Article VI of the collective bargaining agreement, to holiday pay, which he claims is due him as a result of having worked on April 20, which he asserts was Good Friday, and therefore a holiday within the contemplation of the contract.

If we were to break up and simplify this sentence, it might look more like this:

> Article VI does not make Good Friday a holiday. Thus, Grievant is not entitled to holiday pay for working on Good Friday.

The advantage of simple sentences lies chiefly in their directness. They make points forcefully. You can, of course, overuse them. I am not suggesting that you make your brief sound like that grammar school primer in which Dick and Jane watched Spot run. You can be simple without being simplistic.

Avoid Intrusive Phrases and Clauses

When you try to write carefully and accurately, you are often faced with the problem that a flat statement is not quite true. You need to qualify the statement. Sometimes, you even need to qualify your qualification. While this is not generally a problem, it can become a problem if you insist upon doing all your qualification in the same sentence. It becomes impossible for the reader to follow your main thought, since she is so thoroughly distracted by your qualifiers.

Consider, for example, the following sentence:

> The issue before the arbitrator is whether Article VI of the collective bargaining agreement, which is entitled "Holiday Pay," and which provides for the payment of certain premium rates for all hours worked on a holiday regardless of whether they would otherwise be considered overtime, applies to the day in question, April 20, which according to Grievant's allegations (which allegations were not admitted by the company) was Good Friday.

Notice how many phrases intrude upon the main idea. The writer could have stated, "The issue is whether Article VI requires holiday pay for Good Friday." The writer could then have gone on to make all of the appropriate qualifications and to fill in the rest of the detail. If the writer had done this, the arbitrator would have had a clear statement of the issue, followed by an honest qualification of the items before her. Then she could proceed to argue the case. Instead, this one-sentence statement of the issue is filled with so many intrusive phrases and clauses that it is impossible for an arbitrator to quickly read and understand. Rather, the arbitrator must read the sentence repeatedly and untangle its many elements.

If you see that you have written a sentence like this, untangle it. Look for the true subject (in this case, Article VI), the true verb (in this case, applies), and the true object (in this case, Good Friday). Throw out everything that comes between these basic sentence elements, and rewrite the sentence. Then decide which of the "qualifiers" you really need. Put them in separate sentences. Then both you and the arbitrator will know precisely what you are talking about.

Use the Active Voice

The passive voice is a way of changing the focus of the sentence. It is useful when you want to avoid identifying the person who did the action contained in the sentence. It is harmful when it omits information that you need to include. Thus, you should use the passive voice only when it is necessary for making your argument.

An ordinary, active voice English sentence looks like this:

John hit the ball.

In the passive voice, the sentence would look like this:

The ball was hit by John.

Notice that the focus of the second sentence is on the ball, rather than John.

We can take this a step further. Suppose we want to eliminate entirely the responsibility for hitting the ball. We can use what is called a truncated passive, and write:

The ball was hit.

This truncated passive omits an important piece of information: who hit the ball.

Take a look at this sentence:

Grievant was denied holiday pay for Good Friday.

Notice that it does not say who denied holiday pay to grievant. It is easy enough to infer that the company denied him holiday pay. However, it would be more forceful, from the union's point of view, if that denial was made explicit. Thus, we could rewrite the sentence:

The company denied Grievant holiday pay for Good Friday.

If your object is to make the company look like a wrongdoer, you are better off using the second version of the sentence. If you want to make the employer look less culpable, use the first sentence.

The real difficulty with the passive voice comes when you are trying to be clear. If you inadvertently slip into using the passive voice, you can wind up losing important information. For instance, consider the following sentence:

Good Friday was incorporated into the agreement by past practice. It was asserted that there was no reason to be explicit as to all the holidays covered by Article VI.

Notice that the first use of the passive voice in these two sentences is not harmful; that is, it simply serves to emphasize Good Friday. The second use, however, seriously undercuts the writer's argument. It is critical to know who asserted that the holidays did not have to be explicitly enumerated in Article VI. If it was the union negotiator in a caucus with his negotiating team, this is probably not an effective argument. If it was the management negotiator in an across-the-table discussion, this is probably a very significant piece of information. Unfortunately, the arbitrator is left in the dark because the writer has used the passive voice.

Avoid Nominalizations

In the English language, verbs and adjectives can be made into nouns. For instance:

VERB	NOUN
apply	application
resolve	resolution
determine	determination
convert	conversion

ADJECTIVE	NOUN
distinguishable	distinguishability
enforceable	enforceability
applicable	applicability
reasonable	reasonability

When you turn verbs and adjectives into their nouns you weaken the force of the sentence. For instance:

The application of Article VI to Good Friday is clear.

versus

Article VI clearly applies to Good Friday.

or

The importance of the bargaining history is clear.

versus

The bargaining history is clearly important.

In each instance, you have to add two little words, "the" and "of," in order to use the nominalization. This makes the sentence both longer (by only a trivial amount, of course), and less forceful. If you develop a habit of using nominalizations, your arguments will sound like they were written by the people who create government regulations. Reading them, for the arbitrator, is like wading through molasses: slow, sticky, and unpleasant.

Avoid Multiple Negatives

Somewhere in grammar school you probably learned the dubious "rule" that two negatives make a positive. Later on, faced with such double negatives as the "not un-" construction (a construction that is not uncommon in legal writing) you probably discarded the simplistic grammar school rule. Perhaps it seemed more subtle and sophisticated to use clauses such as "burglars are not infrequently heroin addicts," rather than forcing yourself to decide between "frequently" and a word such as "sometimes," which further narrows the number of instances. By using the multiple negative you avoid taking a position, but you do so at the cost of blurring your argument.

Even if two negatives do not make a positive, they do make your sentence more difficult to understand. And what you gain in apparent subtlety may be lost in reader confusion. Research shows that when you have two negatives within a single clause it is *more* than twice as difficult to understand as the corresponding positive statement.[8] Thus, if your goal is persuasion, you should avoid overusing negatives.

Many brief writers have become so accustomed to reading legal documents, however, that they fail to notice words of negation and inadvertently create double and triple negatives. Prefixes such as "un-," "in-," and "mis-" negate the words to which they are attached. Words such as "unless," "until," "except," "failure," "deny," "absent" all indicate negation. If you fail to take into account the way these words work, you may inadvertently write double and triple negatives. For instance, if you say "no employees may leave the pier unless they have the supervisor's permission," you are actually saying, "All employees must have the supervisor's permission to leave the pier." Alternatively, you could say, "Only employees with

---

8. CLEAR AND EFFECTIVE WRITING FOR LAW STUDENTS, American Institutes for Research, Washington, D.C., 60, 1982.

the supervisor's permission can leave the pier." In both instances, you avoid a double negative and make the sentence clearer.

Triple negatives are not infrequent in legal writing, absent caution on the part of the writer. Was it difficult to follow that last sentence? All it really says is, "Cautious legal writers avoid the use of triple negatives." By using a variation on the "not un-" construction and a word of negation ("absent") I built a common legal triple negative—for illustrative purposes only.

Here is a sentence from a brief in a recent case. "No grievance can be found non-arbitrable unless. . . ." I spent quite a bit of time trying to figure out which side of the arbitrability argument this writer was on. The point is simple: the more negatives in a clause, the more difficult it is for the arbitrator to comprehend.

Choose Your Vocabulary with Care

For both lawyers and lay advocates, the temptation to "sound like a lawyer" is nearly overwhelming. Avoid it. "Sounding like a lawyer" usually means using archaic words (like "hereinabove," "hereinafter," "heretofore"), legal jargon (like "subsequent to," "for the reason that," "to the extent that," "null and void"), and technical terms (like "reasonable man," "due process," and "equal protection") in contexts for which they are not suited.

You can always avoid using the first two categories of words. A phrase such as "hereinabove mentioned Grievant" can be replaced by "the previously mentioned Grievant," or, more simply, "Grievant." Instead of using "subsequent to" and "for the reason that," try "after" and "because."[9]

---

9. For excellent lists of archaic words and lawyers' jargon, see WYDICK, PLAIN ENGLISH FOR LAWYERS, or MELLINKOFF, LEGAL WRITING SENSE & NONSENSE.

There are, however, instances in which technical words are required. "Arbitrability" is a word of art and cannot easily be replaced. Be sure that you know when you need words of art and when you are using them to try to impress the arbitrator. Remember, experienced arbitrators are less likely to stand in awe of legal phrases than are neophyte advocates. And if you have used a legal phrase instead of a clever argument, you have probably weakened your case.

I am not arguing against eloquence. As I mentioned earlier, you should strive for the right word, rather than being satisfied with its second cousin. But legal terms are very often not the right word; they are simply the first word that comes to your mind when faced with the difficult task of persuading an arbitrator. The best advice I can give you is to learn to spot your own favorite legalisms. Then use your red pencil to remove them from every brief before it goes out.

I have suggested a number of guidelines for improving your brief writing. If you follow them, you can write concise, well-reasoned briefs that will serve your client's interests well. If you do better than that and achieve eloquence, you have my admiration.

Reopening the Hearing

There are few hard and fast rules about reopening hearings. But the ones that exist are important enough so that you should be aware of them. First, after the arbitrator has issued his award and opinion, he is powerless to reopen the hearing. He is *functus officio*—Latin for "finished in office"—and without further powers under either state or federal law to do more than correct arithmetical or technical defects in the award that do not affect substance. These would include misdescriptions of things, incorrectly spelled names, or miscalculated sums. In all other respects, if you want to modify or challenge an award, you must address yourself to the courts rather than the arbitrator.

A second rule to remember is Rule 32 of the American Arbitration Association Voluntary Labor Arbitration Rules:

> The hearings may be reopened by the arbitrator at will or at the motion of either party, for good cause shown, at any time before the award is made, but if the reopening of the hearings would prevent the making of the award within the specific time agreed upon by the parties in the contract, out of which the controversy has arisen, the matter may not be reopened, unless both parties agree upon the extension of such time limit. When no specific date is fixed in the contract, the arbitrator may reopen the hearings, and the arbitrator shall have 30 days from the closing of the reopened hearings within which to make an award.[10]

The instances in which an arbitrator will reopen a hearing on his own motion are few. Occasionally it becomes obvious that, because of their own familiarity with the practices in the industry, the parties have inadvertently left a gap in the arbitrator's knowledge as to the meaning of an item they have put before him. In that instance, it is appropriate for the arbitrator to request an explanation by the parties and reopen the hearing to receive either a letter, stipulation, or some additional testimony to clear up the problem.

Alternatively, because the arbitrator has decided the case differently from the way that either of the parties anticipated he would decide it, there is an aspect of remedy that has not been addressed by the parties. In that instance, the arbitrator may, without reopening the hearing, take further evidence solely on that aspect of remedy, if the parties agree.

Sometimes, what a party is actually requesting is not a reopening of the hearing but a further hearing. That is, many

---

10. *See* Appendix 3.

arbitrators do not declare the hearing closed until they receive the parties' briefs. Prior to the date on which the briefs are due, if a party requests additional hearing, the arbitrator is likely to apply a different standard than he might have applied if the arbitration hearing had been declared closed. When the hearing has not yet been declared closed, the arbitrator must take into consideration the importance of giving the parties a full opportunity to present all the relevant evidence prior to making his decision.

Where the hearing has been declared closed, the arbitrator should only reopen it for "good cause shown," regardless of whether he is operating under the AAA or some other agency's rules. A useful analogy is provided by the state statutes that permit reopening of a trial where the parties' substantial rights have been materially affected by, for instance, "newly discovered evidence, material for the party making the application, which he could not, with reasonable diligence, have discovered and produced at the trial."[11]

Courts generally disfavor and distrust claims of newly discovered evidence. They wish to avoid reopening trials and wasting judicial efforts. Moreover, there is a policy in favor of finality in trials. This same policy seems appropriate to arbitrations. Evidence that is cumulative, goes solely to credibility, or provides further rebuttal will probably not support reopening the hearing. Moreover, in considering reopening, an arbitrator is likely to hold the parties to high standards of diligence in preparing the case.

If you believe, however, that the hearing should be reopened, your first effort should be directed at your opponent. If the parties agree to a reopened hearing, the arbitrator is unlikely to stand in their way. Even if your opponent does not agree to reopening the hearing, he or she may agree to a stipulation as to

---

11. CAL. CIV. CODE § 657 (West 1976).

what would have come in if the hearing had been reopened. This would then be an additional piece of stipulated evidence for the arbitrator to consider in determining the case.

Finally, if your opponent will agree to none of these things, you should make an offer of proof in a letter to the arbitrator and your party opponent, along with your request for reopening the hearing. You should include an assertion as to why, despite the exercise of due diligence, you were unable to discover this evidence before. Based upon your offer of proof and due diligence, together with his or her own assessment of whether the fact is material to his decision in the case, the arbitrator will be able to determine whether to reopen the hearing. Since only a handful of reported cases in the last ten years have considered this question, and since the hearing was reopened in only one of them, you should not have high expectations about your case being reopened.

Evaluating the Award

Most advocates evaluate arbitration awards by turning to the last page to find out if they won. I have no quibble with that. Indeed, experienced advocates know the likely outcome of a case. When the hearing has gone pretty much as expected, they are not surprised by the award.

If you are surprised by the result in any particular case, there are three preliminary questions you should ask. First, is it possible that you became so convinced by your own rhetoric that you failed to see the flaws in your own case? If so, the weaknesses of your case are likely to be underscored by the arbitrator's discussion of the facts and theories that led to his decision. You may disagree with a theory, but if it is correctly applied, you can not fault the award. On the other hand, you are under no obligation to reemploy an arbitrator if you disagree with the theories he uses in deciding cases.

Second, did you get the evidence that was necessary to your case admitted at the hearing? You can not fault an arbitrator for deciding a case on the record, rather than on what you know are the "true" facts. Third, did the arbitrator believe your key witnesses? Credibility judgments are often based upon the arbitrator's instincts, as well as the consistency and probability of your witness's testimony. As an advocate you often have a bias towards your witnesses that leads you to find them believable. Arbitrators do not share that bias.

But what if you ask all of the questions I have suggested, in a "clear" case, and find that the award is still inexplicable? It is possible that the arbitrator has made a decision based upon extraneous factors. These factors include: the outcomes of this arbitrator's previous cases between these parties, the "importance" of the case to one of the parties as expressed at the hearing, and the arbitrator's perception of his continuing acceptability. None of these factors is ever a proper basis for an award, and, for most arbitrators, none ever is. If you are convinced that the arbitrator made this award on one of these bases, you would do well to avoid using that arbitrator, even if you won the case.

In most instances, you will not have that absolute certainty about the outcome of a case that would lead you to be startled by an arbitrator's deciding it the opposite way. There is time and chance in all. Therefore, in evaluating an arbitration award you will use, in part, the same standards that you used for arbitrator selection. As discussed in Chapter 4, you will want to read the award for directness, elegance, the relation of remedy to breach, and economy in stating facts and argument. You will also want to ask yourself the same questions that you asked your friends in connection with choosing an arbitrator.

There are some things, however, you will be in a much better position to evaluate after having presented the case than if you were simply reading the arbitrator's award. First, you can determine whether the arbitrator's award was prompt. Was it rendered within the time limit imposed upon the arbitrator, or, in any event, soon enough to resolve the case without creating problems with the parties? In answering this question you should be sensitive to your own role as an advocate in achieving prompt awards. Many arbitrators plan their schedules to take into account the need for adequate time to prepare awards and opinions. If you have established a briefing schedule and stuck to it, you can expect the arbitrator to fulfill his responsibilities. Where, however, you and your opponent have granted each other generous extensions on briefs, you may have adjusted the time frame of the case so as to make it impossible for the arbitrator to meet the obligation he originally undertook. That should be taken into consideration when you assess the promptness of the award.

Second, when you have been the advocate in a case, you are in a unique position to assess the arbitrator's statement of the facts. You are aware of what was said by witnesses for both sides and with what conviction and demeanor. Therefore, you can determine whether the arbitrator has been faithful to the proofs that came in from both sides. Even if the arbitrator believed your opponent's witnesses, his statement of fact should be an honest representation of what was proved. Where there was contradictory evidence, the arbitrator should make clear what he believed and why. Finally, you know if there were facts that would tend to undercut the arbitrator's final decision. You should note whether the arbitrator dealt with those facts, or simply ignored them.

Third, did the arbitrator understand and address the parties' principal contentions? You should not expect the arbitrator to repeat your argument sentence by sentence. That is a job for a copying machine. But what is critical is a sufficient treatment of your argument, in abbreviated form, so that you are convinced that the arbitrator understood it. This is different, of course, from having the arbitrator accept your argument. The arbitrator may simply find a particular argument far less valuable than you did.

In addition, in some instances, it is perfectly appropriate for an arbitrator not to address some of your arguments. If the arbitrator's decision on one argument logically obviates the need to address certain other arguments, then he may not address those other arguments. Arbitrators differ on this point. Some suggest that "arbitral economy" and avoiding dicta require that an arbitrator only discuss those arguments that he had to accept or reject in order to reach a decision. Other arbitrators believe that a full exposition of the case requires them to discuss every argument made by the parties, simply because it was made. Regardless of which school of thought your arbitrator belongs to, what is critical in evaluating the award is to feel certain that the arbitrator understood your arguments.

Fourth, was the decision logically reasoned from the facts and the contract obligations? Even where the case was decided in your favor, it is important that it be done so for the proper reason. An illogical interpretation of a contract provision may win this case for you but cause untold harm in the workplace. Harm can also be caused by the arbitrator discussing extraneous matter at length. An arbitrator's tendency to discuss extraneous matters may be helpful to you in this case; it may hurt you in another. If the arbitrator failed to limit himself to the matter before him, you should give that fact significant weight in your evaluation.

Fifth, was the remedy clearly reasoned, definite, and capable of precise application? The arbitrator's opinion should express his reasons for arriving at a particular remedy. That remedy should clearly reflect the arbitrator's resolution of the issue that the parties put before him. The remedy must set forth a verbal or mathematical formula that is finite. It can not direct vague actions such as simply "taking appropriate measures" or leave the parties without any direction whatsoever.

At one extreme, of course, an arbitrator's indefinite award is a failure to resolve the issue before him and can result in vacatur. Even if the failure is not that extreme, however, the parties are entitled to have a remedy that is capable of being executed by the party against whom it is made. Thus, if the arbitrator orders payment of a sum of money to a group of people, the exact people and amounts to be paid must be ascertainable. In some instances the way in which the arbitrator resolves the issue makes insufficient the evidence before him upon which to base a remedy. In those instances, it is appropriate for an arbitrator to issue an "interim award" so as to retain jurisdiction in order to permit the parties to present further facts and argue the appropriate remedy. Otherwise, the remedy should be clear, definite, and capable of precise application.

Evaluating the Bill

Billing is a difficult area for both parties and arbitrators. In part, this results from certain billing conventions that have developed over the years. I will discuss these conventions and how they should be applied in evaluating an arbitrator's bill.

The Code of Professional Responsibility for Arbitrators of Labor-Management Disputes provides that:

> Prior to appointment, the parties should be aware of or be able readily to determine all significant aspects of an arbitrator's bases for charges for fees and expenses.[12]

---

12. *See* Appendix 6.

After the Hearing

Where the arbitrator has filled out a questionnaire provided by a listing agency, he has fulfilled his obligation under the Code of Ethics.

Where the arbitrator is contacted directly by the parties, Paragraph 93 of the Code provides:

> The arbitrator has a professional responsibility to respond to questions by submitting his or her bases for charges for fees and expenses.

The Code of Professional Responsibility also sets forth the categories of fees and expenses about which an arbitrator should indicate his practices. These are: hearing time, study time, travel time, postponement fees, office overhead expenses, and the work of paid assistants or associates. Paragraph 85 of the Code of Ethics specifically notes:

> Any fixed ratio of study days to hearing days, not agreed to specifically by the parties, is inconsistent with the per diem method of charges for services.

Given this background of ethical constraints, we can look at an appropriate method for examining an arbitrator's bill. A little later, we will take a look at the appropriateness of the per diem method.

When you receive an arbitrator's bill, you should first verify the number of hearing days. If there were any postponement or late cancellation fees, you should check to be sure they were charged to the appropriate party. Where the contract does not provide for sharing costs and one party requests a postponement to which the other party objects, if the arbitrator grants a postponement he is likely to charge only the party requesting it. If your arrangements with your opponent include sharing late postponement and cancellation fees, you should make this known to the arbitrator. Otherwise, you may find that you have been charged for the entire late cancellation fee when you thought you only owed half.

It is often difficult to evaluate the arbitrator's charges for study and preparation of the award and opinion. A survey conducted some years ago indicated that most arbitrators billed in units no smaller than one-half a day. Obviously, if this is still the case, the bill may not reflect precisely the amount of study and preparation time the arbitrator spent on your case. This is just one of the difficulties inherent in the per diem fee basis of charging for arbitrations.

Another difficult area is the appropriateness of the overall number of study and preparation days charged for a particular case. You will, of course, be able to easily see a ratio of study days to hearing days. One study shows an average of 1.7 study days to each hearing day. This figure can, however, be terribly misleading. As a famous union negotiator used to put it, "If you have one foot in a block of ice, and the other foot in boiling water, on the average you are comfortable." In the same way, you can be "comfortable" with an arbitrator who charges an average of 1.7 study days to each hearing day. On the other hand, you may be paying too much or too little in a particular case, despite the arbitrator's average.

You can, however, both control the ratio of study days to hearing days and assess its appropriateness. There are three things you should consider. First, you should consider the type of case. That is, disciplinary cases can often take a relatively long time to hear because of conflicting testimony. When the arbitrator decides the case he will have to make some credibility determinations. After he makes them, he will be able to dismiss certain testimony after explaining why he found it incredible—frequently a complex job. Once that is done, the task of writing the award becomes simpler. That is not to say that deciding credibility issues is either quick or easy. Rather, deciding the issue usually does not take as long as hearing the conflicting testimony.

In addition, parties can control the ratio of study days to hearing days in disciplinary cases. I have served on disciplinary panels where the parties have agreed that the award and opinion shall normally be no more than five pages and that the maximum ratio of the study days to hearing days shall be one to one, except in "unusual and compelling circumstances." In my view, if I were to charge more than one study day for each hearing day, I would be obliged to explain the circumstances.

Second, time spent in preparing an award and opinion is directly related to whether there was a transcript and whether the parties submitted briefs and reply briefs. Where you have had a transcript, submitted briefs, and then submitted reply briefs, you can expect at least two study days for each hearing day. The arbitrator must read the transcript and may feel obliged to quote it verbatim where appropriate. Further, the number of study days will be directly related to the approach you have taken in your brief. If you follow the suggestions in the first part of this chapter and limit your brief to the critical arguments to be made, you will save money. On the other hand, if you submit a brief that uses every possible argument that can be made, no matter how remote or attenuated, you can expect to increase your costs. As noted earlier, careful arbitrators will address all the arguments raised by the parties unless there is a logical reason for not addressing one or more of them. The more arguments you include, the more time it will take the arbitrator to decide the case. I am *not* suggesting that you be less than thorough in your presentation of your side's case. I am suggesting that you avoid a "shotgun" approach.

Third, the contractual, legal, or factual complexity of the case will directly affect the ratio of study days to hearing days. A complex argument based on the contract or external law can be time-consuming for an arbitrator to read and decide. Further, where both parties use case law to support their positions, the arbitrator must read the cases himself, especially where the parties contest their meaning. If you rely on cases, you can save yourself some money by attaching them to your brief. That way the arbitrator does not have to go to the library and look them up. The same should be done with arbitral opinions you wish to use for analogies.

It is less obvious that factually complex cases may take a longer time to decide. While the arbitrator may not be reading other cases or other arbitrators' awards, he may be wading through an enormous pile of documents. Indeed, I have had the experience of a single day of hearings in which the parties devoted all of their time to opening statements and introducing documents. When you send the arbitrator home with a brief-case full of documents you can expect the ratio of study days to hearing days to be quite high.

Occasionally you will be surprised not by how much the arbitrator has charged but by how little. The Code of Professional Responsibility[13] requires arbitrators to recognize their obligation to keep the cost of arbitration reasonable. Many leading arbitrators charge less than their normal fee because the parties, or one party, was in a poor position to pay for arbitration. Sometimes a very small local union or a very small employer has a very large problem that must be addressed through arbitration. Thus, an arbitrator's charges may not reflect time actually spent.

There is one other situation where charges may reflect less than the time an arbitrator spent. Deciding cases of unusual novelty, complexity, or difficulty often takes a great deal of time. An arbitrator may find himself endlessly considering and reconsidering the issues and arguments in a complex case while

---

13. *See* Appendix 6.

swimming, jogging, or engaging in some other form of recreation. It is not possible to quantify this time; therefore, arbitrators do not charge the parties for it. Rather, it is part of the joy, stimulation, and, occasionally, torment of being an arbitrator.

You should also consider the appropriateness of any expenses the arbitrator claimed. The story is told of an arbitrator who unexpectedly had to stay overnight for a second day of an out-of-town hearing. He agreed to do so and later charged the parties for a new shirt and socks. When queried, the arbitrator said that he had needed a clean shirt and socks for the next day's hearing, not having brought any because he thought the hearing would last only one day. The parties accepted this explanation but asked that the arbitrator send them each one-half of the shirt and one sock.

This apocryphal story illustrates the somewhat unusual nature of expenses you may incur. Unanticipated complications and inclement weather often intervene to extend out-of-town cases. Since the parties have requested the arbitrator undertake the trip, arbitrators usually feel justified in charging for the additional night's expenses. Since I keep the new shirts (and use them in other cases), I do not bill them to the parties.

Where you have a question about what elements went into an arbitrator's claim for expenses, be sure to raise that question with the arbitrator himself. After all, any arbitrator would prefer to have the opportunity to explain a bill than to have a disgruntled party talk about the arbitrator's "outrageous" billing practices.

Billing forms provided by some administering agencies do not always allow the parties to understand what occurred. For instance, a union fiscal officer once questioned an arbitrator's travel expenses because it appeared the air fare was extremely high. This occurred because the form provided by the administering agency did not permit the arbitrator to indicate that two hearing dates were separated by one month. Thus, two trips were necessary, rather than one. Once the union fiscal officer understood this the entire bill made sense.

There are, of course, errors made on both sides. Many arbitrators have had to send back money to one party because that party misread the bill and paid both its own and its opponents share. In addition, arbitrators often find omitted charges when reviewing bills. Embarrassingly enough, omitted charges usually result from failing to record expenses or late cancellations and to charge them to the parties.

Do not hestitate to question an arbitrator's bill if you do not understand it. You are entitled to an explanation. Where the case is administered by the American Arbitration Association, questions should be raised through the tribunal administrator. Otherwise, it is appropriate to contact the arbitrator directly.

While the tradition of per diem fees for services has become well established in arbitration, it is not clear that it makes sense. Certainly, an argument can be made that there should be a fixed rate for a normal hearing day. Both the arbitrator and the parties have committed that full day in advance.

When it comes to study time, however, the arbitrator is in an unusual position. Many arbitrators are lawyers, as are many of the parties' advocates. Lawyers are accustomed to charging on an hourly basis and keeping detailed records of the time spent on each client's business. There is no obvious reason why arbitrators should not bill by the hour. Nor is there any reason why they should not be held to the same standards of accountability for the time they bill.

In many instances, arbitrators may be billing by the hour but expressing it in "days." Since the daily rate of most arbitrators, divided by six, does not yield an hourly sum equivalent to what a lawyer of similar experience and ability would charge, the number of days may get multiplied to yield an appropriate hourly rate. Or, a single hour beyond the first "day" spent on an award may be billed as an additional day. Much of the "slippage" in billing on a per diem basis would be eliminated if arbitrators billed by the hour for time spent preparing their awards and opinions. The parties would know in advance the arbitrator's hourly rate, and might base their choice of arbitrator on the complexity of the case and the rate charged by the arbitrator. Furthermore, the parties would be entitled to the same careful accounting that they are accustomed to getting from their lawyers.

The only reason for continuing the custom of billing study time on a per diem basis is that it has always been done that way. Not everyone finds that reason compelling, and perhaps it is time to reexamine this convention.

7

Arguing an Interest Arbitration

Introduction

Earlier chapters talked about the most common form of arbitration, rights arbitration, explaining how to prepare for hearings, and how to present your case in the light most favorable to your side. There are, of course, other forms of arbitration, some of which you may become involved in. You do not need to learn an entirely new set of skills for each new type of arbitration. Rather, you can adapt the skills you use in rights arbitration to the specific needs of other forms of arbitration. In this Chapter I assume you have already read Chapters 1 through 6. If you have not, and if you are not an experienced advocate, you may find it difficult to follow the material in this chapter.

On the whole, the techniques and methods used in interest arbitrations are the same as in rights arbitrations. This chapter highlights the differences.

The Difference Between "Rights" and "Interest" Arbitrations

In "rights" arbitration, an arbitrator must decide whether a right established expressly or implicitly in an *existing* contract has been violated. In "interest" arbitration the arbitrator establishes contract rights and obligations between the parties. This distinction is both fundamental and critical, because under most contracts, a "rights" arbitrator is prohibited from adding to, subtracting from, or modifying the agreement through arbitration. In interest arbitration, the arbitrator does precisely that.

Origins of Interest Arbitration

Interest arbitration is largely a creature of public sector collective bargaining. In many jurisdictions, statutes forbid public employees from striking. This creates a perceived imbalance in the negotiating power of the parties. By substituting interest arbitration for raw economic power, some argue, public employees can reduce the difference in bargaining power between themselves and a governmental entity.

When interest arbitration occurs in a political setting, it has certain other advantages. First, it can provide a way out for political figures who have painted themselves into a corner. That is, a politician who ran on a platform of cutting personnel expenditures may find, when faced with the facts of a budget rather than the rhetoric of a campaign, that public employees in the jurisdiction are underpaid rather than overpaid. Without interest arbitration it would be extremely difficult for the politician to reverse field shortly after being elected and acknowledge a legitimate need to raise public employees' salaries. Interest arbitration makes the arbitrator, rather than the political figure, the source of a legitimate pay increase.

Second, given the unacceptability of strikes in much of the public sector, a governmental entity has no incentive to make concessions. It can simply let negotiations drag on indefinitely, knowing that employees are unable to strike in order to motivate a settlement. Unions can also refuse to make concessions, knowing that public opinion limits the employer's ability to change benefits unilaterally. With interest arbitration as a statutorily imposed last step, both sides must weigh the advantages of delay and the strength of their positions against the possibility of an outsider's imposing a potentially unacceptable contract.

Outside of the public sector, interest arbitration provides a mechanism for bringing parties together, or closer together, without having to invoke economic sanctions, litigation, or ultimately strikes to close the deal. In situations where continuing production is more important than an ideal agreement, as was the case in the steel industry during the term of the "experimental negotiating agreement," interest arbitration permits both sides to continue a productive relationship during negotiations. Because they know that there will ultimately be a just determination of their differences, neither feels disadvantaged by continuing the status quo. So, too, with business relationships. When parties have a long-standing relationship, such as that between a cable franchise and the public entities it serves, it is more important to have a smooth resolution of differences than to have the perfect (from either side's view) resolution.

Types of Interest Arbitration

The term "interest arbitration" covers a great variety of arbitration. There are different types of panels and methods of decision-making, each of which has an effect on how a case will be determined. You need to understand these differences to be an effective advocate in different types of interest arbitration.

There are two basic types of panels, single arbitrator and tripartite. In the single arbitrator model, the parties agree upon one arbitrator who runs the hearing and makes the decision. In the tripartite model, each party nominates its own "partisan" arbitrator. Those two choose an impartial chair of the arbitration panel. The chair runs the hearing, but he does not make decisions alone. Rather, all decisions are by majority vote.

Research has shown that the single arbitrator model is more likely to lead to *adjudication* of the dispute. That is, the arbitrator will choose the position of one side or the other on each issue. In some instances, the arbitrator will arrive at a position that simply splits the parties' differences. The single arbitrator model is not likely to produce an innovative decision, since the arbitrator is unable to "pretest" its acceptability. Any ideas about compromise you may want to introduce have to be part of your argument to the arbitrator.

The tripartite model leads to what is called *legislation* as opposed to adjudication. That is, the neutral chair is likely to seek compromises from the party-appointed panelists in order to arrive at a consensus or unanimous decision. Since both of the party-appointed panelists are likely to be well-informed about the issues, the parties' background, and the feasibility of alternative approaches, the panel may be able to reach an innovative decision. The advocate can introduce suggestions for compromise through his party-appointed arbitrator, while still making the most forceful arguments for his original position.

The ability of the panel to innovate depends, of course, upon the type of arbitration the parties have chosen. The most common form of arbitration, conventional arbitration, allows the arbitrator to choose either party's position on an issue or arrive at some compromise. Parties who choose conventional arbitration give the arbitrator the widest possible latitude. So long as he does not stray from the issues submitted to him, he can do whatever the circumstances seem to him to dictate.

Last offer arbitration is the opposite of this. The arbitrator must choose between the last offer of one or the other party. This form of arbitration is generally thought to encourage more energetic bargaining. Because the system forces parties to make more reasonable last offers, you choose it in the hope there will be no award because the parties have reached their own agreement. You also might choose it if the parties have defined their dispute so carefully that a compromise would be worse than choosing your opponent's position.

There are three major variations on last offer arbitration. First, there is last offer "package" arbitration. In this system, the arbitrator is forced to choose between the entire package of proposals of the parties. Second, there is last offer arbitration by "issue." In this system, the parties define broad areas, such as the economic terms of an agreement, to be denominated as "issues." The arbitrator may choose only the position of one of the parties on each issue. Third, there is last offer arbitration by "item." That is, for every single item in dispute, the arbitrator is permitted to choose the position of one of the parties. Obviously, last offer by issue and item can be combined in an almost infinite variety of ways.

You can, of course, combine different panel types with different forms of arbitration. As I noted before, if you choose a tripartite arbitration format you will get more compromise, even when you use last offer arbitration, unless you choose last offer by package. A further complication can be introduced by varying the time at which a last offer can be modified. If the arbitrator may mediate, and if the chosen system permits the parties to modify their last offers up until some final point, the arbitrator can often manipulate the parties' positions so that they move closer to one another. Yet a further complication can be introduced by not permitting either party to modify its last offer without the permission of the other party. This makes it imperative that the parties negotiate with one another.

I could go through many more variations, all of which increase the incentives of the parties to reach their own agreement instead of ultimately submitting their dispute to arbitration. That preserves collective bargaining in the face of interest arbitration. If you are interested in the possibilities, I recommend looking at the Wisconsin statute covering public sector employees. It is so Byzantine the parties would have to be hopelessly unable to reach their own agreement before using it. As a matter of fact, I like the Wisconsin statute precisely for that reason.

Standards in Interest Arbitration

Since interest arbitration requires an arbitrator or panel of arbitrators to arrive at some resolution of economic or other differences between parties, the most obvious and critical issue is the standard that will be used. There are three possibilities. First, where the interest arbitration is required by statute, the statute itself may provide the standards that are to be applied by the arbitrator. The Iowa statute, covering all public employees, is fairly typical in the standards it enunciates. It requires the arbitrator or arbitration panel to consider:

1. Past collective bargaining contracts between the parties including the bargaining that led up to such contracts.
2. Comparison of wages, hours, and conditions of employment of the involved public employees with those other public employees doing comparable work, giving considerations to factors peculiar to the area and the classifications involved.
3. The interest and welfare of the public, the ability of the public employer to finance economic adjustments and the effect of such adjustments on the normal standard of services.
4. The power of the public employer to levy taxes and appropriate funds for the conduct of its operations.

These criteria embody the same types of comparisons that have been made in the private sector when determining "prevailing wage rates." The major difference is that they take into consideration the public employer's ability to pay.

A second way of arriving at standards is through negotiation by the parties. That is, prior to beginning negotiations, the parties can determine that they will ultimately settle their differences through arbitration if negotiations fail. The parties, in their agreement to arbitrate, determine the standards by which each of their positions ultimately will be judged. The parties may choose as standards readily ascertainable future facts. For instance, they may use settlements that have not yet occurred in other industries, national wage averages in their industry, or wage settlements between specified other parties. They may use changes in the cost of living reflected by the consumer price indices as a standard.

Third, the parties may simply avoid agreeing to a standard and leave the determination to the arbitrator. This option may be necessary because both sides recognize that any standards they might agree to will be outcome-determinative. If this is the case, the parties are likely to choose a tripartite arbitration panel, which will enable each side to influence the neutral arbitrator's choice of standards. As discussed below, the type of arbitration and panel that are chosen will significantly affect the way the case is argued and decided, although not necessarily produce a particular outcome.

Arguing a Case in the Absence of Specified Standards

Where there are no established standards, your obligation is twofold. You must first convince the arbitrator of the appropriateness of the standard you advocate and then convince him of the necessity of applying that standard in your favor. While the two processes are intimately related, they can be analyzed separately.

First, your job is to provide a paradigm, or ideal standard for decision, against which your argument can be judged. For instance, if wages are at issue, you might urge that the employees before the arbitrator be paid the same as "comparable" employees. The abstract idea of "comparability" then needs to be fleshed out with more specific standards, such as the precise type of work done, the conditions under which it is done, the geographical location of the work, and other such standards.

Or, suppose you are representing one group of trustees in a section 302(c)(5) trustee deadlock case. The issue over which the deadlock occurred is whether the fund should choose investment advisor X or Y. You must first develop a paradigm of the perfect investment advisor. You will attempt to convince the arbitrator that the perfect advisor has qualities A through M. Your second job is to convince the arbitrator that the investment advisor you are advocating has more of qualities A through M than the advisor advocated by the other trustees.

So, too, with the wage comparability paradigm. Your second job will be to show the arbitrator that employee groups X and Y have more of the characteristics that are comparable to the employees you represent than do employee groups A and B. Since the wages of groups X and Y are higher than the wages of the employees you represent, you argue that "comparability" demands that your employees be paid the same wage rate as employee groups X and Y.

The two processes intimately affect one another. Obviously, you will choose those aspects for the paradigm case that will ultimately prove most favorable to your position. You cannot, however, initially support them on the basis of your ultimate position. Otherwise, you would be making so obvious a circular argument that your opponent will have an easy time discrediting you.

Rather, you must support the paradigm on the basis of arguments that do not have specific reference to your case. For instance, there may be groupings of data provided by neutral agencies that support your paradigm. The Bureau of Labor Statistics, for instance, arrays data on cities of under and over 50,000 population. Thus, if you are arguing wage comparability for a city of 30,000, you can suggest a group of cities that includes those up to the size of 50,000 and point to an objective reason for doing so.

So, too, in the investment advisor example. Magazines such as *Forbes* make comparisons among different investment firms. The criteria they use are, arguably, ones that a panel should use. Again, you are relying on an outside party not concerned with your controversy for establishing the paradigm. As an advocate, you must find the outside parties whose standards, alone or in combination with others, will enable you to effectively support your position.

Except as I specifically indicate otherwise, all of the same principles and techniques apply in interest arbitration as apply in rights arbitration. Thus, you should read each of the following sections in conjunction with the earlier sections with the same title.

Investigation and Preparation

Where statutory or agreed-upon standards exist, one of the most difficult portions of your job has been done. You know the standards that will be used in determining the case. You also know the "essential elements" to be used in your calculation matrices. There is, however, a more difficult problem of allocating the burden of proof.

In general, the burden of proof and the burden of going forward rest upon the proponent of change. For instance, if the union is asking to change the status quo by raising wages, as its advocate you have the burden of going forward and showing why—in accordance with applicable standards—wages should be raised. Supposing, on the other hand, as management you wish to overcome an unfavorable earlier arbitral ruling through a change in contract language. As the proponent of a change in an existing set of affairs (the situation that exists after the arbitrator's ruling), you must go forward and show why it should be changed.

Sometimes you may believe that you are the proponent of the status quo while in fact you are advocating change. For instance, assume the parties' agreement says nothing about how vacation accrues, but the parties have always treated vacation accrual in a consistent manner. If you want to specify that method in the contract, you must go forward. The contract says nothing and you want it to say something. While your proofs may be minimal—indeed the parties may well agree about the way in which the vacation accrual has always been treated—as proponent of change you must still go forward.

The importance of allocating the burden of going forward and the burden of proof lies in the consequences of failure to meet them. Assume, for example, that you seek to have an arbitration panel award a new benefit for the employees you represent. If you fail to bear your burden of showing that comparable employees elsewhere have this benefit, the arbitration panel is unlikely to award it.

Finding Data

There are many sources of proof for advocates preparing an interest arbitration. We will look first at the general sources for data and then the ways you can array these data to present your argument most advantageously.

Here are some sources outside the parties' relationship that provide neutral data for comparison purposes. The Bureau of Labor Statistics (BLS) provides a wealth of information on wages and benefits of public and private sector employees. The BLS's *Monthly Labor Review* provides monthly data in the following categories:

> Employment data from the household survey, employment hours and earnings data from establishment surveys, unemployment insurance data, price data (including nine different consumer price indices) productivity data, wage and compensation data, work stoppage data.

Population data are available from the Bureau of the Census, as well as from the *Statistical Abstract of the United States*. In any industry there are often employer or (in the public sector) union consortia that provide data on that industry. For instance, the International Association of Firefighters has a computerized data base on firefighter salary and benefits. In the private sector, the Conference Board, Personnel Policies Forum, and such organizations as the Bureau of National Affairs and Commerce Clearing House provide data on collective bargaining agreements, contract clauses, and current wage settlements. Probably the most current and useful resource is the Bureau of National Affairs' *Daily Labor Report*.

There are also data resources within the parties' relationship. In the private sector, the interest arbitration agreement should address the extent to which an employer will open its books to the union for relevant proofs. In the public sector, the employer may already have a statutory disclosure obligation. For instance, school districts must frequently file financial reports with a state comptroller or a state department of education. Municipalities usually must submit to state auditors. In each instance, the data are quickly available as public documents, and they give a union the opportunity to scrutinize a current budget in light of what a particular political entity has done in the past.

Employers, too, normally have undisputed and reasonably available data on their own employees. Data on job classifications, length of service, distribution by age, marital status, and educational level—any or all of these items of information may be important in determining the cost of particular proposals. Ordinarily, both sides have an interest in providing cost data to an arbitrator or interest arbitration panel. There may, however, be some differences in the way each side gathers and computes this data.

Choosing Data

Both statutory and agreed-upon standards are usually somewhat abstract. For instance, the Iowa statute previously quoted requires the arbitrator to compare the "wages, hours, and conditions of employment of the involved public employee with those other public employees doing comparable work, giving consideration to factors peculiar to the area and the classifications involved." This standard does not enumerate specific proofs for the parties to adduce.

To determine what specific evidence you should present under this statutory standard, consider using "feedback loops." The first step is to survey all available economic data for employees doing the same job (for instance, engineers running sewage treatment plants) in your local area, your state, and neighboring states, keeping two standards in mind: favorability and supportability. Favorability is obvious. You are going to use the data that are most favorable to your position.

Favorability may, however, conflict with supportability. If, for instance, you chose all cities under 50,000, a choice that is supportable because it is a grouping BLS uses, you might find data that both support and contradict your position. You should therefore redefine your standard to excise the unfavorable cities. You might, for instance, choose only cities between 25,000 and 50,000, asserting (if it is indeed a fact) that smaller cities are not appropriate for comparison because they usually share sewage treatment plants on a county-wide basis and thus tend to skew the sample. Again, the key issue is whether you can legitimately support the comparison group you have chosen.

New advocates often succumb to the temptation to omit unfavorable examples that clearly fall within the comparison group. This is usually a mistake. You should assume that your opponent will catch the omission, for he probably has available the same data as you. If not, and if he challenges your data at the hearing, the arbitrator will require you to provide the sources from which you abstracted your data. Your witness may be embarrassed when confronted with the omitted data. Beyond embarrassment, you will have seriously damaged your own credibility with the decision maker. Even if he ultimately accepts the supportability of your comparison group, he will probably find it significantly less favorable than you asserted it to be.

Preparing Your Proofs

Although your basic considerations are the same in creating exhibits as when you looked for relevant data (that is, the data should be both favorable and supportable) there are many effective ways in which you can put information before the arbitrator.

Tables summarize relevant underlying documents. For example, you may have a number of cities in the same size range as yours, among which you want to compare salaries for sanitary engineers, the group involved in the arbitration. There are various ways you could array the data. You could use alphabetical order, city size order, salary order, or geographical location.

The real question is what you want the data to show. If you want to emphasize how low the salaries are in your city, you might want to array the data with the highest paid employees on the top of the chart and your city in bold print at or near the bottom.

It may be that salary data would show your city has salaries around the center of the salary range. Another way of putting this is that your city's salary is close to median. If there are some cities with very high salaries, you may want to compute an average. The average salary, which may well be somewhere above your city's salary, indicated in boldface above your city's salary, would show that your city is below average. Obviously, including cities with high salaries raises the average. But this is not always apparent at first glance. If you represented the city, you might well want to use the median salary, which would provide data more favorable to your position, or an average salary computed by first eliminating the highest and the lowest as distorting factors and then calculating an average.

In some instances, the absolute data may not be terribly favorable to your position. In that case, you might consider evidence on change, for example, the average increase for sanitary engineers in comparable districts over the last five or ten years (depending on which period is more favorable to your position). You would then argue that your group has not had comparable increases during the same time. A simple table comparing percentage salary increases over time could serve that same purpose.

Among the more impressive employer comparisons I have seen are those showing "total employer costs" and "total taxpayer burdens." In the first category are all the costs that an employer pays for both direct wages and benefits. A chart of this sort credits the employer for increases in health care costs, retirement costs, and social security that may have outstripped direct wage increases. Similarly, though the employer may have no way to affect the taxes that its citizens pay to such other entities as the state and county, comparing the total tax burden of citizens in the municipality involved in the arbitration against those in other municipalities can be instructive.

All of these comparisons can be done by tables. There are many other visual formats that can dramatize the points you are making. Graphs, bar graphs, and pictograms can all be used to illustrate differences. The magnitude of a particular distance is controlled by the scale that the advocate chooses. For instance, a bar graph (showing the compounded percentage pay increases received by a group) of employees over the last five years could have a scale from zero to fifty or zero to one hundred. Obviously, a scale of zero to fifty will show a far more dramatic percentage increase.

I have seen a pictogram that employed a cartoon of a police officer and a criminal. The criminal represented reported crime while the police officer represented police compensation. Each grew by a quarter-inch graph square for each 1 percent increase in the items they represented. Predictably enough, since it was an employer exhibit, the police officer grew far faster and fatter than the criminal. According to the employer, this showed that police were being paid more for doing a total job that the employer asserted was shrinking. I am not certain that it proved that point, but it did make a significant impression on the panel. Remember, the ways you can effectively present the data supporting your position are limited only by your imagination.

Preparing your proofs of your proposal's costs and impact also requires supportable choices of computational methods. In showing costs employers generally seek to incorporate all wage-driven costs into their calculation of the cost of a salary increase. Unions, on the other hand, generally urge omitting those costs.

Some costs present a range of arguable values. For instance, what is the cost of an additional day's vacation for a clerical employee? You could argue equally well any of these alternatives: (1) one day's pay at the average pay in the unit for the employee on vacation; (2) one day's overtime pay at the average pay in the unit that the employer must pay a replacement to do the work; or (3) nothing, because the employer may incur no additional expense. This is a matter about which there is significant dispute.

In proving the impact of a change, you must again be specific. For example, an employer can show that a certain percentage increase in the police department will result in a specific increase in cost for the existing force. This increase in cost can be translated into personnel terms by dividing the increased cost by the average cost of a police officer. These data would tend to show that absent any other changes, only a smaller force could be maintained within present budgetary constraints. This assumes, of course, an inability of the employer to raise taxes or shift budget priorities. Rarely is that the case. The point to be remembered is that you must be prepared to support the determination you made as to how costs could be computed.

Using Experts

Presenting your case effectively will often require that you employ experts to testify on behalf of your position. The experts you choose, their demeanor and their ability to respond to the arbitrator's questions—are all critical to your case. Arbitrators like to think of themselves as educable, so that a truly expert witness can explain complex scientific, medical, actuarial, and other technical data *so that they can understand.* Most appealing to an arbitrator is a conclusion about the meaning of data that he had reached himself. Arbitrators prefer being educated to being told that they must believe something because of the authority of the expert. All of the criteria for selecting experts and techniques for preparing their testimony discussed in Chapter 3 apply in interest arbitrations. They are, however, even more critical because a far larger proportion of your case is likely to be built upon expert testimony.

Tailoring Your Demands for Relief

In interest arbitration it is vitally important to have very specific demands. This is true regardless of the composition of the panel or the format of the arbitration. If you are proposing new contract language, you should draft the specific language you want. If you are proposing year-by-year percentage salary increases, you should make clear when they will begin, on what base they will be computed, and whether they are fully retroactive. Never leave any of this to the arbitrator's imagination. While the arbitrator may not ultimately award your position, he will at least know the proper way to word the increases you do get. Since an arbitration award is enforceable by the courts, it must be specific and definite to avoid modification or risks of vacatur.

Pre-hearing Briefs

In an interest arbitration there is far less apparent structure than in a rights arbitration. Ordinarily, in a rights arbitration, the moving party must cite the section of the contract that it believes was violated. This limits the hearing's scope and enables both parties to prepare for likely areas of factual controversy.

In an interest arbitration, on the other hand, it is difficult to know beforehand what precise standards each party will be relying upon, so there are mixed questions of fact and argument. Consequently, I think a pre-hearing brief makes excellent sense. I have often been successful in public sector interest arbitrations in getting parties to agree to pre-hearing briefs filed two weeks before the scheduled hearing. The brief contains all of the party's arguments, based upon whatever standards it is arguing are most applicable, a statement of the facts it intends to prove at the hearing, and the marked documents it intends to move into evidence. I tell the parties that factual allegations of their memoranda will be deemed true unless challenged by the opponent. In that case, the proponent of the fact will have to prove it in the normal fashion at the hearing. In some instances the parties agree to submit answering briefs, and these may be helpful to define precise areas of dispute.

There are many advantages to the pre-hearing brief in interest arbitration. First, it avoids hearing delays caused by surprise. Since each side is aware of what the other will be arguing, both can prepare to refute those arguments. Second, it provides a sharp focus for the hearing. Quite often, the briefs confirm that the parties do not dispute key facts (for instance, the dollar cost of a 1 percent increase), just their significance. Third, since fewer facts are in dispute, less testimony is necessary. This produces a speedier hearing and a shorter record, important factors in reducing costs. Fourth, since the arbitrator or arbitrators have had an adequate chance to study the brief, it makes for a "hot bench." Arbitrators are better able to understand and question witnesses and to advise the advocates what troubling issues they would like them to address. Finally, as a result of the pre-hearing brief, you will be better prepared and your arguments more focused. Consequently, posthearing briefs are usually unnecessary. Where parties do file them, they are always quite short.

Because of all these advantages, I am convinced of the efficacy of pre-hearing briefs and employ them in interest arbitration cases whenever the parties agree. I think, too, that pre-hearing briefs have substantially reduced the costs of interest arbitrations.

At the Hearing

As I noted earlier, the proponent of change bears both the burden of going forward and the burden of proof. Usually this is the union—as to most of the changes. As to those changes that the employer seeks, it has the burden both of going forward and proof on those issues. What is unusual about an interest arbitration is that the moving party must argue both for the standard or paradigm that it believes the panel should apply, and for the result it seeks through applying the facts to that paradigm. Since both sides know each other's arguments, and since the standard of decision is itself part of the argument, there is no real disadvantage in going forward first.

Inquire to be sure that the panel has read your brief. Then concentrate on the remaining factual disputes. These will often involve expert testimony. The expert may testify as to economic data, standards of comparison, or appropriate actuarial standards. Your job as an advocate is to keep the expert carefully focused on the issues before the panel. You must be conscious of the level of comprehension of the panel, stopping your expert witness whenever it appears that the panel's eyes are, collectively, glazing over. If your expert is rebutting your opponent's expert, you must be sure that he explains the preferability of his approach to the other, rather than touting his greater expertise. Remember, the arbitrator is not interested solely in counting the number of books each expert has written. He is more interested in whether his or her explanations make sense.

In this same vein, it wastes everyone's time to use your expert simply to nitpick the other expert. Concentrate on operative facts. Ignore those small errors that only make your expert look pedantic. If there are errors, however, that make your expert look more thorough, pounce upon them.

Throughout the testimony, be sure to keep focusing the arbitrator's attention on where new proof fits into your structure of the case. Your goal is to have the arbitrator or panel accept your structure of the case, including your definition of the paradigm. It is far more important for you to do this than to win a dispute over last year's percentage increase in health care costs.

If you are appearing before a tripartite panel, you must instruct your party-appointed arbitrator in how to best help your case. At the hearing, the party-appointed arbitrator can ask questions of witnesses. While the party-appointed arbitrator ought not to operate as an advocate at the hearing, there is no prohibition on asking easy questions of your witnesses that will underscore points you are trying to make. He can also ask tough, nonargumentative questions of your adversary's witnesses that underscore the weakness of their position. In both instances, moderation is the best guide.

Your party-appointed arbitrator can also serve the important function of keeping the neutral arbitrator focused on the matters before him. If he sees doodling or signs of daydreaming or even actual sleep, your arbitrator can bring the neutral arbitrator back to the real world. In discussions at lunch, he can reiterate major points. He should not, however, argue about the credibility of witnesses to the extent of appearing so partisan that his opinion seems suspect.

After the Hearing

The major job of the party-appointed arbitrator occurs in the posthearing executive session. That is when the panel decides the case. Since advocates are often given that role (although not in the same case in which they act as advocate) it will be worthwhile to describe that task. Prior to this session the party-appointed arbitrator should have carefully reviewed the transcript, if there is one, the briefs, and his own notes. When he goes into the executive session he should be able to point to specific evidence in the record that supports your view as to both standards and facts. He must remember that the executive session is not a place where new evidence may be introduced. Indeed, if new evidence were introduced at an executive session, and the panel relied upon that new evidence for its determination, that would probably be ground for vacatur. Finally, if you are involved in conventional interest arbitration, the party-appointed arbitrator should have a series of fallback positions in case your main position has not convinced the arbitrator.

Trustee Deadlocks Under Labor Management Relations Act (LMRA) 302(c)(5)

I have touched briefly on arbitrations over trustee deadlocks in the previous sections of this chapter. What I said about preparing and presenting your case in interest arbitrations holds true for trustee deadlock arbitrations. There are, however, some special considerations that need more careful attention.

Statutory Authority

For joint funds set up under the authority of the LMRA arbitration is statutorily required to break trustee deadlocks. The statutory language is contained in LMRA section 302(c)(5), which reads:

> [i]n the event the employer and employee groups deadlock on the administration of such funds and there are no neutral persons empowered to break such deadlock, such agreement provides that the two groups shall agree on an impartial umpire to decide such dispute. . . .

There are, however, neither statutory standards nor procedures for the arbitrator to decide how to break the deadlock.[1] This obviously increases the importance of your developing paradigms in arguing trustee deadlock cases, and I will devote some further attention to that later in this section. What is important to note here is that there is another statutory consideration that plays a part in arbitrators' decision making processes in these cases. The arbitrator is considered a fiduciary when he meets any of the definitions contained in section 3(21)(A) of ERISA. They are:

1. He exercises any discretionary control respecting management or disposition of its assets.
2. He renders investment advice for a fee or other compensation, direct or indirect, with respect to any moneys or other property of such plan, or has any authority or responsibility to do so, or
3. He has any discretionary authority or discretionary responsibility in the administration of such plan.

In most trustee deadlock cases the arbitrator will be considered a fiduciary. Consequently, the arbitrator will be acting as

---

1. Voluntary procedures are contained in the AAA Impasse Rules. *See* Appendix 5.

though he were another trustee, with the power to break the deadlock through his "vote." The primary obligation of trustees is to manage the plan for the sole benefit of its participants. Thus, in breaking the deadlock the arbitrator is obliged to have the benefit of the participants as his guiding principle. In arguing the case, you must always show the arbitrator how what you propose will benefit the participants.

Choosing the Arbitrator

Experience and Type

In choosing an arbitrator for a trustee deadlock you need to pay close attention to three considerations: the arbitrator's experience in resolving trustee deadlocks or other interest disputes, the arbitrator's reputation for managing complex cases, and the arbitrator's ability to cope with complex mathematical issues. Few arbitrators have, as a large part of their practice, trustee deadlock cases. They are not frequently heard cases and they are not amenable to the processes normally used in rights arbitration. Some arbitrators have done trustee deadlock arbitrations. Other arbitrators have done interest arbitrations of various sorts. Both are likely to be qualified to do trustee deadlock arbitrations. You need to select someone who is comfortable deciding both what standards are applicable and how the facts fit those standards.

You also need someone who is capable of managing a case. Earlier I talked about pre-hearing case management and provided an example. It is absolutely critical in trustee deadlocks to have an arbitrator who will push the parties to do substantial work before the hearing. Otherwise, the hearing will be both formless and endless.

Finally, it is important to choose an arbitrator who is highly educable. Trustee deadlocks most frequently involve issues of

medical disabilities or investment decisions. In both areas the
expert testimony is likely to be detailed and difficult. The
arbitrator must be capable of assimilating technical matters so
that he can choose between the testimony of competing experts.
In particular, if you are going to need actuarial testimony, be
sure you select an arbitrator who is comfortable with mathematical concepts. It is sometimes the case that otherwise excellent arbitrators have their eyes glaze over as soon as your
expert witness begins explaining the assumptions that went into
determining whether the fund could increase current benefits
without increasing employer contributions.

Insurance

The arbitrator is usually a fiduciary when breaking trustee
deadlocks. This is the net result of a series of Department of
Labor decisions beginning in about 1978. The significance of
the arbitrator's fiduciary status is that he has the same liability
as the trustees to a suit by a beneficiary for breach of his
fiduciary duty. He is probably not covered by the normal,
quasi-judicial common law immunity that arbitrators otherwise enjoy.[2] I say "probably" because there is one decision that
said an arbitrator in a trustee deadlock case had common law
immunity.[3] The reasoning in that decision is suspect, however,
since it states the issue in the following way:

> Our view of the issue, however, is whether the duties and liabili-
> ties that arise under ERISA are enforceable against an arbitra-
> tor who is acting in his official capacity and, as such, entitled to
> arbitral immunity.[4]

---

2. In California arbitrators enjoy statutory immunity from civil liability.
3. International Union, United Auto., Aerospace, & Agric. Implement
   Workers of Am., Locals 656 & 985 v. Greyhound Lines, Inc., 701 F.2d
   1181 (6th Cir. 1983).
4. *Id.* at 1184-85.

The court goes on to assume the arbitrator has arbitral immunity. On that basis it avoids deciding whether the arbitrator is a fiduciary. It then declares, without recourse to legislative intent, that ERISA was not intended to abrogate arbitral immunity. While every arbitrator applauds the court's effort to provide common law quasi-judicial immunity to arbitrators in trustee deadlocks, few rely upon it. As a consequence, you are likely to be faced with the issue of insuring the arbitrator.[5]

You probably have never before been confronted with an arbitrator insisting that he be insured before he will serve on one of your cases. In trustee deadlock arbitrations it is commonplace. Most arbitrators, faced with the possibility of being sued for breach of their fiduciary duty by any beneficiary of the plan, require the plan to insure them for the year of the case and the next six years, the statutory period during which suit can be brought. The customary coverage that arbitrators are likely to require is $10 million. There are two ways you can provide this coverage.

First, some plans find that it is cheapest to add the arbitrator to their existing trustee errors and omissions coverage. Most insurance companies are willing to do this, although the cost varies enormously. It appears that insurers do not have a uniform way of rating this coverage so the variations in cost are more a function of the insurance carrier than the amount in issue. In addition to being added to the plan's trustee coverage, most arbitrators ask for "waiver of recourse" insurance from the insurer. The arbitrator will pay for this insurance himself, since it violates ERISA for the plan to pay for it. If you intend to use this method of insuring the arbitrator, be sure to have the insurance company send him a copy of the rider adding him to

---

5. There are some arbitrators who are either unaware of their potential liability, or willing to go uninsured in these cases despite the potential liability.

the plan's coverage well in advance of the hearing. You should also send the arbitrator a commitment letter indicating that the plan will be continuing his coverage for the six years following the year in which he hears the case.

A second method of insuring the arbitrator is to have him do it himself. Some arbitrators carry their own liability insurance for ERISA cases. The insurance is quite expensive, and usually carries a substantial deductible that is applicable to the insurance company's cost of defending any suit. One reason arbitrators carry this insurance is their fear that a plan will cease to keep their insurance in force for the full six years. Since it is claims-made insurance, it covers the tail of liability from earlier cases, as well. Arbitrators who have insurance will ask the plan or the parties (in a withdrawal liability case) to pay an amount that is this case's share of the annual cost of the insurance and its continuation. Most arbitrators will give the parties a choice of using his insurance, or buying insurance for him. In general, it is far cheaper to use the arbitrator's insurance.

Creating an Appropriate Issue for the Arbitrator

In most forms of interest arbitration the issue for the arbitrator is framed by the demands of the parties. Their negotiating strategy leads them to a point where, for political or practical reasons, they do not believe further compromise is possible. In "last offer" arbitration, the arbitrator is limited to choosing between the last offer of each party. One of the reasons for using "last offer" arbitration is that it prevents the arbitrator from damaging the parties by creating a compromise that is less palatable to the parties than either choice.

For trustee deadlock arbitrations the "last offer" model is most appropriate. When the deadlock is over plan administration, or the denial of a benefit claim, or plan investments, both groups of trustees see their proposals as an expression of what is in the best interest of plan participants. Presumably, they have tried to resolve their differences and examined compromises, but they are left with an honest difference of opinion. When that occurs, there is a danger of giving too much authority to the arbitrator.

Limiting Jurisdiction

It is usually in the best interest of the plan to limit the jurisdiction of the arbitrator, for two reasons: first, the less the arbitrator has to decide, the less chance there is of his erring; second, the management of the fund is properly in the hands of the trustees, not an outside arbitrator. The arbitrator, coming in to break a single deadlock, is never in as good a position as the trustees to shape the ongoing affairs of the plan.

Jurisdiction can be limited in two ways. First, you can draft language in the plan documents that limits the jurisdiction of the arbitrator in deadlock cases. If the parties had done that, you probably would not be reading this section. More typically, the language in a plan looks like this:

> If, by unit vote, the trustees deadlock on any matter arising in connection with this trust agreement of the plan. . .any matters in dispute shall be submitted to the impartial arbitrator in writing. If the trustees cannot jointly agree upon a statement submitting the matter to arbitration, the employer trustees and the union trustees shall each prepare and forward in writing their versions of the dispute and the question or questions involved.

Under this language, if the trustees do not agree, it is possible for one group of trustees to give the arbitrator extraordinarily broad jurisdiction by wording its version of the dispute as, for instance, "Shall the plan involve itself in innovative investment vehicles?" Thus, limiting jurisdiction in plan language may not be sufficient.

Second, you can limit the arbitrator's jurisdiction by narrowly drawing the resolution upon which the trustees deadlock. This has the dual advantage of conforming with the mandate of section 302(c)(5) and allowing the trustees to use parliamentary methods to shape the resolution. Sometimes, you want no more than a "yes" or "no" answer from the arbitrator. At other times, a simple "yes" or "no" will lead you to a series of further deadlocks. In those situations, you want to shape the arbitrator's jurisdiction, through a series of resolutions, so that you have a single arbitration, rather than a series of them.

Shaping the Deadlock

The jurisdiction of the arbitrator is limited by the wording of the resolution upon which the trustees deadlock. The wording of the resolution will, in turn, be shaped by what you want the arbitration to accomplish. For instance, in a disability case the dispute may be over when a participant became totally disabled, not whether he is totally disabled. The trustees could agree to deadlock on two resolutions, each one containing the date that one group believes the participant became totally disabled. The arbitrator would then have jurisdiction to decide on which of those dates the disability became total. There are, of course, two potential problems. First, the wording of the resolution may obscure the question and limit the arbitrator's ability to decide correctly. For instance, if the resolution reads:

> RESOLVED, that Jones shall receive total disability benefits as of December 11, 1986.

the arbitrator is limited to deciding whether Jones gets the benefits of that date. If a second deadlocked resolution reads:

> RESOLVED, that Jones shall receive total disability benefits as of April 15, 1986.

the arbitrator has two choices. But it may be that there were events or medical examinations between those two dates which, legitimately, could have shown that Jones was totally disabled on some other date. Because of the way you have phrased the issue, the arbitrator can not decide that total disability occurred on that other date.

You could agree not to submit the deadlocked resolution itself and stipulate as the issue: "When did Jones become entitled to total disability benefits?" In a situation of this simplicity you may feel quite comfortable with that formulation. Alternatively, if the trustees are worried about the arbitrator splitting the baby and fuzzing up some important principles, you can offer a series of dates (each offered as a resolution if necessary), so that the arbitrator must say "no" to all but one. These dates would, of course, conform to the examinations or other events that could have marked the beginning of the period of total disability. The arbitrator will justify his choice in the award, offering the trustees an operational principle for the future.

If the dispute is over an investment, you want to strictly limit the arbitrator's ability to decide how plan assets shall be used. This can be done by a crisply worded resolution. For instance:

> RESOLVED, that the fund shall invest $10,000,000 in the Series 37 bonds of the Development Authority of the City of East Buffalo Chip.

If this is the deadlocked resolution, the arbitrator can not decide what else is to be done with the money. Nor should he, if he is cognizant of his jurisdiction, decide that the fund should invest some lesser amount. If the dispute is actually over the amount to be invested in these bonds, you should offer a series of resolutions, similar to those on the disability issue.

A third type of deadlock involves noninvestment, plan administration decisions. These may include such matters as where the fund's headquarters should be. For instance, suppose one group of trustees would like to see the offices moved to the new Taj Mahal center in downtown. The other group thinks the headquarters is fine exactly where it is, but in no event should it be moved to the Taj Mahal center. If any move were to be made it should be to the Watergate center.

The proponent of change, the group of trustees advocating moving the offices, will have the burden of going forward in the arbitration and proving that a change should be made. If it prevails, the next question will be whether the change should be to the Taj Mahal or Watergate center. If the trustees wish to limit the arbitrator's jurisdiction, so as to decrease their exposure to an inappropriate decision, they can deadlock on the following series of resolutions:

a. RESOLVED, that the plan's headquarters shall be moved.
b. RESOLVED, if the plan's headquarters is moved it shall be to the Taj Mahal center.
c. RESOLVED, if the plan's headquarters is moved, and it is not moved to the Taj Mahal center, it shall be moved to the Watergate center.

As to the first two resolutions, the trustees wanting the move must first convince the arbitrator that a move is appropriate, and then convince him that a move to the Taj Mahal center is appropriate. If they do not succeed on the first resolution, the arbitrator will not have to consider the second. If they succeed on the first and second, the arbitrator will not have to consider the third. If they succeed on the first, but not the second resolution, the arbitrator will have to consider the third. The other trustees will now have the burden of convincing the arbitrator of the propriety of locating the plan headquarters at the

Watergate center. If they fail, the trustees are left with a decision that a move should be made, but the discretion to determine where the headquarters should go.

Creating Standards in a Trustee Deadlock Arbitration

Earlier in this Chapter I talked about creating standards, or paradigm cases, for interest arbitrations in which there were neither statutory nor agreed upon standards. This is particularly important in trustee deadlocks, since there will often be no specific standards that can be used. In most instances the plan will define, for instance, "total disability," either in specific terms or through reference to a Social Security definition. But it will not define the criteria for locating the offices, or choosing an administrator. Rather, it will be your job, if a trustee deadlock occurs, to define the criteria in a way that is both convincing and consistent with the choice you advocate.

For instance, let us suppose that you represent the trustees who want to move the plan headquarters to the Taj Mahal center. Your first task is to construct a paradigm, that is, determine what standards define the "ideal" headquarters location. In doing this you might take into consideration such factors as:

1. The location—Is it convenient for plan participants to get to? Is there public transportation nearby? Is there convenient parking? Is the neighborhood considered safe? Is it in a location (such as a union hall) where participants already come to transact other business?
2. The cost—How much does the current location cost, per square foot? What percentage of the plan's administrative costs go to rent? What services (such as cleaning) are included in the rent? What amenities (such as parking) are included in the rent?

3. The physical plant—Is there currently enough space for equipment, records, and employees of the plan? Is the space maintained in adequate physical condition, including climate control? Are there amenities for the employees, such as lunch or break rooms?

Each of the questions posed under the three considerations suggests an answer that would be "ideal." For instance, the headquarters should be easily accessible to participants who either drive or take public transportation, in a place where they already come for some other purpose, in a neighborhood where they are not afraid to go, etc. Before these considerations could become part of a paradigm, however, you need to find some support for an assertion that these are relevant factors.

There are many places where you might find support. For instance, the International Foundation of Employee Benefit Plans (IF) reviews articles and books on plan management. It would be a source of information on what other plans spend, as a percentage of their administrative costs, on physical plant. In addition, you might well find studies on locations of plan headquarters, or reasons for staff turnover at various plans. All of these data would go to supporting your paradigm. The proof that these are relevant considerations would be contained in the research, and articles from sources such as IF, as well as any studies the plan itself may have done among its participants.

It would be naive to suggest that, as an advocate, you would create this paradigm without reference to its impact on your position in the trustee deadlock. Obviously, you want to create a paradigm that supports your position. The art is in doing it subtly. For instance, if you represent the trustees who want to move the plan to the Taj Mahal center, you may find that the cost per square foot is much higher than your current location. You would want to know the percentage of administrative costs represented by both your current rental price and the proposed rental price. You could then compare these to a median (or average, depending upon which is more favorable to your position) of costs for other plans, as shown in IF data. In creating the paradigm you would include both absolute costs and percentage costs, so that you do not look foolish when your opponent shows absolute costs. In your argument, however, you would assert that the percentage is currently among the lowest and the move would bring it only up to the average. Consequently, in terms of operating the plan for the benefit of the participants, the trustees could not be faulted for moving to a new location, if other reasons for the move exist.

You can use the evaluation matrix in Chapter 1 for identifying the essential elements of your paradigm, and for determining how to prove that they are essential. In addition, you can use the evaluation matrix to apply each of the standards from the paradigm to the case you are arguing. Thus, while trustee deadlock arbitrations require you to create and support a paradigm, after that what you do is essentially similar to what you have already learned.

Withdrawal Liability Arbitrations Under Multi-employer Pension Plan Amendment Act (MPPAA)

Under MPPAA,[6] arbitration is required for disputes over withdrawal liability determinations made by the plan. These arbitrations may be jointly initiated, or demanded by the withdrawing employer.[7] The arbitrable issues are: whether a withdrawal has occurred, whether the De Minimis Rule should be

---

6. 29 U.S.C. § 1401.
7. MPPAA § 4219(b)(2)(A), (B).

applied, whether withdrawal liability was correctly computed, and when payments must be made and in what amount. These arbitrations are unique and require some special consideration.

The system of arbitration created by the statute contains a series of important time limits and presumptions. The time limits are a matter of procedure that is best covered by the statute itself.[8] For purposes of preparing for a withdrawal liability arbitration the presumptions are most important. It is presumed that the plan's determinations are correct and the party contesting the determination has the obligation of showing, by a preponderance of the evidence, "that the determination was unreasonable or clearly erroneous."[9] As for the plan's calculation of the unfunded vested liability owed by the withdrawing employer, there is a presumption that the calculation is correct unless the employer can show "by a preponderance of the evidence—

1. The actuarial assumptions and methods used in the determination were, in the aggregate, unreasonable (taking into account the experience of the plan and reasonable expectations), or
2. The plan's actuary made a significant error in applying the actuarial assumptions or methods.[10]

---

8. Section 4219(b) requires the plan to notify an employer who has completely or partially withdrawn of its liability for unfunded vested benefits. The employer must request a review by the plan "no later than 90 days" after receiving the demand. Arbitration must be demanded either 60 days after the plan has responded to the employer's request for review, or 120 days after the request is made, whichever is earlier. Section 4221(a)(1)(A)&(B). The parties can jointly initiate an arbitration within 180 days of the plan's demand to the employer.
9. MPPAA § 4221(a)(3)(A).
10. MPPAA § 4221(a)(3)(B).

In addition, on appeal there is the further presumption, "rebuttable only by a clear preponderance of the evidence, that the findings of fact made by the arbitrator were correct."[11]

These presumptions severely limit the scope of the arbitration. In effect, it is a review of the plan's determinations, rather than an independent judgment by the arbitrator of the appropriateness of the plan's determinations. Thus, you will not have much success with arguments that there are better assumptions that could have been made in determining withdrawal liability, or that the equities favor your client. Rather, if you represent an employer you are limited to showing that the plan was wrong. That is a difficult task. Moreover, the arbitrator has statutory authority to assess arbitrator's fees (if the parties have not previously agreed on them) and to award "reasonable attorney's fees."[12]

If you become involved with a withdrawal liability arbitration, you should be aware that the Pension Benefit Guaranty Corporation has approved the procedural rules jointly promulgated by the American Arbitration Association and the International Foundation of Employee Benefit Plans.[13] Those rules provide for the appointment of an arbitrator (AAA maintains a special list of arbitrators who are qualified to hear withdrawal liability disputes), pre-hearing procedures to expedite the case, and ex parte hearings if they should become necessary. Thus, if you adopt those rules, you can be assured that your procedure conforms with the fair procedure requirements of the law, and contains rules that provide for most contingencies.[14]

The major difference in the way in which you prepare for and handle a withdrawal liability arbitration is a result of the

---

11. MPPAA § 4221(c).

12. MPPAA § 4221(a)(2).

13. *See* Appendix 4.

14. MPPAA § 4221(a)(2).

presumptions and the statutory mechanism for appealing arbitrator's awards to the federal courts. The presumptions require you to make the essential elements of your evaluation matrix the various ways in which the plan erred in its determinations. The appeal mechanism has led to a significant body of case law, which provides the basis for an "appeal to authority" in your brief that is not otherwise available in arbitrations. Consequently, you should include applicable law in your brief to the arbitrator. In some instances, it provides definitive guidance on what actuarial assumptions are reasonable and what methods for determining withdrawal liability are correct.

Conclusion

There are many varieties of arbitration other than rights arbitration. While I have dealt with the major types in the labor-management context in this chapter, you should not think I have provided an exhaustive list. In the areas of commercial, construction, consumer, and judicial arbitration there are new statutes in many different states. There is a strong interest in arbitration as a means of resolving disputes in a wide variety of settings. While this book is devoted to the labor-management setting, I have operated in other settings as well, and feel comfortable saying the lessons of the earlier chapters are applicable, with appropriate modifications for unique statutes or rules, to most forms of arbitration. Thus, in mastering the skills emphasized in this book you will have made yourself competent in many arbitration settings.

8

Ancillary Litigation

Introduction

Arbitration is a creature of statute. The first modern arbitration statute was adopted in New York in 1920; a few years later the United States Arbitration Act[1] was passed. Since that time, approximately forty-four states have passed modern arbitration statutes, usually modeled on the Uniform Arbitration Act.[2] The purpose of these statutes is to overcome the perceived common law hostility to arbitration, to enforce agreements to arbitrate future disputes, to give arbitrators the power to hold hearings that provide essential due process rights, and to enforce arbitration awards through the judicial machinery.[3] Although arbitration is generally conceived of as a substitute for litigation, there are times when you will be obliged to litigate in order to enforce your arbitration agreement.

There are separate bodies of law that apply, depending upon whether the dispute is covered by the National Labor Relations

---

1. *See* Appendix 2.
2. *See* Appendix 1.
3. Much has been written about the common law's "hostility" to arbitration. It was allegedly based upon a theory that arbitration "ousts jurisdiction of the courts." It is not at all clear that any such theory was ever articulated. Rather, courts repeated that phrase without analyzing it. As Judge Frank put it in Kulukundis Shipping Co. v. Amtorg Trading Corp., 126 F.2d 978 (2d Cir. 1942): "Give a bad dogma a good name and its bite may become as bad as its bark."

Act (ordinarily the case in private sector cases), by a state act (ordinarily the case in public sector cases), or by the Federal Service Labor-Management Relations Statute, which covers federal employees.[4] In drawing a distinction between federal and state enforcement, I do not suggest that the differences are outcome determinative. In many private sector cases, one of the parties will go into a state court, which will apply federal substantive law. In states with modern arbitration statutes, the result will usually be the same whether the matter is heard by a federal court applying federal law, a state court applying federal law, or a state court applying state law. There are, however, some differences that are worth noting. I will compare the federal,[5] New York,[6] and California[7] schemes to give you some idea of the similarities and differences.

It is important to remember that states with public sector bargaining usually have specific collective bargaining laws that may impact on arbitration in ways that are not apparent through examining the arbitration statutes. For instance, public sector interest arbitration, where it exists, is usually covered by the state's collective bargaining statute. Awards may be subject to different standards of review, on a vacatur motion, than ordinary arbitration awards. In New York, where the public sector bargaining statute does not precisely define the scope of bargaining, the courts have expanded the statutory vacatur grounds to include "public policy," in order to insulate certain governmental decisions from the collective bargaining

---

4. *See* Appendix 10. The federal sector scheme for reviewing arbitration awards is unique. These general comments about statutory mechanisms are not intended to apply to the federal sector, which is covered in the last section of this Chapter.

5. *See* Appendix 10.

6. *See* Appendix 12. (New York Arbitration Act, CPLR 7500 *et seq.*).

7. *See* Appendix 13 (California Arbitration Act, CAL. CIV. PROC. CODE § 1280 *et seq.*).

272

process.[8] Thus, while I can provide a general outline of types of ancillary litigation, you must check your own state's laws before proceeding.

I do not intend to provide a step-by-step guide for litigating, but only an outline of the areas of law involved in labor arbitrations. As with any textual material on the law, some of what is said in this book will be out of date by the time you read it. Consequently, you should regard this chapter as a map. And you should not mistake the map for the territory.

Coverage of Arbitration Statutes

There are three general areas that the arbitration statutes address: first, enforcing the parties' choice of forum; second, providing the arbitrator with the powers needed to hold a due process hearing; third, enforcing or vacating an arbitrator's award.

Enforcing the Parties' Choice of Forum

In the first area, the courts concern themselves both with requiring the parties to live up to their arbitration agreement, and staying pending litigation. For instance, the New York law reads:

> A written agreement to submit any controversy thereafter arising or any existing controversy to arbitration is enforceable without regard to the justiciable character of the controversy and confers jurisdiction on the courts of the state to enforce it and to enter judgment on an award. In determining any matter arising under this article, the court shall not consider whether the claim with respect to which arbitration is sought is tenable, or otherwise pass upon the merits of the dispute.[9]

---

8. *See, e.g.,* Cohoes v. Cohoes Teachers Ass'n, 40 N.Y.2d 774, 358 N.E.2d 878, 390 N.Y.S.2d 53 (1976).
9. N.Y. CIV. PRAC. L. & R. 7501 (McKinney 1980). *See* Appendix 12.

To someone unfamiliar with the history of the arbitration acts, this language may be misleading. There is a long history of litigation dealing with fraud in the inducement, and other such equitable grounds for contract rescission. Both federal and state courts have made it clear that there must be legal or equitable grounds to revoke the arbitration agreement itself, since it is regarded as a separate "contract," with the mutual promises to arbitrate being sufficient consideration for each other.[10] Thus, on a motion to compel arbitration (or to stay pending litigation), the courts only consider whether an agreement to arbitrate has been made by the parties, and whether it covers this controversy.

In deciding whether a controversy is covered by the arbitration agreement, the courts are reluctant to involve themselves in close interpretation of the language at issue. The reason is obvious; parties to an arbitration agreement contracted to have an arbitrator, not the court, interpret their contract. Consequently, when there is a broad arbitration clause, and the matter is arguably covered by the arbitration clause, the courts indulge in a presumption of arbitrability and leave interpretation of the contract to the arbitrator. Upon the request of a party, the arbitrator is free to determine if the controversy is arbitrable. As the Supreme Court recently made clear, however, the courts can not abdicate their responsibility to determine whether there was an agreement to arbitrate this particular dispute, and allow an arbitrator to determine his own jurisdiction.[11]

---

10. *See, e.g.,* Prima Paint Corp. v. Flood & Conklin Mfg. Co, 388 U.S. 395 (1967); *In re* Weinrott, 32 N.Y.2d 198, 290 N.E.2d 42, 344 N.Y.S.2d 848 (1973).

11. *See,* AT&T Technologies v. Communication Workers, 475 U.S. 643, 89 L. Ed. 2d 648, 106 S. Ct. 1415 (1986). In this case the Court saw the issue as whether the court must determine whether the parties intended

Finally, in the first area of enforcing the parties' agreement to arbitrate, the state statutes provide for courts to appoint an arbitrator when the parties have either failed to choose a method of appointment, or that method itself has failed. The standard provision requires the court to appoint, upon application of a party, a single arbitrator, unless the agreement provides for more. The Uniform Act provides:

> If the arbitration agreement provides a method of appointment of arbitrators, this method shall be followed. In the absence thereof, or if the agreed method fails or for any reason cannot be followed, or when an arbitrator appointed fails or is unable to act and his successor has not been duly appointed, the court on application of a party shall appoint one or more arbitrators.[12]

The state acts that vary from the Uniform Act usually accomplish the same end, regardless of their specific language. The courts also recognize that where the parties have provided for tripartite arbitration the right of a party to appoint its own arbitrator is an important one, not to be eliminated by the court unilaterally appointing a single arbitrator.[13]

Providing the Arbitrator with Power to Conduct a Due Process Hearing

The second area covered by statutes, providing the arbitrator with power to conduct a due process hearing, generally involves the power to administer oaths, issue enforceable subpoenas, and compel the production of documents. Most state acts specifically empower the arbitrator to administer oaths. More

---

to arbitrate a dispute, or whether that was properly left for the arbitrator. It decided that the courts can not abdicate their responsibility to decide whether the parties agreed to arbitrate a dispute.

12. UNIF. ARB. ACT § 3. *See* Appendix 1.

13. *See, e.g., In re* Lipschutz, 304 N.Y. 58, 106 N.E.2d 8 (1952).

importantly, all of the statutes provide an arbitrator with sub-poena power. Although methods of enforcement vary, it is ordinarily the courts that enforce subpoenas, not arbitrators. The exceptions will be discussed below.

Enforcing or Vacating Arbitral Awards

The third area with which statutes concern themselves, is enforcing (or vacating) arbitral awards. The statutes generally provide for minimal review of the award, in order to avoid making arbitration a mere prelude to litigation. In fact, this subject has generated a great deal of litigation. There are three general types of controversy. First, there are controversies about whether the award should be vacated on any of the grounds specified in the statute. Second, there are controversies over whether an award should be vacated because of a failure of the union to fairly represent an individual. Third, there are controversies over the preclusive effect of an arbitration award in other settings. Each of these will be discussed more fully below.

Compelling and Staying Arbitration

Private Sector

Many agreements to arbitrate are contained in private sector collective bargaining agreements between unions and employers subject to the National Labor Relations Act. These parties have the federal courts available to enforce their arbitration agreements. Under section 301 of the Labor Management Relations Act, a party who is aggrieved by the failure of the other party to arbitrate a dispute subject to an arbitration agreement contained in a collective bargaining agreement can bring an action to compel arbitration in the federal district court. The court will apply federal law in enforcing the arbitration agreement.[14]

Compelling Arbitration

The court will decide the motion to compel under the standards set forth in what has come to be known as the "trilogy." These three decisions by the Supreme Court, announced on the same day, set the standards of federal law for compelling or staying arbitration.[15] In *American Manufacturing* the Court of Appeals had rejected the Union's request to compel arbitration because it was "frivolous." The Court reversed, holding that where the dispute is, on its face, governed by the arbitration clause, the courts have no business weighing the merits of the grievance. Rather, "the agreement is to submit all grievances to arbitration, not merely ones a court may deem to be meritorious."[16] In *Warrior & Gulf,* after hearing evidence, the district court refused to compel arbitration because the contract excluded matters that were "strictly a function of management" from an otherwise broad arbitration clause. It determined that the matter sought to be arbitrated was "strictly a

---

14. *See,* Textile Workers Union v. Lincoln Mills, 353 U.S. 448 (1957).
15. United Steelworkers v. American Mfg. Co., 363 U.S. 564 (1960); United Steelworkers v. Warrior & Gulf Navigation Co., 363 U.S. 574 (1960); United Steelworkers v. Enterprise Wheel & Car Corp., 363 U.S. 593 (1960).
16. The Court noted the mischievous effect of deciding otherwise, citing a New York decision which found the matter to be arbitrated "beyond dispute" and dismissed the motion to compel. New York later added the following language to CPLR 7501: "In determining any matter arising under this article, the court shall not consider whether the claim with respect to which arbitration is sought is tenable, or otherwise pass on the merits of the dispute."

function of management," as that term was used in the contract. Consequently, it declined to compel arbitration. The Court held:

> An order to arbitrate the particular grievance should not be denied unless it may be said with positive assurance that the arbitration clause is not susceptible of an interpretation that covers the asserted dispute. Doubts should be resolved in favor of coverage.

This has come to be known as the "presumption of arbitrability." It deals, of course, with "substantive arbitrability," the question of whether the parties agreed to submit this dispute to arbitration. "Procedural arbitrability," the question of whether the parties have met the contractual conditions precedent to invoking arbitration, is decided by the arbitrator.[17] Since *Enterprise Wheel* dealt with the enforcement of arbitral awards, it will be dealt with in the section on that topic.

Resisting Arbitration

If you want to resist arbitration because you do not believe the matter is covered by the arbitration agreement, you have three choices. First, you can bring a section 301 action in federal district court, for a declaration that you are not required by your agreement to arbitrate the dispute.[18] The court will decide the issue and you will either proceed with the arbitration or have a definitive decision that you do not have to arbitrate the dispute. Second, you can refuse to respond to your opponent's demand for arbitration and force your opponent to bring a motion to compel in district court. On that motion you

---

17. *See, e.g.,* John Wiley & Sons, Inc. v. Livingston, 376 U.S. 543 (1964), *and* Operating Engineers Local 150 v. Flair Builders, Inc., 406 U.S. 487 (1972).

18. *See,* Black-Clawson Co. v. IAM Lodge 355, 313 F.2d 179 (2d Cir. 1962).

will have an opportunity to argue whether you agreed to arbitrate the dispute. This course of action has certain risks. In federal court you risk paying the other side's attorney fees and costs if the court decides your refusal to arbitrate was in bad faith.[19] In California, if the other side prevails in the action to compel arbitration, under Labor Code section 1128, you will be required to pay attorney fees, unless you raised "substantial and credible issues involving complex or significant questions of law or fact regarding whether or not the dispute is arbitrable under the agreement."[20]

Second, if you have already chosen an arbitrator—through naming him in the contract—you can advise the arbitrator that you do not believe the matter is arbitrable and, if a hearing is held, you can appear and put on the record that you do not submit the arbitrability issue to the arbitrator.[21] If the arbitrator issues an award, you may have to raise the arbitrability issue on a motion to vacate. If the award is against your opponent, of course, you have nothing further to do. But if the award is for your opponent, you must move to vacate the award.

---

19. International Longshoremen's & Warehousemen's Union, Local 6 v. Cutter Laboratories, 552 F. Supp. 979 (D.C. Cal. 1982).
20. The statute provides the same remedy to a prevailing party in an action to "compel compliance" with an arbitration award. The statute specifically exempts public employment from its coverage.
21. The safer route, of course, is to move for a declaratory judgment. If you do not, you may be foreclosed from any other course of action. As this book is being written, the authority for saying that you will have a later chance to raise arbitrability is Day Constr. Co. v. Carpenters Local 354, 722 F.2d 1471, 115 L.R.R.M. 2459 (9th Cir. 1984). In light of *AT&T Technologies, (see supra* note 11), that case may no longer be good law. Whether that means you will always be given an opportunity to have your arbitrability argument heard by the courts, or that you must raise your argument before the arbitration in order to have it heard by the courts, remains to be seen.

If the court vacates the award because there was no agreement to arbitrate that dispute, and, therefore the arbitrator had no jurisdiction, the arbitrator's remedy will be nullified. If you lose the vacatur motion, you will have a confirmed award against you, which your opponent can then have made a judgment of the court. This last is the most perilous method, since if you lose on your jurisdictional argument you will have foreclosed any opportunity to be heard on the merits. Moreover, given the reluctance of the courts to permit parties to an arbitration agreement to avoid their obligations, once an award has issued your chances of prevailing are quite slim.

Public Sector

Under the Uniform Arbitration Act, an arbitration can be compelled by a party to the arbitration agreement, or stayed by a party that has been threatened with arbitration but contends there is no agreement to arbitrate. In addition, any pending court action can be stayed by a party who has successfully compelled arbitration by showing there is an agreement to arbitrate the controversy.[22] If you are in a state that has adopted the Uniform Act, you can have the question of whether there is an agreement requiring arbitration of the dispute decided expeditiously. In other states, there can be complications.

The California statute, for example, contains no provision for staying an arbitration.[23] Thus, a party who believes that there is no agreement to arbitrate a dispute is left without a statutory method for rapidly resolving the question. Although

---

22. Unif. Arb. Act § 2. *See* Appendix 1.
23. Cal. Civ. Proc. Code § 1280 *et seq.* (West 1982). *See* Appendix 13.

the statute contains no explicit provision for ex parte proceedings, if the arbitration agreement of the parties is "self-executing," that is it incorporates rules of procedure, one party may go ahead with the arbitration unilaterally. If, for instance, the parties have incorporated the American Arbitration Association's Voluntary Labor Arbitration Rules, after giving proper notice, an arbitrator can hold an ex parte hearing.[24] Under the rules, or a state statute that expressly permits ex parte hearings, an arbitrator does not exceed his powers (which means that an award cannot be vacated on that ground) by holding an ex parte hearing and rendering an award.[25] The party that believes there is no agreement to arbitrate can, of course, move to vacate the award after it has been rendered, on the ground that the arbitrator was without jurisdiction. If, however, the arbitrator had jurisdiction to hear the matter, there would be no ground for vacating the ex parte award.

The New York statute has a unique provision for handling the question of substantive arbitrability. In addition to permitting an objecting party to move to stay an arbitration,[26] it allows the party initiating an arbitration to force an early determination of substantive arbitrability. Under section 7503(c) of the CPLR, a party demanding arbitration may serve a notice (in the same manner as a summons) on the other party, specifying certain information and stating that:

---

24. Rule 27, "Arbitration in the Absence of a Party" reads: Unless the law provides to the contrary, the arbitration may proceed in the absence of any party who, after due notice, fails to be present or fails to obtain an adjournment. An award shall not be made solely on the default of a party. The Arbitrator shall require the other party to submit such evidence as may be required for the making of an award. *See* Appendix 3.

25. Northern Cal. Dist. Hod Carriers v. P A Pipeline, 103 Cal. App. 3d 163, 162 Cal. Rptr. 851 (1980). The court applied federal law.

26. N.Y. CIV. PRAC. L. & R. 7503(b) (McKinney 1980). *See* Appendix 12.

unless the party served applies to stay the arbitration within twenty days after such service he shall thereafter be precluded from objecting that a valid agreement was not made or has not been complied with and from asserting in court the bar of a limitation of time.[27]

This unique provision has been stringently enforced by the courts. It will not, of course, be enforced against a party who is a stranger to any agreement with the moving party.[28] If you are served with what is called a 7503(c) notice, you must respond within twenty days, or lose any right to contest arbitrability.

The major advantage of the New York procedure is that it avoids the uncertainty associated with not knowing whether the other party intends to raise a question of arbitrability. It is particularly important in the New York scheme, since the statute itself gives an arbitrator the power to conduct an ex parte hearing.[29] Thus, it avoids the possibility of a party going through an arbitration only to learn later, on a vacatur motion, that his opponent contends the matter is not arbitrable.

State statutes that follow the Uniform Act, including the New York statute, all contain provisions permitting the court to name an arbitrator, or arbitrators.[30] This can be done if the parties cannot agree upon an arbitrator, or if the method of selection agreed to by the parties fails. In those cases where the parties have incorporated AAA's Voluntary Labor Arbitration

---

27. N.Y. CIV. PRAC. L. & R. 7503(c) (McKinney 1980). *See* Appendix 12.
28. *See,* Glasser v. Price, 35 A.D.2d 98, 313 N.Y.S.2d 1 (1970).
29. The Uniform Act also gives the arbitrator power to conduct a hearing in the absence of a party. UNIF. ARB. ACT § 5(a). *See* Appendix 1. The California statute gives the arbitrator power to hold an *ex parte* hearing only after a court has compelled arbitration. CAL. CIV. PROC. CODE § 1282.2(e) (West 1982). *See* Appendix 13.
30. UNIF. ARB. ACT § 3. *See* Appendix 1. N.Y. CIV. PRAC. L. & R. 7504 (McKinney 1980). *See* Appendix 12.

Rules, no court action is necessary, since the Association is given the power to appoint an arbitrator when the parties fail to do so.[31]

Enforcing the Due Process Hearing

Private Sector

As I noted earlier, there is a body of federal substantive law under section 301. Although federal and state courts have concurrent jurisdiction over section 301 actions, both apply the same substantive law. To enforce the due process hearing there must be a mechanism for appointing an arbitrator, compelling the attendance of witnesses, requiring the production of documents, and providing sworn testimony. If the section 301 action is brought in a state court, it may apply its own procedural law to matters involved in enforcing the due process hearing, so long as that does not frustrate the substantive federal law. Federal courts have available the procedural mechanisms contained in the United States Arbitration Act for enforcing the due process hearing, but they may not be applied to section 301 actions by all federal courts.[32] Thus, while I will note the mechanisms, a fuller discussion will be reserved for state procedural mechanisms.

The United States Arbitration Act provides for appointing an arbitrator where the methods chosen by the parties have

---

31. AAA Voluntary Labor Arbitration Rule 12. *See* Appendix 3.
32. There is a split in authority as to whether the United States Arbitration Act applies in section 301 actions, because of the exclusion in 9 U.S.C. section 1 of "contracts of employment of seamen, railroad employees, or any other class of workers engaged in foreign or interstate commerce." *See* Appendix 2 (United States Arbitration Act).

failed, or in the absence of any method.[33] While the Act does not specifically grant the arbitrator power to administer oaths, it does give him subpoena powers.[34] Arbitrators may require the attendance of witnesses or compel the production of documents through "summonses," which are issued "in the same manner as subpoenas to appear and testify before the court." Subpoenas are enforced by a petition to the district court of the district in which the arbitrators are sitting. The court "may" compel attendance or punish contempt in the same manner as it would in a court action.

There is an important tactical decision you must make if your opponent has refused to obey a subpoena issued by the arbitrator.[35] In order to obtain court enforcement of a subpoena, you need to have the arbitrator determine whether the person or document you have subpoenaed is relevant and material to the case. The burden is on the party not obeying the subpoena—both before the arbitrator and the court—to explain why it failed to produce people or documents in its control.[36] If your opponent has failed to produce, and the arbitrator has ruled the witness or material subpoenaed is relevant evidence, you need not proceed by court enforcement of the subpoena. Instead, you can ask the arbitrator to draw an adverse inference from your opponent's failure to produce.

---

33. 9 U.S.C. § 5. *See* Appendix 2.

34. 9 U.S.C. § 7. *See* Appendix 2.

35. Arbitrators or AAA may issue signed subpoenas in blank, to be filled out by the person requesting them. Some arbitrators will ask you to provide an affidavit in support of your request for subpoenas, to avoid being used in a tactical effort to harass one party.

36. Where the subpoena is to be a third party, of course, there may be no one at the hearing to explain why a person has not appeared or a document was not produced. If a third party is involved, you will be obliged to use court enforcement mechanisms to produce the person or document.

That is, you ask the arbitrator to infer that the witness would have testified favorably to your side, or that the document would have supported your case. Many arbitrators will draw such an inference, rather than require the party on whose behalf the subpoena was issued to go to court. This is particularly so where the burden on the party refusing to respond to the subpoena is relatively light, and the requested documents or witness are material but not crucial. Or, when the inference to be drawn is "bad faith." It is not often appropriate for an arbitrator to decide the crucial issues in a case based upon an adverse inference. But it is certainly possible.

If you ask the arbitrator to draw an adverse inference, there may be further problems. For instance, if the arbitrator gives the party against whom the inference is drawn an opportunity to overcome that inference during the hearing, through secondary materials, you may be worse off than if you had pursued enforcement of the subpoena. Your opponent may get to use secondary evidence to overcome the inference while you have been denied the primary evidence necessary for your case. Thus, before being satisfied with having the arbitrator draw an adverse inference you must ascertain whether your opponent will be allowed to overcome the inference with secondary material. If so, you may want to pursue enforcement of the subpoena.

Public Sector

State arbitration statutes generally give the arbitrator the right to administer oaths and issue subpoenas to compel attendance of witnesses and production of documents.[37] If your case is not administered by AAA, you should request subpoenas

---

37. *See, e.g.,* UNIF. ARB. ACT § 7. *See* Appendix 1. N.Y. CIV. PRAC. LAW § 7505 (McKinney 1980). *See* Appendix 12. CAL. CIV. PROC. CODE §§ 1282.6 (West Supp. 1987), 1282.8 (West 1982). *See* Appendix 13.

directly from the arbitrator, well in advance of the hearing. Arbitral subpoenas are generally served in the same manner as subpoenas in civil actions under the state's civil procedure law. The party subpoenaing a witness must pay the normal witness and mileage fees. Enforcement of arbitral subpoenas varies according to the civil procedure law of the state involved. Two examples may be instructive.

California's arbitration statute specifically provides for serving and enforcing arbitral subpoenas in accordance with specified sections of its civil procedure law.[38] Three types of enforcement are provided. First, the arbitrator can report disobedience of a subpoena to the superior court of the county in which attendance was required. The court has the power to order the person to perform the omitted act. Any refusal to comply is punishable as contempt of court.[39] Second, a witness disobeying a subpoena forfeits $500 to the aggrieved party *and,* through a civil action, may be required to pay the damages sustained by the witness's failure to attend.[40] Third, the arbitrator may, upon proof of service and failure of the witness to attend, issue a warrant to the sheriff of the county to arrest the witness and bring him before the arbitrator.[41] There are no reported cases in which the arbitrator had a witness arrested. Nor does it seem likely an arbitrator would issue a warrant. It is, however, an amusing prospect to liven up an otherwise dull discourse on enforcement.

The New York statute permits either the arbitrator, or any attorney of record in the arbitration proceeding, to issue a subpoena.[42] The CPLR provides that either the issuer of the

---

38. CAL. CIV. PROC. CODE § 1282.6 (West Supp. 1987). *See* Appendix 13.
39. CAL. CIV. PROC. CODE § 1991 (West 1983).
40. CAL. CIV. PROC. CODE § 1992 (West 1983).
41. CAL. CIV. PROC. CODE § 1993 (West 1983).
42. N.Y. CIV. PRAC. L. & R. 7505 (McKinney 1980). *See* Appendix 12.

subpoena, or the person on whose behalf it was issued, may move in Supreme Court (the trial level court) to compel compliance. You should not expect the arbitrator to take on the adversarial role of forcing compliance with a subpoena; you will have to do it yourself. If the court determines the subpoena was authorized, it orders compliance and can impose costs of up to $50, a penalty of $50, and the damages sustained by the failure to comply with the original subpoena. The court can also issue a warrant for the sheriff to arrest the person and bring him before the arbitrator. Finally, the court can order a witness who still refuses to answer proper questions, or produce required documents, committed to jail until he does the required act.[43] The sanctions are rigorous, but they are imposed by a court that passes upon the propriety of the subpoena before taking further action.

Enforcing or Vacating the Arbitration Award

Private Sector

Arbitration awards are, almost without exception, final and binding. There are, however, three narrow grounds upon which, under federal law, the award may be vacated. First, there may be vacatur grounds under substantive federal law. Second, there may be a contention that the arbitration process was ineffective because the union failed in its "duty of fair representation." Third, there are nonwaivable federal statutory rights that benefit individuals, and an arbitration award deciding these rights may not preclude subsequent litigation.

---

43. N.Y. Civ. Prac. L. & R. 2308(b) (McKinney Supp. 1987).

First, when I discussed the "trilogy" in an earlier section I omitted a discussion of *Enterprise Wheel*.[44] It was there that the Supreme Court examined the standard by which federal courts would determine whether to vacate an award. The Court announced a strong federal policy of limiting judicial inquiry into the "merits" of the award, so long as the award "draw[s] its essence from the collective bargaining agreement." It noted that there is an "industrial common law," which is not contained in the agreement, but is background to it. Furthermore, the Court made it clear that an ambiguity in the award that permitted an inference that the arbitrator might have exceeded his authority would not be sufficient grounds to vacate an award. Finally, as a limitation on the authority of the arbitrator to go beyond the collective bargaining agreement, the Court noted that the arbitrator "does not sit to dispense his own brand of industrial justice."

In general, the federal courts have followed the spirit of the Court's pronouncement in *Enterprise Wheel*. In a later decision the Ninth Circuit noted that "[i]f, on its face, the award represents a plausible interpretation of the contract in the context of the parties' conduct, judicial inquiry ceases and the award must be affirmed."[45] This means that there is little chance of having an award vacated because you think its reasoning faulty, its application of the law erroneous, or its interpretation of the contract idiosyncratic. The "substantive" federal ground for vacating an award is that it fails to draw its essence from the collective bargaining agreement.[46] There are,

---

44. United Steelworkers v. Enterprise Wheel & Car Corp., 363 U.S. 593 (1960).

45. Holly Sugar Corp. v. Distillery Workers, 412 F.2d 899, 902-03 (9th Cir. 1969).

46. It is not always clear why a particular award does or does not "draw its essence" from the collective bargaining agreement. In general, the federal courts are reluctant to substitute their judgment for that of an

however, other grounds for vacating an award that have become part of federal law. They are, essentially, the grounds contained in the United States Arbitration Act and state statutes.[47] They will be discussed below.

Second, an award may be vacated because the union failed in its "duty of fair representation." The essence of this duty is that a union must serve the interests of all its members without hostility or discrimination; it must act in complete good faith and honesty, avoiding arbitrary conduct.[48] When the union breaches this duty in its representation of an employee in the grievance procedure, the arbitration award can be vacated in a section 301 action, despite the contractual commitment of the parties that the award will be final and binding.[49] The employee who alleges the union's breach of the duty of fair representation, in a "hybrid" section 301 action against both the union and the employer (for violation of the collective bargaining agreement), must bring the action within six months of the award.[50] In those instances in which the employee sucessfully

---

arbitrator appointed by the parties. There are times, however, when a court will vacate an award, saying that the arbitrator "does not sit to dispense his own brand of industrial justice." Students of contract law will recognize that the distinction between an award "drawing its essence" from the contract, or an arbitrator dispensing "his own brand of industrial justice," is similar to the difference between "liquidated damages" and "penalty clause." In each instance, the use of a phrase is outcome determinative.

47. *See* Appendixes 2, 12, 13.
48. Vaca v. Sipes, 386 U.S. 171 (1967).
49. Hines v. Anchor Motor Freight, 424 U.S. 554 (1976).
50. Del Costello v. International Bhd. of Teamsters, 462 U.S. 151 (1983). If the employee's claim is solely against the employer, the applicable limitation period is found in the state arbitration statute's time limit for vacatur of arbitration awards. United Parcel Serv. v. Mitchell, 451 U.S.

argues that the union breached its duty of fair representation, the arbitration award will not be final and binding on the parties.

Third, if an overriding federal statutory right that is deemed nonwaivable is involved, an arbitration award will not prevent litigation of the same matter. Two areas have clearly been identified. Where there is a claim of racial discrimination, even though the collective bargaining agreement has an anti-discrimination clause, an arbitration on the merits of the claim will not preclude a title VII action.[51] Where the collective bargaining agreement permits a violation of the Fair Labor Standards Act (FLSA), an arbitration award finding the violation is permitted by the negotiated agreement will not prevent an action under the FLSA.[52] Where a "whistleblower" provision in a federal statute is invoked, it appears that an arbitration award on the same issue may not preclude review by the appropriate federal official.[53] While only these areas have been litigated to the Supreme Court, the principle involved is an important one. There are nonwaivable rights, which a union has no authority to bargain away. To the extent the union negotiates an agreement that either includes those rights or replaces them with greater rights, a contract arbitration award does not prevent a disgruntled employee from pursuing statutory rights.[54] This is the private sector corollary of the public sector's "public policy" vacatur.

---

56 (1981). If the employee wants to recover that portion of the damages attributable to the union, he would have to sue both. Bowen v. United States Postal Serv., 459 U.S. 212 (1983).

51. Alexander v. Gardner-Denver Co., 415 U.S. 36 (1974).

52. Barrentine v. Arkansas-Best Freight Sys., Inc., 450 U.S. 728 (1981).

53. Brock v. Roadway Express, Inc., No. 85-1530 (April 22, 1987).

54. There are, for instance, rights granted by the National Labor Relations Act, which can not be finally decided in an arbitral forum.

While the award may not have a preclusive effect, it still may have some effect on the later litigation. A court may give great weight to the arbitrator's initial finding of facts. Or, it may permit one side to use the award as a means of shifting the burden of going forward back to the other side.[55] For instance, in a case of alleged racial discrimination the employee-plaintiff may make out a prima facie case by statistical means. The employer-defendant may then use the arbitration award to show a bona fide business justification for its actions (e.g., an arbitration award showing the employee was fired for sleeping on the job.) Thus, even in a situation where the award does not have a preclusive effect on litigation, it may still be extremely influential.

Outside of matters covered by federal law, there may be additional vacatur grounds under state law. For instance, "unconscionability" is a vacatur ground under California law.[56] A court may find that the contract containing the arbitration agreement is a contract of adhesion, which is also unconscionable. Recent cases have demonstrated that unconscionability may be a matter of the tribunal, not the process. That is, it is not arbitration itself that is unconscionable, but having the arbitration heard by an arbitrator or panel that is likely to be

---

55. *See, e.g.,* Becton v. Detroit Terminal of Consol. Freightways, 687 F.2d 140 (6th Cir. 1982).

56. In saying that it is a vacatur ground, I am really using a shorthand description of longer reasoning. Under California's arbitration statute, there is no motion to stay arbitration. *See* Appendix 13. It is possible, of course, to seek declaratory relief in a contract action asserting that there is no agreement to arbitrate. That is, ordinarily, the posture in which "unconscionability" should come up. If, however, there is a self-executing arbitration clause, it is more likely that the question will come up on a vacatur motion. I have followed that possibility in the rest of this section.

biased.[57] Even if a term of the arbitration agreement is unconscionable, the agreement itself may be enforced while removing the unconscionable term.

Public Sector

Your purpose in confirming an award is to gain the postjudgment remedies ordinarily available in civil actions. Statutes generally provide that once the award is confirmed it has the same dignity as a judgment in a civil action.[58] The procedures for confirmation and vacatur focus on the due process aspects of the hearing and the jurisdiction of the arbitrator, rather than the content of the award. The function of the court is not to review the award to make sure it is correct, but to scrutinize the process to be sure it was what the parties bargained for.

The statutes are generally written so as to require confirmation of an award unless it is corrected or vacated within the applicable time limits.[59] The New York statute is representative

---

57. *See* Graham v. Scissor-Tail, 28 Cal. 3d 807, 623 P.2d 165, 171 Cal. Rptr. 6 (1981).

58. *See, e.g.,* UNIF. ARB. ACT § 14. *See* Appendix 1. N.Y. CIV. PRAC. L. & R. 7514 (McKinney 1980). *See* Appendix 12. The California statute is typical. It provides:

> If an award is confirmed, judgment shall be entered in conformity therewith. The judgment so entered has the same force and effect as, and is subject to all the provisions of law relating to, a judgment in a civil action; and it may be enforced like any other judgment of the court in which it is entered. CAL. CIV. PROC. CODE § 1287.4 (West 1982). *See* Appendix 13.

59. The statutes generally provide for correction or modification of an award by the arbitrator or the court. The grounds for modification generally include matters that are ministerial. Asking an arbitrator or court to modify an award is not an opportunity to re-argue your case. Typical grounds for court modification are:

in its catalogue of the grounds upon which a party who has participated in the arbitration can seek vacatur. It permits vacatur where the rights of that party were prejudiced by:

1. corruption, fraud, or misconduct in procuring the award; or
2. partiality of an arbitrator appointed as a neutral, except where the award was by confession; or
3. an arbitrator, or agency or person making the award exceeded his power or so imperfectly executed it that a final and definite award upon the subject matter submitted was not made; or
4. failure to follow the procedure of this article, unless the party applying to vacate the award continued with the arbitration with notice of the defect and without objection.[60]

There is, of course, an enormous body of law on each of these typical points in state statutes. While it would be futile to attempt to cover all of the law, you can get some flavor, from decided cases in different jurisdictions, of what facts permit vacatur under the various sections.

Procuring an award through corruption, fraud, or other misconduct can involve an undisclosed business relationship between the neutral arbitrator and one of the parties, ex parte communications between the arbitrator and one of the parties

---

1. There was an evident miscalculation of figures or an evident mistake in the description of any person, thing, or property referred to in the award;
2. The arbitrators have awarded upon a matter not submitted to them and the award may be corrected without affecting the merits of the decision upon the issues submitted; or
3. The award is imperfect in a matter of form, not affecting the merits of the controversy. UNIF. ARB. ACT § 13(a). *See* Appendix 1.

60. N.Y. CIV. PRAC. L. & R. 7511(b) (McKinney 1980). *See* Appendix 12.

(on matters material to the case), deciding the case on the basis of material not presented at the hearing, failing to permit an adjournment on good cause shown,[61] or giving a default award where one party fails to appear at the hearing. The partiality of an arbitrator can be shown by a failure to disclose a substantial business relationship with one of the parties, failure to reveal that he has any ownership or similar interest in the matter he is deciding, or a failure to disclose facts that may reasonably support an inference of bias. You should note that when you proceed with the arbitration after full disclosure by the arbitrator of relationships or facts from which bias might be inferred, you are later estopped from raising those facts as grounds for vacatur.

An arbitrator can be found to have exceeded his powers or imperfectly executed them when he awards upon a matter not submitted to him, renders an award that does not state any sum for the remedy or formula from which it can be ascertained, or fails to answer the questions posed by the parties in their submission. In dealing with failures to follow the statutory arbitration procedures the courts indulge every intendment in favor of supporting the award.

It may be somewhat misleading to focus on the reasons that awards have been vacated. The vast majority of cases in which one party sought to vacate the award resulted in the award being confirmed. Of the cases in which an award was vacated, many were reinstated on appeal. The lesson is clear, your best opportunity to argue the case is before the arbitrator, not in a vacatur motion to a court.

---

61. Under some statutes, the failure of an arbitrator to grant a postponement for good cause shown is a separately stated ground for vacatur.

Suing the Arbitrator

In most arbitrations there is a winner and a loser. The loser is usually unhappy with the way the arbitration turned out. Sometimes the loser is sufficiently unhappy with the arbitrator to attempt a civil suit. As a matter of public policy, courts have found that to exercise their quasi-judicial function arbitrators must be free from any fear of reprisals by litigants. In *Babylon Milk & Cream Co. v. Horvitz,*[62] the New York Supreme Court found that "the same rule of immunity should apply to arbitrators as applies to the judiciary, inasmuch as the same reasons of public policy are applicable." This decision was later affirmed by the Appellate Division, and subsequently followed by other courts. There matters stood, with most commentators believing that arbitrators had quasi-judicial immunity for their acts as arbitrators, until *Baar v. Tigerman.*[63]

In *Baar*, the court fashioned an exception to the general rule of arbitrator immunity. The arbitrator had failed to render a timely award and before an award was made one of the parties to the arbitration sued on a breach of contract theory for "nonfeasance." The court found that the complaint stated a cause of action, and that the arbitrator's failure to act was not shielded by arbitral immunity. As a result of the case, California added a new section to its Code of Civil Procedure. It reads:

> An arbitrator has the immunity of a judicial officer from civil liability when acting in the capacity of arbitrator under any statute or contract.[64]

As a consequence of this section, and the common law immunity enjoyed by arbitrators in other jurisdictions, there does not

---

62. 151 N.Y.S.2d 221, 224 (1956).
63. 140 Cal. App. 3d 979, 211 Cal. Rptr. 426 (1983).
64. CAL. CIV. PROC. CODE § 1280.1 (West Supp. 1987). *See* Appendix 13.

seem much point in attempting to hold an arbitrator civilly liable for perceived defects in the proceeding, either in California or elsewhere.

Closely related to questions of arbitrator immunity is the problem of the delayed award. There have been cases where parties have waited as long as two years for an award. Fortunately, that is aberrational, rather than common. There are several types of sanction that may be imposed upon an arbitrator who is late with awards. The first is the most effective. Do not continue to use that arbitrator and tell the arbitrator why you are unhappy. Second, if the arbitrator was selected from a Federal Mediation and Conciliation Service (FMCS) panel and the award is issued more than sixty days after the close of the hearing, inform FMCS. Repeated failures to issue timely awards will result in the arbitrator's name being temporarily removed from the panel. Third, you can adopt specific, reasonable time limits for awards in your arbitration agreement. The time limits can be jurisdictional, with the arbitrator losing authority to decide the case after a specific length of time. If you adopt that type of guideline, and if an arbitrator is late, you must inform the arbitrator of your position that jurisdiction has been lost, *before* the award is issued. If you wait to see if you won, a reviewing court would probably find that you waived your right to object. If you do stand on your rights to have a timely award, you will still be obliged to go through the time and expense of having the case heard by another arbitrator. Thus, it may be something of a Pyrrhic victory.

Federal Sector

An increasing number of arbitrations are being done in the federal sector. While most are done by specialists (both on the government and union side), there may be times when a non-specialist is called upon to handle an arbitration in a federal sector case. The purpose of this section is simply to alert advocates to the unique system of federal sector arbitration, without attempting to make them instant experts.

The Federal Service Labor-Management Relations Statute (FSLMRS), a portion of the Civil Service Reform Act of 1978, provides the statutory basis for bargaining and dispute resolution in the federal sector.[65] What distinguishes ancillary litigation in the federal sector is the relative lack of finality in arbitral awards. The system has an extremely broad definition of grievances, a unique choice of forum provision, no provision for the arbitrator to enforce the due process hearing, and an appellate procedure that enables the parties to have a court, or the Federal Labor Relations Authority (FLRA), review the substantive basis of an arbitrator's award. A brief exploration of these provisions will highlight the differences between the federal sector and the rest of the public sector.

Definition of Grievance

The FSLMRS defines a "grievance" as "any complaint":

(A) by any employee concerning any matter relating to the employment of the employee;

(B) by any labor organization concerning any matter relating to the employment of any employee; or

(C) by any employee, labor organization, or agency concerning—

(i) the effect or interpretation, or a claim of breach, of a collective bargaining agreement; or

---

65. 5 U.S.C. § 7101 *et seq. See* Appendix 10.

(ii) any claimed violation, misinterpretation, or misapplication of any law, rule, or regulation affecting conditions of employment.[66]

This definition commits to the grievance procedure both employment related complaints and the interpretation of the myriad laws, rules, and regulations that affect governmental employment. It would be difficult to conceive of a broader definition of a grievance.

The FSLMRS also requires that these broadly defined grievances shall be settled by an exclusive procedure contained in the collective bargaining agreement.[67] Among other characteristics, this exclusive procedure must:

provide that any grievance not satisfactorily settled under the negotiated grievance procedure shall be subject to binding arbitration which may be invoked by either the exclusive representative or the agency.[68]

Thus, the FSLMRS defines grievances quite broadly and commits them to a procedure that is capped by "binding arbitration."[69]

---

66. 5 U.S.C. § 7103(a)(9). This definition of a grievance applies only to bargaining unit employees (those recognized as such by the FLRA, after an election of an exclusive representative) who are covered by a collective bargaining agreement. *See* Appendix 10.

67. 5 U.S.C. § 7121(a). There are certain exclusions from this grievance procedure either through negotiations (5 U.S.C. § 7121(a)(2)), or operation of the statute (5 U.S.C. § 7121(c), (d), (e)). *See* Appendix 10.

68. 5 U.S.C. § 7121(b)(3)(C). *See* Appendix 10.

69. As in other sectors, ordinarily the collective bargaining agreement provides that only the union can appeal a grievance to arbitration. An agency can also file a grievance and bring a case to arbitration. It is possible, although not clearly decided, that a grievant can appeal an adverse arbitration award.

Choice of Forum

The FSLMRS also provides both employees and exclusive representatives with a series of forum choices, depending upon the nature of the complaint.[70] Discrimination complaints[71] can be raised either under the available statutory procedures or negotiated procedures. An employee can only choose one route, and this is determined by where he or she first files a timely action.[72] So, too, with certain "personnel actions" that an employee is unhappy with.[73] These can be appealed through the negotiated procedure, or directly to the Merit Systems Protection Board (MSPB)[74], and the employee makes the choice by filing a timely appeal or grievance.[75] These forum choices do not affect the standards of decision, but they do affect the forum for appeal.

Power to Enforce Due Process Hearing

The FSLMRS is silent about the powers of an arbitrator to enforce a due process hearing. It does not specifically provide the arbitrator with power to administer an oath, compel the

70. The astute reader will note a shift from "grievance" to "complaint" in certain sentences. This is upon the advice of counsel. In the federal sector the term "grievance" is ordinarily restricted to complaints brought by bargaining unit employees under the negotiated agreement.
71. I use the term broadly to cover prohibited personnel practices under 5 U.S.C. section 2302(b)(1).
72. 5 U.S.C. § 7121(d). *See* Appendix 10.
73. I use the term broadly, to include matters covered by 5 U.S.C. section 4303 ("chapter 43 actions," or "performance actions") and 5 U.S.C. section 7512 ("chapter 75 actions," or "adverse actions"), as well as other matters.
74. Having just used the term broadly, I must narrow it to say that complaints which include discrimination issues may be appealed to MSPB, although chapters 43 and 75 actions can not.
75. 5 U.S.C. § 7121(e)(1). *See* Appendix 10.

attendance of witnesses, or require the production of documents. Whether there is some inherent arbitral power to conduct a due process hearing has not been decided by the courts. Nor does the FSLMRS provide a mechanism for the union to compel the agency to participate in the arbitration. If the agency chooses not to participate, however, it will not prevent an arbitration, since the aribitrator may hold an ex parte hearing.[76] If an agency failed to produce witnesses or relevant documents, there would appear to be two choices. First, the exclusive representative could ask the arbitrator to draw an adverse inference from the agency's failure to provide the witness or documents. (Obviously, it could do this in an ex parte hearing, as well as one at which the employer appeared.) Second, the exclusive representative could file an unfair labor practice with the Federal Labor Relations Authority (FLRA), alleging a failure to provide documents as required by 5 U.S.C. section 7114(b)(4). Neither method is entirely satisfactory, but the FSLMRS fails to give the arbitrator compulsive power.[77]

Review of Awards

The employee choice of forum does not affect the standards under which a grievance will be heard or an award reviewed. Discrimination claims that are handled through the negotiated procedure leave the parties with an award of an arbitrator that can be reviewed by the MSPB (if they involve an appealable personnel action), the FLRA (except for chapter 43/75 actions), the Equal Employment Opportunity Commission,

---

76. *FAA Alaskan Regional Office and Professional Air Traffic Controllers Organization, MEBA, AFL-CIO, Pacific Region* 7 FLRA No. 23.

77. The U.S. Arbitration Act excludes federal agencies from its coverage. 9 U.S.C. § 7. *See* Appendix 2.

and ultimately the courts.[78] The appellate procedure is so extensive that those outside the federal sector may have difficulty understanding why an employee would go through the negotiated grievance procedure. There are three reasons.

First, the employee gets more than one "bite at the apple" since de novo reviews are involved. Second, the processing time is much faster, since it may take two years or more before an agency decision is rendered in a statutory EEO process. Third, there may be contractual issues involved that an arbitrator can decide on the merits, while the statutory EEO procedure will settle questions of intent. EEO cases are usually not taken through arbitration, and the confusing, cross-agency system is rarely used. Rather, the parties prefer the straightforward arbitral aspects of the system because they have an interest in an expeditious process.

Complaints about certain personnel actions (chiefly "adverse actions," which are normally disciplines for improper behavior, and "performance actions," which are disciplines for poor performance) may be appealed to arbitration or the MSPB. If they are appealed to arbitration, the arbitrator must apply the same evidentiary standards as the MSPB in determining whether to sustain the agency's action.[79] The action must be sustained if it:

> (A) in the case of an action based on unacceptable performance described in section 4303 of this title, is supported by substantial evidence, or

---

78. 5 U.S.C. §§ 7702, 7121(d). *See* Appendix 10. Charts of appellate routes are included in Appendixes 8 and 9. They will be best understood by those who practice in the federal sector and most appreciated by chess afficionados. The number of known appellate routes is staggering. And it is not clear that all have been discovered.

79. 5 U.S.C. § 7121(e)(2). *See* Appendix 10.

(B) in any other case, is supported by a preponderance of the evidence.[80]

The arbitrator's award, in turn, may be reviewed by the United States Court of Appeals for the Federal Circuit "in the same manner and under the same conditions as if the matter had been decided by the Board."[81] This review mechanism imports into the arbitration procedure the same "substantive statutory standards" as would be applied if the case had gone through MSPB.[82] Thus, the arbitrator cannot sustain the agency decision if the employee:

---

80. 5 U.S.C. § 7701(c)(1). *See* Appendix 10.
81. 5 U.S.C. § 7121(f). *See* Appendix 10. Chapter 43 and 75 actions go to the Federal Circuit *unless* they involve allegations of discrimination, in which case they go to federal district court. 5 U.S.C. § 7702. Arbitration awards that do not involve chapters 43, 75, or title VII are appealable only to the FLRA. 5 U.S.C. §§ 7122, 7123(a). *See* Appendix 10.

It should be noted that only the employee, not the Agency, has the right to appeal. If the Office of Personnel Management determines that an arbitrator erred as a matter of law "in interpreting the civil service law, rule, or regulation affecting personnel management" *and* that the erroneous "decision will have a substantial impact on a civil service law, rule, regulation, or policy directive," it may seek judicial review. The courts, however, must make an independent evaluation of the impact of the error on civil service law. Devine v. White, 697 F.2d 421 (D.C. Cir. 1983).

82. Devine v. White, 697 F.2d 421 (D.C. Cir. 1983). Cornelius v. Nutt, 105 S. Ct. 2882 (1985). Before *Cornelius*, the Federal Circuit held that the traditional deference to arbitration awards required that it give more careful scrutiny to an OPM appeal of an arbitration award, as opposed to an MSPB decision. Devine V. Sutermeister, 724 F.2d 1558 (Fed. Cir. 1983). I am told that the Federal Circuit continues to require a showing that the arbitration award is exceptional in both the error in civil service law it embodies, and the substantial impact it has on government-wide labor relations. Moreover, the Federal Circuit continues to reject mere factual disputes and cases involving only mitigation.

(A) shows harmful error in the application of the agency's procedures in arriving at such decision;
(B) shows that the decision was based on any prohibited personnel practice described in section 2302 (b) of this title; or

(C) shows that the decision was not in accordance with law.[83]

What is more significant, however, is the expanded standard of review this section provides for arbitral awards.
The court reviews the record and sets aside any:

findings or conlcusions found to be —
(1) arbitrary, capricious, an abuse of discretion, or otherwise not in accordance with law;
(2) obtained without procedures required by law, rule, or regulation having been followed; or
(3) unsupported by substantial evidence;[84]

This standard is far different from the normal standard of federal court review of private sector cases, and far more expansive than the rest of the public sector. It permits the court to determine whether there was substantial evidence for an arbitrator's decision, which invites a review on the merits. Moreover, since failure to be "in accordance with the law" is a criterion, legal principles that may never have been raised before the arbitrator may become grounds for refusing to confirm the award on appeal.[85]

There is a second appellate route for reviewing arbitration awards. If the award does not involve chapter 43/75 personnel actions, either party can file an exception to the award with the FLRA. There are two bases for overturning an arbitration award:

---

83. 5 U.S.C. § 7701(c)(2). *See* Appendix 10.
84. 5 U.S.C. § 7703(c). *See* Appendix 10.
85. In Devine v. White, 697 F.2d 421 n.68 (D.C. Cir. 1983), Judge Edwards indicated that the appropriate role of the courts is to be reluctant to delve deeply into arbitration awards.

(1) because it is contrary to any law, rule, or regulation; or

(2) on other grounds similar to those applied by Federal courts in private sector labor-management relations;[86]

Any exceptions must be filed within thirty days after the award is served on the party.[87] From January 1979 through May 1985, there were approximately 4,800 federal sector arbitrations, involving both personnel actions and other matters. Of that number, 987 were appealed to the FLRA, 60 percent by the unions and 40 percent by the agencies.[88] Since the gross number of arbitrations includes those personnel actions that are appealable to the federal courts, it appears that in excess of 20 percent of the arbitration awards are appealed to the FLRA. Of the 857 cases closed by the FLRA from January 1979 through June 1985, the arbitration award was modified or set aside in 115 cases. In 96 percent of the instances it was because the award "was found to be deficient as contrary to law, rule, or regulations."[89]

To advocates outside the federal sector, these numbers will seem extremely high. Whether they reflect the relative novelty of arbitration in the federal sector, or a different approach to the finality of arbitration awards remains to be seen. What is important for the advocate to realize is that litigation is hardly "ancillary" in the federal sector. Rather, it is almost to be expected. Given the overwhelming percentage of cases found deficient because they were contrary to laws, rules, or regulations, and since they can be argued on appeal regardless of

---

86. 5 U.S.C. § 7122(a). *See* Appendix 10.

87. 5 U.S.C. § 7122(b). *See* Appendix 10.

88. Frazier, *Arbitration in the Federal Sector,* 41 ARB. J. 70, 71 (Mar. 1986).

89. *Id.* at 71.

whether they were argued before the arbitrator, it is in the parties' interest to raise laws, rules, and regulations before the arbitrator.

Conclusion

In the vast majority of arbitrations, there is no need for ancillary litigation. Where it is needed, however, the courts have shown a bias towards enforcing arbitration agreements and upholding arbitration awards.

Index

A

A fortiori argument used in arbitration briefs...205-06

Absenteeism and tardiness, employer's just cause obligation and...65-66

Active voice used in arbitration briefs...214-15

Actual evidence of intent...60-61

Adjudication, single arbitration model and...238

Admissions of fact...3

"Adverse actions"
appealable to Merit Systems Protection Board (MSPB)...301-03
generally...301

Adverse inference drawn from failure to comply with subpoena...284-85

After the hearing...185-233

Agreed outcomes...180-82

Alcohol use...65

Ambiguous contract language, *see* Contractual ambiguity

Amblyopia, witness demeanor and...92

American Arbitration Association (AAA)
as neutral agency for designating arbitrators, how arbitrators are designated...113
generally...129, 130
Voluntary Labor Arbitration Rules...115, 144

Analogies used in arbitration briefs...202-03

Analyzing claims, *see* Claims, analyzing

Analyzing contract language...33-71

Analyzing facts...16-17

Analyzing your case...1-31

Ancillary litigation...271-305

Annual review of arbitrators...106

Antagonistic witnesses...94

Apologies from witnesses...90

Appeal mechanism for withdrawal liability cases...269-70

Appeal to arbitration, as a pleading...150

Appeals from arbitration in the federal sector...301-05

Appeals to Merit Systems Protection Board (MSPB)
evidentiary standards applied to...301-02
generally...301

Appeals to the U.S. Court of Appeals for the Federal Circuit, standards for...302-03

Appearance of impropriety shown by arbitrator's disclosure...137

Appearance of neutrality, setting location of hearing and...141

Appointing an arbitrator...109-10

Appointment of arbitrator where parties fail to do so...275

Arbitrability, *see also* Resisting arbitration; Compelling arbitration
7503(c) notice...281-82

Arbitrability of claims, determining...3

Arbitration
compelling, *see* Compelling arbitration
date of, parties unable to agree...114-15
demand for...4

307

specializing in withdrawal liability
cases...269
suing, *see* Suing the arbitrator
treated as fiduciaries in trustee deadlock...256-57, 258
Arbitrator's behavior at hearings used
as guide to selecting an
arbitrator...123-24
Arbitrator's bill
as consideration in selecting
arbitrator...125-26
charges for study and preparation of
award and opinion...228-29
Code of Professional Responsibility
obligations...226-27
evaluating...226-33
examining...227
fees and expenses and...227, 231
hourly billing...232, 233
late postponement and cancellation
fees...227-28
questioning...232
Arbitrators' immunity...258-59,
295-96
Arbitrators' Qualification Reports
Service...130-31
Arguing an interest arbitration, *see*
Interest arbitration, arguing
Argument
based on troublesome consequences
used in arbitration briefs...204-05
used in arbitration briefs...199-210
Argumentative witnesses...90
Assumptions used to interpret contract language
assumptions about how parties draft
contracts...58
assumptions about how parties normally act...59-60
assumptions of things arbitrator
assumes parties did not
intend...59-60
avoid internal conflicts...58

canons of construction...56-57
construe all parts of a contract
together...58
construe all words of a section
together...58
dictionary meanings...54-55
different meanings for different
word...55
drafters' intent...55-56
generally...54-61
ordinary meaning...54
same meaning for same word...55
technical meaning...54
Attorneys' fees and costs, resisting
arbitration and...279
Authorization, issues of...20-21, 23,
26, 28, 29
Availability of witnesses...139

B

Between-hearing delays,
avoiding...138
Bill, *see* Arbitrator's bill
Billing forms...231-32
Bolstering credibility...12
Breaks
during hearings...146-47
excessive...64-65
Burden
of going forward
generally...243-44, 253
in trustee deadlock cases...264
proponents of change as parties
burdened...264
of proof
generally...253
in interest arbitration...243-44
on party not complying with
subpoena...284
Bureau of Labor Statistics (BLS) as
source of data for interest
arbitration...245

cutting the witness off...170
generally...167-70
leading questions and...167-70
of antagonistic witnesses...94
rehearsals with witnesses...91-92
scope...167
strategy...28
Cumulative evidence...77-78

D

Daily Labor Reports...245
Damages
for failure to comply with
subpoena...286
money, securing...179
Data
choosing, for preparing an interest
arbitration...246-47
concerning witnesses and grievants,
identifying...5
sources for, for preparing an interest
arbitration...244-47
Date of arbitration, parties unable to
agree...114-15
De minimis rule...267
Deadlocks, *see* Trustee deadlocks
Defense, shaping...7
Deferring your opening
statement...156
Defining the issue in arbitration hearings...135, 151-53
Delayed award...296
Delays between hearings,
avoiding...138
Demands
for arbitration...4
for relief, tailoring...251
Demeanor
evidence...92
of witness as evidence...95-96
Dependability of employee...65-66

Description of all events and objects
relating to grievance...6
Destruction of property, employer's
just cause obligation and...69
Determinations at the grievance procedure's earlier steps, as a
pleading...150
Dictionary meaning used to interpret
contract language...54-55
Different meaning for different word
used to interpret contract
language...55
Direct evidence...11, 12
Direct examination
checklists of facts to be proved as
guide to...163
cutting a witness off...164
evaluation matrix as guide to...163
generally...159-67
hostile witnesses...165-67
leading questions and...159-63,
165-66
preparing witnesses for...162-63
recasting a witness's
testimony...164-65
rehearsals with witnesses...91
sidetracking the examiner...163
Directory of U.S. Arbitrators...128
Disability case as trustee deadlock
dispute...261-62
Discharge cases
arbitrator selection and...132
generally...121
scheduling hearings for...138
Discharge of employee
cause for...64
employer's just cause obligation
and...70
unfitness to perform job as
grounds...70
Disciplinary cases
arbitrator selection and...132

negotiated, in federal sector
  arbitrations...301
pre-arbitration steps...3
when occurred...5
where occurred...6
written responses to...3-4
Grievant
demands of, identifying...7
identifying...4-5
Grievant evaluation matrixes, *see also*
  Evaluation matrix
essential elements...16, 22, 24, 25,
  30, 31
how to use...13-31
necessary facts...17, 22, 24, 25, 30,
  31
persuasive impact...19-21, 22, 24,
  25, 30, 31
probative value...19-21, 22, 24, 25,
  30, 31
sources of proof...17-18, 22, 24, 25,
  30, 31
Grounds for vacating arbitration
  award...293-94
Grumbling...67

H

Health problems, employer's just
  cause obligation and...65
Hearing dates
for recurring disciplinary
  matters...115
notifying parties of...139-40
setting...139-40
Hearing location...140-41
Hearing rooms
amenities...143
selecting...141-43
Hearings
audio tape recording of...144-45
breaks during...147
conduct at...253-54
elements of

generally...154-76
opening statements, *See* Opening
  statements
generally...135-83
lunch breaks during...146-47
preliminary problems encountered at
defining the issue...151-53
disqualification of arbitrator for
  impartiality...149
generally...149-54
motion to quash subpoena...149
sequestering witnesses...153-54
providing witnesses directions or
  transportation to...96-97
reopening, *see* Reopening the hearing
running overtime...146
scheduling
complex, multi-hearing
  cases...138-39
consecutive hearing dates...139
discharge cases...138
expedited as condition imposed on
  arbitrator...107
generally...137-39
high exposure cases...138
spectator seating at...142
when to schedule...137-38
starting and ending times...146
table arrangement at...142-43
time arrangements for...146-47
to quash subpoena...100
High exposure cases, scheduling hearings for...138
Hourly billing by arbitrators...232,
  233
Human Resource Information Network or Dialog...128

I

Identifying
data concerning witnesses and
  grievants...5

converting contract language into
  essential elements...45-53
flowcharts...50-53
generally...45-61
just cause...63-70
list algorithms...48-50
negotiations as proof of
  intent...60-61
past practice...61-63
structured enumeration...46-48
Investigating a claim
documents to be collected...2-4
generally...2-9
purpose...2
Investigating and analyzing a case,
  past practice and...62-63
Investigating your case...1-31
Investigation and preparation of an
  interest arbitration, *see* Interest
  arbitration, investigation and
  preparation
Investments as trustee deadlock
  dispute...262
Iowa statute covering interest
  arbitration...240-41
IRAC organization used in arbitration
  briefs...200-02
Issues
defining
  at arbitration hearings...151-53
  generally...135
  of timing...27
stated in arbitration brief...191-92

J

Joint exhibits, stipulation to...150-51
Judicial review of arbitration decisions, absence of...186
Jurisdiction
generally...3
of the arbitrator, limiting, in trustee
  deadlock cases...261-62, 263

retained by arbitrator...119-20,
  175-76
Just cause clauses
in contracts...63-70
Just cause obligation
discharge of employees and...70
discharge of employees for conduct
  off the job...69-70
employee's destruction of
  property...69
employee's failure to perform job
  and...63-64
employee's fighting on the job
  and...68
employee's health problems
  and...65
employee's insubordination
  and...66-67
employee's neglect of duty
  and...64-65
employee's personal hygiene
  and...67-68
employee's stealing and...68
employee's tardiness and absenteeism
  and...65-66
employee's work performance
  and...63-64
employee's work rule violations
  and...66
establishing...64
warnings to employees...63-64

L

Labor Arbitration Awards...116, 128
*Labor Arbitration Information Sys-
  tem* (LAIS)...129
*Labor Arbitration in Govern-
  ment*...116, 129
Labor Arbitration Reports...116,
  127-28
Labor Management Relations Act
  (LMRA)...276
LAIRS system...127

O

Index

Multi-employer Pension Plan Amendment Act (MPPAA)...268-69
Presentation of documents...135
Presumptions, withdrawal liability arbitrations under Multi-employer Pension Plan Amendment Act (MPPAA) and...268-69
Private sector cases, federal court review of...303
Private sector collective bargaining agreements...276-80
Probative value
generally...11
of real evidence...12-13
of testimony, assessing...77
Production of documents
arbitrator's power to compel...275, 284
court's power to compel...287
Proleptical arguments used in arbitration briefs...207-09
Promptness of arbitrator's award...224
Proof
failure of...21
problems with...20-21, 28, 29
of facts...10-11
sources of...17-20
witness demeanor as...20-21, 26, 27-28
Proofs, preparing for interest arbitration, *see* Interest arbitration, preparing your proofs
Proofs, preparing, *see* Preparing the proofs
Proponents of change as parties with burden of going forward...264
Providing the arbitrator the power to conduct a due process hearing...275-76
Publication of arbitration awards...127

Punctuation errors...39
Punitive damages as grounds for vacatur...210

Q

Qualifying language used in arbitration briefs...212-13
Questioning the arbitrator's bill...232
Questions, how witness should respond when unclear...89
Questions to ask colleagues when selecting an arbitrator...122-26
Quotation marks used in arbitration briefs...194

R

R.C. Simpson Co....130
Ratio of study days to hearing days...228-29
Real evidence
assembling for use at hearing...101
documents, preparing copies to distribute at hearing...100-01
examples of...98
generally...11
in the hands of adversaries...99-100
inspecting...100
locating and securing...99-100
originals of...100
preparing...98-101
preparing witness to authenticate...100
presentation of...171
probative value of...12-13
selecting...98-99
Rebuttal...136, 174
Recollection, refreshing...163
Recross-examination...170-71
Recurring disciplinary matters, designating hearing dates for...115
Redirect examination...170-71

323

Timeliness of arbitration award as
consideration in selecting an
arbitrator...125
Timely grievance evaluation
matrix...30
Timing, as issue...27
Title page of arbitration
brief...189-90
Transcripts
appropriateness of case for...145
as evidence...143
costs of, sharing...144-45
generally...143-47
impact of...145
time required to prepare...145
whether to order...143-44
Transportation of witnesses to
hearings...96-97
"Trilogy" standard for compelling or
staying arbitration...277, 288
Tripartite model of interest
arbitration...237-38
Trivial evidence...77, 78
Troublesome consequences as argument used in arbitration
briefs...204-05
Trustee deadlocks under Labor Management Relations Act (LMRA)
302(c)(5)
arbitrators treated as
fiduciaries...256-57
burden of going forward...264
choosing the arbitrator...257-60
generally...255-67
insuring the arbitrator...259
last offer arbitration and...260
limiting jurisdiction of the arbitrator...261-62, 263
shaping the deadlock...262-65
standards for, creating...265-67
types of...262-64
waiver of recourse insurance for the
arbitrator...259-60

U

Undisclosed
outcomes...182
settlements...182
Unfitness to perform job as grounds
for discharge...70
Uniform Arbitration Act
generally...271, 275, 280, 282
subpoenas duces tecum
and...99-100
U.S. Arbitration Act...271
U.S. Court of Appeals for the Federal
Circuit, standard for appeals
to...302-03
Untimely grievance evaluation
matrix...31

V

Vacating the arbitrator's award, *see*
Enforcing or vacating the arbitration award
Vacation of award for lack of
disclosure...136-37
Vacatur
arbitrator's indefinite award resulting in...226
demand for relief sufficient to
avoid...251
generally...189
grounds for
generally...293-94
in New York...272-73
motion, arbitrability and...282
motion for...272
motion, resisting arbitration
and...279-80, 281
of arbitration awards...292-94
panels' reliance on new evidence
introduced at executive session as
grounds for...255
punitive damages as grounds
for...210

state law grounds for...291-92

Vocabulary use in arbitration
briefs...218-19

Voir dire to authenticate evidence...171, 172-74

Voluntary Arbitration Rules...115,
144

W

Waiver of
opening statements...155
recourse insurance for the arbitrator
in trustee deadlock cases...259-60

Warning by employer
of consequences of employee's failure
to meet production
obligations...64
to employee regarding employee's
conduct...63-64

When grievance occurred...5

Withdrawal liability arbitrations
under Multi-employer Pension Plan
Amendment Act (MPPAA)
AAA list of special arbitrators qualified for...269
appeal mechanisms for...269-70
citing law in...270
generally...267-70
issues to be arbitrated...267-68
preparing for and handling...269-70
presumptions...268-69

Witness credibility
antagonistic witness...94
generally...92-96
long-winded witness...92-93
loss of...95
problems with credibility...77
reevaluating...96
short-winded witness...93-94

Witness preparation
apologies and...90
argumentative witnesses and...90
demeanor problems...92, 95-96

directions to the hearing,
providing...96-97
educating witnesses...82-91
evaluation matrixes and...82
generally...82-98
"good buddy" witnesses...95
how to act...89
how to dress...89
how witness should speak...89
list describing how to be a good
witness...89-91
memory lapses and...90
nervousness...92
outlines...82, 83-88, 89-91
preparing witness to authenticate
real evidence...100
rehearsals...91-96
scripts...84
self-control of witness...90
sequestration and...97-98
speculation, warning witness
against...95
telling the truth...88
understanding questions propounded
by interrogator...89
what to say when a question is
objected to...90
witnesses that qualify their
answers...94-95

Witnesses
antagonistic...94
availability of...139
convenience of as factor in setting
location of hearing...140-41
demeanor of as evidence...95-96
educating...82-91
evasiveness of...20-21
examination of, *see* Examination of
witnesses
excluding from hearing room...91
expert, *see* Expert witnesses
fees for subpoenaed witnesses...286
"good buddy" witnesses...95

CPSIA information can be obtained at www.ICGtesting.com
Printed in the USA
BVOW050424021111

275092BV00002B/74/A

9 780977 813407